# THE CRAFT OF
# LITERARY BIOGRAPHY

*Edited by*
Jeffrey Meyers

Schocken Books · New York

First American edition published by Schocken Books 1985
10 9 8 7 6 5 4 3 2 1    85 86 87 88

Printed in Hong Kong

Library of Congress Cataloging in Publication Data
Main entry under title:
The Craft of literary biography.
  Bibliography: p.
  Includes index.
  1. Biography (as a literary form) – Addresses,
essays, lectures.    I. Meyers, Jeffrey.
CT21.C69  1984    808'.06692    84–5614
ISBN 0–8052–3943–X

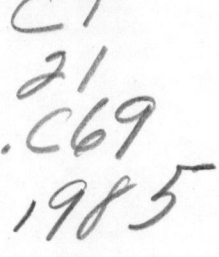

*For Laurence and Polly*

# Contents

# Notes on Contributors

**Deirdre Bair** is the author of *Samuel Beckett: A Biography* (1978), which received the 1981 American Book Award for Biography. She is currently writing the biography of Simone de Beauvoir. She has published many articles and reviews on twentieth-century British and French writers, has lectured extensively in Europe, and has been Visiting Professor at the Institute for Modern Biography of Griffith University in Australia. She is Associate Professor of English at the University of Pennsylvania.

**Lyndall Gordon** is a Senior Research Fellow of Jesus College, Oxford, and author of *Eliot's Early Years* (1977), which won the British Academy's Rose Mary Crawshay prize. She has recently completed a critical biography of Virginia Woolf.

**Donald Greene** is Bing Professor of English at the University of Southern California. He has published extensively on Samuel Johnson and eighteenth-century English literature in general, including *The Politics of Samuel Johnson* (1960) and an edition of *The Political Writings of Samuel Johnson* (1977).

**Nigel Hamilton** wrote (with Olive Hamilton) and published *Royal Greenwich* (1969), the first guide and history of Greenwich for over a century. His *Brothers Mann* was published in 1978 and *Monty: The Making of a General, 1887–1942* followed in 1981, winning the Whitbread Literary Award for the best biography of that year. *Monty: Master of the Battlefield, 1942–1944* appeared in 1983.

**Ronald Hayman** has written biographies of *Artaud* (1977), *De Sade* (1978), *Nietzsche* (1980), *Kafka* (1981), *Brecht* (1983), and many books on the theater. He is now writing a life of Jean-Paul Sartre.

**Mark Holloway** is the author of *Heavens on Earth*, a history of utopian communities in the USA in the eighteenth and nineteenth centuries, which was published in 1951 and reissued in a revised edition in 1966. It is generally considered to be the best popular account of the subject. His biography *Norman Douglas* was published in 1976. In the following year he was elected a Fellow of the Royal Society of Literature.

**Frederick R. Karl** is Professor of English at New York University, author of several books on the novel and of *Joseph Conrad: The Three Lives* (1979). He is general editor of the *Collected Letters of Joseph Conrad* and co-editor of the first volume; he is also advisory editor for the Cambridge University Press edition of Conrad's novels and stories. His book on the American novel, *American Fictions: 1940–1980*, appeared in 1983. He is at present working on a book called *Modern and Modernism*.

**Phillip Knightley**, member of the "Insight Team" of the *Sunday Times* and English journalist of the year in 1981, is the author of *Philby* (1968), *The Secret Lives of Lawrence of Arabia* (1969), *The Pearl of Days* (1972), *The First Casualty* (1975), *The Death of Venice* (1976), *Suffer the Children* (1979) and *The Vestey Affair* (1982).

**Elizabeth, Countess of Longford**, C.B.E., is the author of *Jameson's Raid* (1960), *Queen Victoria* (1964), *Wellington* (1969–72), *Byron* (1976), *A Pilgrimage of Passion: A Life of Wilfrid Scawen Blunt* (1979), *Eminent Victorian Women* (1981) and *The Queen Mother* (1981).

**Paul Mariani**, Professor of English at the University of Massachusetts, is the author of *A Commentary on the Complete Poems of G. M. Hopkins* (1970), *W. C. Williams: The Poet and His Critics* (1975) and *W. C. Williams: A Biography* (1981).

**Patrick McCarthy** has taught politics and literature at Cambridge, Cornell and the Johns Hopkins Bologna Center, and is at present Associate Professor at Haverford College. He is the author of *Céline* (1976) and *Camus* (1982). He is now working on a book on writers and politics in contemporary Europe.

**Jeffrey Meyers**, Professor of English at the University of Colorado, is the author and editor of many books on modern literature, including several works on T. E. Lawrence and George Orwell; biographies of Katherine Mansfield (1978) and Wyndham Lewis (1980); *Wyndham Lewis: A Revaluation* (1980), *Fiction and the Colonial Experience* (1973), *Painting and the Novel* (1975), *A Fever at the Core* (1976), *Married to Genius* (1977), *Homosexuality and Literature* (1977), *Hemingway: The Critical Heritage* (1982) and *D. H. Lawrence and the Experience of Italy* (1982). He has recently completed a life of Hemingway.

**William M. Murphy** is the Thomas Lamont Professor of Ancient and Modern Literature at Union College, Schenectady, New York. His *Prodigal Father: The Life of John Butler Yeats, 1839–1922* (1978) was one of five finalists for the National Book Award in Biography in 1979.

# Introduction

## JEFFREY MEYERS

### I

Biography has become one of the major literary genres of the twentieth century. There is now considerable interest not only in the history of life writing but also in how a biography comes into being, how the biographer captures the essence of an artist's inner life. *The Craft of Literary Biography* describes the problems of writing a modern literary biography from thirteen different viewpoints. It considers, among many other questions, how the biographer chooses a subject, uses biographical models, does archival research, conducts interviews, interprets evidence, establishes chronology, organizes material into a meaningful pattern and illuminates an author's work through a discussion of his life.[1]

The ideal circumstances for selecting a modern literary subject are the existence of significant unpublished material, of family and friends who can be interviewed as well as the absence of an obstructive executor or a recently completed life. Most contemporary readers expect to learn the whole truth about the psychological, sexual and medical aspects of the subject. For this reason, writers like Kafka, Eliot, Orwell and Auden vainly tried to protect their posthumous privacy by requesting that no biography be written about them. Auden asserted that "Biographies of writers, whether written by others or by themselves,[2] are always superfluous and usually in bad taste. . . . His private life is, or should be, of no concern to anybody except himself, his family and his friends."[3] But Samuel Johnson's belief (expressed in *The Rambler* of October 13, 1750), "There has rarely passed a life of which a judicious and faithful narrative would not be useful," has prevailed from his time until our own.

The traditional aim of the literary biographer—to discover,

define and depict the mind as well as the life of the artist—has been rejected by a superficial school of life writing, exemplified by Carlos Baker's *Ernest Hemingway* and Bernard Crick's *George Orwell*, which prefer to present an external view through an encyclopedic accumulation of facts. Baker defends this defeatist approach by maintaining: "No biography can portray a man as he actually was. The best that can be hoped for is an approximation, from which all that is false has been expunged and in which most of what is true has been set forth. . . . If Ernest Hemingway is to be made to live again, it must be by virtue of a thousand pictures, both still and moving, a thousand scenes."[4] Crick also rejects the great tradition of life writing and confesses: "I grew to be sceptical of much of the fine writing, balanced appraisal and psychological insight that is the hallmark of the English tradition of biography. . . . None of us can enter another person's mind; to believe so is fiction. We can only know an actual person by observing their [sic] behaviour in a variety of different situations and through different perspectives."[5] The predictable result of these self-imposed constraints is a clumsy style, an absence of interpretation and a lack of perception. Both books fail to present a convincing and meaningful pattern in the author's life; an exploration of character, an evaluation of relationships, a comprehension of motives.

The more ambitious and successful biographer is an investigative reporter of the spirit. He must reveal evolution and development, present the numerous selves and multiple lives of his subject; for as Henry James observed: "To live over people's lives is nothing unless we live over their perceptions, live over the growth, the change, the varying intensity of the same—since it was *by* these things they themselves lived."[6] The literary biographer must utilize original research that casts new light on the subject; have a thorough mastery of the material; give a complete and accurate synthesis of all the facts about the private as well as the public life: friendships, conversation, dress, habits, tastes, food, money. He should make a selection—not merely a collection—of significant and convincing details, and possess a lively narrative style. He should form a sympathetic identification with the subject, and present a perceptive interpretation of character. He must create a dramatic structure that focuses the pattern of crises in the life, and effectively portray the social and political background. He ought to provide a sensitive evaluation of the subject's achievement—which is the justification of the book. Finally, as Somerset Maugham (who was trained as a doctor) noted, he must also do justice to the end and extinction of the life: "In most biographies it is the subject's death which is most interesting. The last inevitable step has a fascination and even a practical interest which no previous event can equal. I cannot understand why a biographer, having undertaken to give the world details of a famous man's life, should hesitate, as so often happens, to give details of his death."[7]

Modern biography reached its peak in the 1950's with an impressive series of monumental works: Isaac Deutscher's *Trotsky*, Ernest Jones' *Freud*, Erik Erikson's *Luther*, Leslie Marchand's *Byron*, Leon Edel's *Henry James* and, most notably, George Painter's *Marcel Proust* (2 volumes, 1959, 1965) and Richard Ellmann's *James Joyce* (1959, revised edition 1982). Painter and Ellmann, who have influenced most subsequent literary biographies, fulfill the ideal of sympathetic intuition and recreate their subjects' lives by intimately reliving (as James suggested) their perceptions, their growth and their change. Through this essential process and with great psychological penetration, both beautifully written biographies reveal how these two major novelists were drawn to their literary vocation—to the religion of art. They also show how these writers imaginatively transformed the raw material of their lives—the sickness and the squalor—into the symbolic reality of *Remembrance of Things Past* and *Ulysses*. Painter expressed his own aesthetic ideal in his discussion of Proust's absorption with Sainte-Beuve: the biographer "must discover, beneath the mask of the artist's every-day, objective life, the secret from which he extracted his work; show how, in the apparently sterile persons and places of that external life, he found the hidden, universal meanings which are the themes of his book; and reveal the drama of the contrast and interaction between his daily existence and his incommensurably deeper life as a creator."[8]

## II

The twelve other contributors to this volume were chosen because I admired—and sometimes reviewed—their definitive biographies.[9] Five of the authors are American, five are English, one is

Canadian, one is Australian, one is South African. Their birth dates range from 1906 to 1944, but their biographies (apart from Knightley, 1969) were all published between 1976 and 1983. The essays are arranged by chronological order of their subjects—English, Irish, American, German and French—and express a diversity rather than unanimity of theory, technique and style.

Donald Greene—who is now completing the late James Clifford's biography with a third volume on the last two decades of Samuel Johnson's life—offers a learned, fierce and witty demolition of the cherished myth of quaint old "Doctor Sam Johnson" as well as a reconstruction of a less quirky and much more intellectual man. He scrutinizes the limitations of Boswell's *Life of Johnson*, generally considered the greatest biography in English; argues that "the Boswellian Johnson is one of the most successful hatchet jobs in the history of biography"; and concludes that the duty of the modern life writer is "to search out the truth and plead for its acceptance" even when well-established falsehood is more psychologically attractive.

William Murphy is "the only biographer who owns the corpse of his subject." His lucid, elegant essay concerns the influence of irony and fate—of haphazard events developing into a fixed plan—and the interpenetration of his own personal and political life with that of John Butler Yeats: father of the poet, painter, letter-writer, conversationalist and conspicuous failure. Murphy recounts his relations with William Yeats' widow and son, the slow accumulation of material and insight, the crucial decisions about inclusion and form, the gradual shaping of his massive work.

Elizabeth Longford—Catholic, aristocrat and biographer of Byron, Wellington and Queen Victoria—was perfectly suited to write the life of Wilfrid Scawen Blunt: "sportsman, artist, political agitator, poet, amorist." Intimate with the world of her subject and aware of all its subtleties, she was commissioned to write the official life and given access to the sealed Secret Diaries. She believes it was essential to make Blunt's life "visible" by visiting his houses in Sussex, following his travels in the Middle East and India, and recreating what Lawrence called the "spirit of place." She analyzes the difficulties of dealing with Blunt's sexual life, the disparity between the defects of his character and the nobility of his work.

Frederick Karl raises theoretical as well as practical questions, notes the differences between literary and historical biography. He emphasizes the use of psychoanalysis, the transformation of clinical illness into aesthetic form, and the inadequacies (not to mention the absurdities) of semiotic theory. After discussing Joseph Conrad's way of "seeing" and choice of English as his fictional language, Karl concentrates on the split between Conrad's desire for action and emphasis on languor, on his recreation of disastrous Polish memories to nourish his literary imagination. He concludes by stressing not the damaging psychological aspects of Conrad's childhood, but the importance of his individual adult will.

Mark Holloway was forced to endure the horrifying experience of having precious documents torn up before his eyes. His graceful essay on the genesis of his life of Norman Douglas considers his rather delicate relations with Kenneth Macpherson, who owned the most valuable material on Douglas; the difficulties of dealing with Douglas' homosexuality, and of distinguishing between Douglas' real self and the persona of his misleading autobiography. Holloway properly stresses the need for endless patience and persistence, the eccentric memory of the aged, the fruitful cooperation with other scholars, the obsession with a project that has no natural termination, and the redemptive pleasures of learning, travel and friendship.

Nigel Hamilton has written both a dual literary life of Thomas and Heinrich Mann and a military life of Field Marshal Bernard Montgomery. He contrasts Franco-German with Anglo-American biography, concentrates on the moral development and radical change in Thomas Mann's political ideas, and reveals how the writing of the book affected his own values and goals. Hamilton differs from most biographers in three respects. He feels it is dangerous to sympathize with one's subject (though he followed Mann's work habits and was heartened, when his publishers requested cuts, by Mann's refusal to sacrifice a word of *Buddenbrooks*), does his research and writing in sections rather than completing the former before beginning the latter, and thinks that literary biography should separate rather than unify the subject and his work. Hamilton sees biography as a matter of life and death, believes that it penetrates "to the very heart of civilized, free and democratic society."

My own claim to distinction is that I found and held in my

*Jeffrey Meyers*

hands the brain of Wyndham Lewis. My essay begins with an extended comparison of Katherine Mansfield and Wyndham Lewis as biographical subjects. It discusses the problems of gaining access to unpublished material in university libraries and grappling with the legal complexities of the estate; the techniques of interviewing aged informants; and the solution of the major mysteries of Lewis' life: his parents' separation, his mistresses and five illegitimate children, his secret marriage and his medical history. I conclude that at the fag-end of literary criticism, a biography based on unpublished material "is perhaps the most valuable contribution to modern scholarship."

Paul Mariani's passionate *apologia* of William Carlos Williams considers the art of the biographer: his strategies of selection and scope, the proper language to recreate the world of the poet, the search for the best way to commence and conclude, the need for subjective identification and sympathy. Throughout the creation of his work Mariani sought the epiphany of insight and break-through: "that moment of light when the inner life of the subject was suddenly revealed."

Phillip Knightley—who was not a specialist in the Middle East, military history or modern literature—became the biographer of T. E. Lawrence by accident rather than by design. The fascinating account of how he wrote his popular and controversial though serious and accurate book concerns his problems as co-author; how he employed a team of Arabic and psychiatric experts; investigated the story of Lawrence's flagellation which became the basis of his work; wrote under the extreme pressure of a tight deadline; and grappled with tortuous and exasperating legal restrictions. He enjoyed, however, the enormous resources of the *Sunday Times*, the publicity of newspaper serialization and considerable financial rewards.

Lyndall Gordon had to circumvent Eliot's decree, rigidly enforced by his widow and publisher, that no biography be written about him. She began her search for the elusive, "invisible" poet by asking: "Who were Eliot's models? What was his native tradition? . . . What does Eliot's work tell us about his life?"; by questioning the impersonality of the poetry, the absence of an American tradition and the monstrousness of his first wife. She experienced a "detective excitement" in the unpublished manuscripts and gradually discovered the story of a psychic nightmare that became a visionary triumph.

Ronald Hayman's subject, Bertolt Brecht, seems the least appealing author considered in this volume. Brecht thought literature could be useful and was more interested in power than in truth. He was misleading about his own life, callous with women, double-dealing with friends, opportunistic in politics. Hayman—a former actor and director—describes the "actorish feeling of being able to assume [another's] character"; the problems of dealing with the nuances of a foreign language; the passive—as well as active—absorption of knowledge. In contrast to the long gestation period of Murphy, Holloway and Mariani, Hayman (like Knightley and myself) completed his book rapidly. He concludes by pondering the rather questionable enterprise of biography, in which one man "gives up a substantial part of his life to reconstructing another's."

Deirdre Bair, in contrast to the more fortunate authorized biographer, Elizabeth Longford, struggled to find a Ph.D. subject and to justify her endeavor—though she eventually transformed her dissertation into a best-seller. Mark Holloway and Ronald Hayman had briefly met their subjects; Deirdre Bair came to know Samuel Beckett intimately during their six years of conversation. The ambiguous statement that he would "neither help nor hinder" her work ultimately provided the necessary freedom to complete her book. She abandoned the idea of a unifying thesis, was extraordinarily scrupulous in requiring three sources to confirm each fact, and learned that her personal feelings about the people she interviewed "had very little to do with their reliability as a biographical resource."

Patrick McCarthy wanted to show how Albert Camus was "shaped by and also shaped the intellectual and political forces his age." He was conscious from the outset of Camus' origins in the now vanished French Algeria and his prime aim was to reconstruct that country for his readers. He believes "writers are changed by the books they write and still more by the way they are read"; feels the mixture of irony and self-righteousness is the key to Camus' character; and sees his life as "a series of public victories and secret defeats."

Several significant themes emerge from these essays: the change from paralysis when faced with the apparently over-whelming task to a moment of insight and a confident conviction that one can successfully complete the book; the need to replace the myth with the facts; the joys of detection and discovery; the reliance on help from others and importance of (well-deserved) luck; the creative process that demands the same imaginative qualities as fiction and drama; the struggle (in authors like Murphy, Holloway, Hamilton and Mariani) to preserve the integrity of their work when confronted with the compromising expediency of publishers. All the biographers attempted to define themselves while exploring the lives of their subjects, placing them in the proper context and illuminating their art. The contributors to *The Craft of Literary Biography*, who present a retrospective view of their own works as well as a penetrating analysis of the state of contemporary biography, confirm Lytton Strachey's observation: "It is perhaps as difficult to write a good life as to live one."

CHAPTER ONE

# Samuel Johnson

## DONALD GREENE

## I. SOME SMALLER PROBLEMS

It may sound strange, but a modern biographer of Samuel
Johnson envies the contributors to this volume who deal with
writers who lived and flourished in the present century. After all,
much of the basic research still has to be done on these more
recent subjects. The authentic records of their births, ancestry,
marriages, families, residences, illnesses, finances, and the rest
have to be collected from the four corners of the earth; interviews
with their many surviving acquaintances have to be negotiated;
correspondence by and with them has to be dug out and
assembled; a full and accurate bibliography of their writings has
to be compiled, and, when it has been, those writings have to be
carefully read, digested, and placed in context.

For Johnson, on the other hand, all this arduous labor was
surely done long ago. The bicentenary of his death falls in 1984. In
the intervening two centuries, a huge output of biographies,
bibliographies, editions of his writings and correspondence, and
critical studies about him has been published. The listing—a
selective, not a comprehensive, one—of works concerning Johnson compiled by the late James L. Clifford and myself[1] contains
some four thousand titles, from Johnson's own lifetime up to 1969,
and in the dozen years since it was published, a host of additional
studies have appeared. What more is there to do for anyone who
undertakes a new biography of Johnson than to skim the cream of
all this devoted effort, and put it together in pleasantly readable
form? That, indeed, is just what the authors of many recent
popular, sometimes best-selling and award-winning, books about
Johnson have done (no names, no pack-drill, as they say in the
British army), and what their successors will no doubt go on

9

doing. Nothing is a surer bet for the lucrative Christmas coffee-table trade than another attractive fat book about dear, quaint old "Doctor Sam Johnson," retailing for the thousandth time such perennially entertaining sayings of his as "A second marriage is the triumph of hope over experience," and such delightful anecdotes as that about his kicking the stone in refutation of Berkeley—a splendid example of the way the commonsensical, if not too penetrating, mind of the typical John Bull works.

The problem for the conscientious modern biographer is that too much of this kind of thing is myth, and, to make it harder for him, dearly cherished myth. What are the facts—assuming that facts are a concern of the biographer, though there is a recent school of Johnsonian biography which holds that they need not, and perhaps even should not, be? (More about this later.) The quip about second marriages occurs in a collection of miscellaneous anecdotes of no particular date furnished by a friend, which Boswell used to help fill up his grievously thin account of the year 1770, when Boswell did not come up to London to visit Johnson and had no correspondence with him. A number of such unverified anecdotes in Boswell's *Life*—for instance, the one about his retorting to an abusive boatman, "Sir, your wife, under pretence of keeping a bawdy-house, is a receiver of stolen goods"—have been discovered in popular jest-books published long before Johnson or Boswell was heard of:[2] "the Joe Miller syndrome," as historians have called it, in which long familiar jokes are attached to the names of people in the public eye, such as Abraham Lincoln and Winston Churchill—and Johnson. As for Johnson's real attitude toward second marriages, Boswell reports that on another occasion he heard from Johnson's own lips, "By taking a second wife, [a widower] pays the highest compliment to the first, by shewing that she made him so happy as a married man that he wishes to be so a second time." A passage in Johnson's diaries records that on the first anniversary of his wife Tetty's death he proposed "on Monday to seek a new wife." This memorandum, which turned up in the 1950's, was suppressed by Boswell[3]: it did not fit the image he wanted to create of Johnson's undying devotion to Tetty—an image perhaps constructed to ease Boswell's guilt about his compulsive infidelity to his own wife. But the old chestnut about the triumph of hope over experience continues to be cited as an example of "the withering wit of Doctor Johnson,"[4] and no doubt will long do so. Although the stone-kicking incident did take place in Boswell's presence, it may not be such a display of philosophical naïveté as has been supposed. Some time ago, one of the most respected professional journals of philosophy published an article defending, in a highly technical argument, the validity of Johnson's "refutation,"[5] and, so far as I know, no attempt to rebut it has appeared. The epistemological issues involved are rather over the head of the average literary scholar.

Then there is the matter of nomenclature. Recently a talk of mine was introduced by a distinguished scholar who called attention, with the familiar warm chuckle, to the amusing phenomenon that dear, quaint old Sam Johnson, unlike other writers, is always referred to as "Doctor" (responsive warm chuckles from the audience). Probably no one except his relations and school friends when he was a boy addressed or thought of the mature Johnson as "Sam." The mistake comes from Johnson's practice of signing his letters "Sam: Johnson," the colon, or sometimes period, indicating that the expression is an abbreviation, as, until quite recently, many letter-writers signed themselves "Jas:" for James or "Geo:" for George. Probably no more of his acquaintances addressed the mature Johnson as "Sam" than addressed Wordsworth as "Bill" or Tennyson as "Alf." But somehow regularly calling him "Sam" helps us to cut him down to our own size, and perhaps that is the unconscious object of the exercise. Why Johnson is so disturbing to many readers that this cutting-down-to-size, or defanging, operation seems necessary is a question the serious modern student of Johnson cannot avoid grappling with.

As for the obligatory "Doctor," Johnson was no more in the habit of using the title of his honorary doctorates from Oxford and Dublin than most other sensible writers who have been similarly honored. William Wordsworth and T. S. Eliot, to mention two, were also awarded honorary doctoral degrees from Oxford, but never thought of referring to themselves as "Doctor Wordsworth" or "Doctor Eliot," and modern students respect their practice in this. The point, presumably, is that their writings have conferred so much distinction on the bare surnames of "Wordsworth" and "Eliot" that additional honorifics would be not only superfluous but impertinent.[6] It is true that in the eighteenth century "Doctor" was used more frequently than it is now: Jonathan

Swift, D.D., was often referred to by his contemporaries as "Doctor Swift," and Oliver Goldsmith, M.D. (perhaps), as "Doctor Goldsmith." But modern students of these writers have abandoned those doctorates, no doubt for the same reason that they do not use them for Wordsworth and Eliot. Yet the perpetual doctorate seems to be immovably affixed to Johnson.

Why? If one asks a habitual user of it, he is likely to reply something to the effect that it is a special token of admiration for a great man (though, if asked why he does not also bestow it on other writers whom he admires and who are equally entitled to it, such as Eliot, he may have a hard time answering). Of course, Boswell hallowed the usage by carefully changing each reference to "Mr. Johnson" in his manuscript journal of his tour to the Hebrides with Johnson to "Dr. Johnson" when it was printed, twelve years later, after Johnson's death. (As he likewise inserted dozens of "Sirs" at the beginning of many of the speeches by Johnson that he printed.) And we know how greatly Boswell worshipped Johnson, so much so that the adjective "Boswellian" has become a synonym for hero-worshipping.

Or did he? The question will be raised again below; meanwhile, let us look at a note on the matter appended by Boswell to his *Life of Johnson* in 1791. He has just recorded the bestowal of the honorary degree on Johnson by Oxford:

> It is remarkable that he never, so far as I know, assumed his title of *Doctor*, but called himself *Mr.* Johnson, as appears from many of his cards or notes to myself, and I have seen many from him to other persons, in which he uniformly takes that designation.—I once observed on his table a letter directed to him with the addition of *Esquire*, and objected to it as being a designation inferiour to that of Doctor; but he checked me, and seemed pleased with it, because, as I conjectured, he liked to be sometimes taken out of the class of literary men, and to be merely *genteel—un gentilhomme comme un autre*.[7]

*Comme* James Boswell, Laird of Auchinleck, for instance, who as a young man had striven so hard for an entrée into fashionable London society—"Boswell d'Auchinleck," as he signed his letters to Continental correspondents as if he were a member of the nobility (although his father, who, as a Scottish judge, held the non-peerage and non-hereditary title of "Lord Auchinleck," signed his letters merely "Alexr. Boswell")? The naïveté, and snobbery, in this is complex. Is there not more than a hint that "literary men" ought generally to remain in their proper place, though an occasional flight into the class of *gentilhomme* may sometimes be viewed with amused toleration? Boswell's "*sometimes* taken out" flatly contradicts his previous statement that Johnson *never* used the title of "Doctor." And considering that in 1773, two years before Oxford University got around to bestowing the degree on Johnson, its newly elected chancellor, Prime Minister Lord North, had at one blow awarded no fewer than sixty-eight honorary doctorates, mostly on minor politicians and obsequious supporters of North in Parliament such as Henry Thrale,[8] we may find it less remarkable than Boswell that Johnson was not enthusiastic about the title. For all Boswell's contention that "Doctor" is superior to "Esquire," it is worth noting that the Laird of Auchinleck never refers to the wealthy laird of Streatham Park as "Doctor Thrale." *Perhaps* his inflicting the perpetual doctorate on Johnson, who disdained the epithet, was the result of Boswell's high regard for him, but it seems an odd way of showing it.

These may seem small points. But the adventitious "Doctors" and "Sirs" are a significant part of what may be called the "Great Cham" or "literary dictator" syndrome (and, as good democrats, are we not all entitled at least to smile a little superciliously at anyone who sets himself up as a literary dictator?). "Great Cham" was a quip in a letter from Tobias Smollett, no great friend of Johnson's. Boswell, failing to recognize the word as a variant spelling of "Khan," misread it as "Chum"—literally "a chamber companion" or "room-mate"—and so printed it in the first edition of his *Life*; after it was pointed out that this made little sense, he apologetically corrected it in a later edition. The myth is excellently illustrated in a recent Charles Addams cartoon in *The New Yorker*,[9] copies of which various colleagues of mine, especially those teaching the Romantic and Victorian periods, were good enough to send me, expecting no doubt that I would share in their chuckling at it. It is captioned "Dr."—of course—"Johnson gets off a good one," and shows an obese figure with a mad gleam in his eye, a cousin of many earlier Addams ogres, pronouncing to an excruciatingly bored group of denizens of what looks like a nineteenth-century English working-class pub, "So I say, 'You *have* Lord Kames. Keep him; ha, ha, ha!' ". Perhaps not too much should be made of this sort of thing, but it might be pointed out—apart from the unlikelihood that the mature Johnson, any more than Queen Victoria, would have been found in the milieu depicted—that though he was certainly noted for acerbic repartee in company, there is no evidence that he was in the habit of inflicting it gratuitously on strangers. Indeed, those who enjoyed his quips had—as with many other public figures famous for witty talk—to exert themselves to get him to perform, to "draw him out." "No one was . . . less willing to begin any discourse than himself; his friend Mr. Thomas Tyers"—manager of the Vauxhall pleasure gardens, and so a connoisseur of the habits of celebrities—"said he was like the ghosts, who never speak till they are spoken to; and he liked the expression so well that he often repeated it." [10] Other acquaintances of Johnson noted the same trait. The acquaintance who most persistently worked at "drawing him out" was, of course, James Boswell, and sometimes he succeeded only too well, to his own discomfiture. Trying, as he so often did, to badger Johnson into modifying his "prejudice against Scotland"—much of which was a conventional pose for conversational amusement; Scotch jokes, then as later, were the English equivalent of Polish jokes in modern American humor—and, after harping unsuccessfully on "our advancement in literature," Boswell was reduced to the pathetic argument, "But, Sir, we have Lord Kames." [11] Johnson's irritated injunction to Boswell to keep him is perhaps understandable. There is of course no evidence that he ever repeated it out of context.

The origin and growth of the notion that Johnson was, or tried or wished to be, the "literary dictator" of "an age of Johnson" needs some investigation. Book reviewing formed a very small fraction of his total output as a writer, and most of it took place in his younger, journalistic years before his name was well known. Essays on purely literary topics form a relatively small proportion of his *Rambler*, *Idler*, and *Adventurer* pieces, and very seldom, if at all, deal with living writers. The *Prefaces, Biographical and Critical, to the Works of the English Poets* ("The Lives of the Poets" is a misnomer) excluded living writers, and the most outspoken of them, those on Milton, Gray, and Lyttelton, were immediately violently controverted in print—as so many of Johnson's opinions were by his contemporaries. [12]

A generation or so after Johnson's death, Wordsworth was to pronounce, apropos of Bishop Percy's *Reliques of Ancient English*

*Poetry*, published in 1765, "The compilation was however ill-suited to the then existing taste of city society; and Dr. Johnson, 'mid the little senate to which he gave laws, was not sparing in his exertions to make it an object of contempt."[13] Wordsworth was unaware that, in fact, Johnson had spent two months in Percy's home just before the publication of the *Reliques*, helping his friend—secretly, as he helped many other writers of his acquaintance[14]—to prepare it for the press, providing lexicographical help with its glossary of older English words, and writing for it the fine dedication to Elizabeth Percy, Countess of Northumberland, to whom Thomas Percy somewhat vainly hoped to prove his relationship. Far from exerting himself to make the publication an object of contempt, Johnson helped Percy to find a publisher for it, and gave the "ingenious collector" of the old ballads much favorable publicity in his edition of Shakespeare, published the same year.[15]

Wordsworth, like so many, seemed to believe that an acquaintance with Boswell's *Life* provided him with full familiarity with every part of Johnson's life and works. To be sure, in the pages of the *Life*, we often see Johnson at meetings of "The Club," which he and Reynolds founded in 1767, pronouncing—after he had been "spoken to"—decided opinions pro or con current literary productions. But if a literary dictator is one whose decrees are assented to without demur, "The Club" was certainly no individual's "little senate," and such strong-minded members of it as Burke, Gibbon, and Reynolds, at least as important in the public eye as Johnson, were by no means ready to accept Johnsonian "laws" without question. Boswell's own reports tell us the contrary. No doubt Johnson's opinions were often sought. But his old friend Tom Tyers gives us an account similar to that given of many well-known leading literary figures of many times:

He declared that the perpetual task of reading was as bad as the slavery of the mine, or the labour at the oar. He did not always give his opinion unconditionally of the pieces he had even perused and was competent to decide on. He did not choose to have his sentiments generally known; for there was a great eagerness, especially in those who had not the pole-star of judgment to direct them, to be taught what to think or to say on literary performances.[16]

Hardly the attitude, one might think, of a would-be literary dictator. But a study of Johnson's massive output of journalism, including literary critical works, leads to the conclusion that in such writing he was not so much interested in teaching his readers "what to think" as in encouraging them to think for themselves.[17]

## II. THE BIG PROBLEM

The notion that one of the chief occupations of Johnson during his mature life was making dictatorial pronouncements to other members of "The Club" comes of course from the work which James Boswell published under the name of *The Life of Samuel Johnson, LL.D.*—the work which Lord Macaulay was to declare entitled Boswell to the designation of the first of biographers as decidedly as Shakespeare was entitled to that of the first of dramatists and Homer to that of the first of epic poets.[18] Let it be said, by way of exculpation of Macaulay, that few full-length works purporting to be biographies of a literary figure had been in existence before Boswell's; it was, more or less, the first of its *genre*, and no one will deny that it has merits, though not perhaps the precise merits usually ascribed to it. But a volume of essays concerned with the problems of literary biography seems the appropriate place to raise the question whether the judgment that Boswell's is the greatest literary biographies, or even, by modern standards, a competent biography at all, can be any longer maintained.

Consider only the matter of proportion: what would be the modern attitude toward a biography of which only one-sixth deals with the first fifty-four years of its subject's life—in Johnson's case, from his birth in 1709 until the year in which Boswell first met him, 1763—while five-sixths are devoted to the remaining twenty-two years, until his death in 1784?[19] If Johnson's activities during those twenty-two years were recorded in full detail in that substantial space, we should have less reason to complain. But this is far from being the case. Such is the power of the Boswellian myth that many modern readers, even those who profess to be *aficionados* of Boswell and Johnson, are astounded when they are told that Boswell in fact did not spend most of his time during those twenty-two years after his first meeting with Johnson running after him with notebook in hand recording his day-to-day, even hour-to-hour, doings and sayings. The plain fact is that Johnson lived in London, whereas Boswell's home and place of work in his profession of lawyer was in Edinburgh, four hundred miles to the north; that in eight of those years Boswell never saw London or Johnson at all, and that in each of the remaining fourteen years he visited London for only two or three months (sometimes much less), and by no means saw Johnson every day during those visits, or even more than a few hours in the days when he did see him. It has been calculated that Boswell and Johnson were in each other's company, at most, on a total of 425 days during the twenty-two years (to be precise, 7,783 days) between the dates of Boswell's first meeting with Johnson and Johnson's death—100 of those during their Scottish tour, when they were together continuously for three months. And even of these estimated 425 days, a fair number are not recorded in the *Life*.

It is difficult to deny that, whatever title Boswell decided to give his book, the five-sixths of it purporting to describe Johnson's life during his last twenty-two years can only with the utmost courtesy be called, by modern standards, a biography, a serious attempt to provide a connected narrative of an individual's life. The vast bulk of this, the best-known section of the book, consists of excerpts from Boswell's voluminous diary, which he kept from his youth to the end of his life, excerpts—a small fraction of the enormous whole—containing his accounts of the occasions when he was in Johnson's company. There are huge gaps in the chronology, as in the years 1770 and 1780, when no meetings took place, which Boswell tries to fill with pages of miscellaneous, undated, and sometimes dubious anecdotes supplied to him by various friends. Surely a modern biographer would be expected to do a better job of continuity and completeness than this. Ironically, Boswell's first Johnsonian publication, his *Journal of a Tour to the Hebrides with Samuel Johnson, LL.D.*, 1785, which does provide a continuous day-to-day account of what Johnson was doing for three months, has a better claim, on this score, to be called a biography. Yet at the close of it, Boswell enters a plea for its friendly reception on the ground that it belongs to the respectable *genre* of *ana*—of "Table Talk," *Tischreden*, *Gespräche*, like those of Luther, Ménage, and Selden (to be followed by those of Goethe and Coleridge): not biography, but valuable material for the biographer to draw on, though subject to his assessment for relevance and authenticity.

As *ana*, Boswell's 1791 work is superb, in at least the same class as Eckermann's. But it might have been better—it would certainly have been better for later knowledge and understanding of Johnson—if he had called it *A Journal of My Encounters with Johnson Between 1763 and 1784*, or even (like Eckermann) merely *Conversations with Johnson*. But somewhere along the way he was persuaded that by calling it *The Life of Johnson*, he would win immortal fame for himself, something that, near the end of a life of frustration, he desperately wanted. By the time he set to work in earnest on putting it together, he was a tired and sick man.[20] The hardest effort he gave to it was in its initial one-sixth, dealing with the fifty-four years of Johnson's life before Boswell met him. A good deal of information about that half-century was already available to Boswell in earlier published biographical accounts, but the record of Boswell's research on those early years,[21] even though it resulted in the perpetuation of a number of unfortunate mistakes, is impressive. The perfunctory attempts in the later section to plug large gaps in the narrative with desultory collections of second- or third-hand anecdotes seem to indicate a slackening of energy or motivation.

Yet even as a compiler of *ana* Boswell could not resist the temptation—from which, to be sure, other recorders of the lives and personalities of their subjects are not immune—to edit his original reports of Johnson's sayings and doings so as to conform with a preconceived "image" which gives comfort to the writer's longings and insecurities. Boswell was, as they say, a "pre-romantic," who liked to preserve the notion of some early mythical stable and authoritarian social structure, a notion which he wanted Johnson to symbolize. In his original journal in 1763 he reports Johnson explaining to Goldsmith the venerable legal maxim "The King can do no wrong"—that is, that the Crown, the executive, cannot without its express permission be sued, which was indeed the practice in both British and American courts until quite recently: "Johnson showed that in our Constitution the King is the head, and that there is no power by which he can be tried; and that therefore it is that redress is always to be had against oppression by punishing the intermediate agents." In the *Life*, 1791, this becomes "Sir, you are to consider, that in our constitution, *according to its true principles*, the King is the head; *he is supreme; he is above everything*; and there is no power by which he can be tried. Therefore it is, Sir, that we hold the King can do no wrong; that *whatever may happen to be wrong in government* may not be above our reach, by *being ascribed to Majesty*."[22] The additions and changes ("oppression" watered down to "whatever may happen to be wrong in government")—one might also note the sprinkling of added "Sirs"—suggest some sort of blind adoration by Johnson of an anointed monarch; whereas it is perfectly clear from Johnson's own writings that he had very little respect for monarchs as a class,[23] although Boswell, who prided himself on his descent from the Stuarts, did.

Johnson, at Oxford, toasted "the next rebellion of the blacks in the West Indies," virtually adopted as a son the young former West Indian slave, Frank Barber, and made him the residuary legatee to his estate. Boswell devotes much space in the *Life* to arguing heatedly against Johnson that slavery is proven in the Bible to be the will of God, and that the abolition of slavery would be a grievous crime, being the theft of their property from the slave-owners. There is such speculative editorializing as the description of Johnson, in Boswell's company, approaching Oxford after a long day's journey from London a few months before his death: "He seemed to feel himself elevated as we approached Oxford, that magnificent and venerable seat of Learning, Orthodoxy, and Toryism."[24] Perhaps the ideology Boswell attributes to Johnson had something to do with his heightening of spirits. Yet even a Whig and agnostic might have displayed some signs of relief at nearing the end of a weary journey in the public coach, to the accompaniment of Boswell's chatter, and punctuated by a meal in which the roast mutton was "ill-fed, ill-kept, ill-killed, and ill-drest." In such passages, and other comparable ones, readers of the *Life* have somehow assimilated Boswell's views to Johnson's entirely contrary ones.[25]

Has the net result of Boswell's presentation of Johnson been to inspire admiration for him among readers of the *Life*? For some, perhaps, whose attitudes in politics and religion are similar to Boswell's. But certainly not for all, as the Charles Addams cartoon indicates; and the picture many intelligent young students have derived from the work has been that of the same obese, pompous, and not very bright figure of fun who appears there—the picture of "the Great Clubman," as F. R. Leavis satirically called it, lamenting that it has obscured the too little-known Johnson "the great highbrow." Trivial as they may seem, the many "Sirs" and "Doctors" added to the *Life* by Boswell must have reinforced it, giving the reader the impression that Johnson did in fact preface most of his pronouncements with "Sir," and, if he did not actually insist on being addressed as "Doctor," at least complacently accepted the designation.

Throughout the book, Boswell has a curious way of inserting quite unnecessary apologies for Johnson's "weaknesses," something which, if done deliberately, might seem akin to Swift's brilliant satiric technique of damnation by inadequate defence, as in the *Argument against the Abolishing of Christianity*. For instance, after several pages of praise of Johnson's achievement in his *Dictionary*, Boswell feels it necessary to add, "A few of his definitions must be admitted to be erroneous. . . . His definition of *Network* has often been quoted with sportive malignity. . . . His introducing his own opinions, and even prejudices . . . cannot be fully defended,"[26] though Boswell then enters a feeble attempt at a defence of them. In, of all places, his account of Johnson's deathbed, culminating in a fine panegyric on his character, Boswell feels it necessary to call attention to Johnson's "great fear of death," and attribute it to guilt over his "uncommonly strong and impetuous amorous inclinations" having "sometimes overcome" him when he was a young man just come to London. Boswell magnanimously forgives Johnson these slips—as well he might, given the results of Boswell's own amorous inclinations. But the passage makes even Boswell's editor, L. F. Powell, normally the mildest of commentators, lose his temper: "Boswell had no evidence for any irregularity on the part of Johnson. . . . No man's life has been subjected to so microscopic an investigation as his has. What is the result? Nothing but vague insinuations."[27]

There is a good deal more vague insinuation of one kind or another at other places in the *Life*. If this is Boswellian adulation and hero-worship, one is tempted to say, "Spare me from it." What we seem to have here is the well-known pattern of the disciple, the "candid friend," cutting down the Master, in the most reverent way of course, to a little closer to his own size, or even a little below it—as Bruno Bettelheim complained that Ernest Jones did in his monumental, seemingly laudatory biography of his teacher Freud.[28] To use psychiatric jargon, Johnson certainly served as a "father-figure" for Boswell, and the fate of father-figures at the hands of their children, however seemingly respectful, is often an ambiguous one. A full-dress psychoanalysis of Boswell still has to be done: there is no lack of material for it in the voluminous diaries in which he recorded the minutest details of his life and his psyche. But what is more distressing is how, for perhaps similar reasons, this construct has continued to appeal, over generations of readers, to the great "middlebrow" audience whose reactions and values Virginia Woolf described so well.[29] While paying lip-service to "highbrows" in art and literature, the middlebrow in fact likes nothing better than to be able to view them with condescension: "Admirable in their way, of course, but *we* superior solid citizens would not be guilty of such follies and eccentricities." In some ways, the Boswellian Johnson is one of the most successful hatchet jobs in the history of biography.

The great "P.R." man for Boswell's book was, of course, Macaulay. Innumerable printings of his 1831 review of J. W. Croker's edition of the *Life* appeared in the nineteenth and early twentieth centuries—sometimes under the title of *Macaulay's Life of Johnson*—and were distributed to all parts of the English-speaking world as school textbooks. Certainly it is effective prose, written by one of the masters of journalistic persuasion. The circumstances of the review were unusual. The editor of the *Life*, John Wilson Croker, a Tory politician, was a determined adversary of the Reform Bill of 1832, of which Macaulay was one of the most stalwart and voluble proponents. Macaulay made no secret that, for this and similar reasons, his chief motive in his blistering attack on the book was personal animosity against Croker, and much of that animosity rubbed off as well on both the biographer and the biographee. The result is a hilarious and brilliantly readable diatribe against an incompetent editor of a moronic biographer's treatment of a worthless or at best ludicrously overrated subject. Boswell stressed what he thought to be Johnson's "Toryism": "Tory" in the violent battles over the Reform Bill was the proverbial red rag to the Macaulayan bull, and anything to which the label Tory might be attached had to be anathematized, however inconsistent what Macaulay conceived as Toryism might be with Johnson's actual complex of attitudes to political and social issues of the previous century.[30]

But Macaulay manages to brush off Johnson's manifold and acute comments on politics by informing us that he was not really interested in politics at all; that he was a blind and bigoted Tory John Bull who detested foreigners and foreign travel; despised history and historians—Macaulay, of course, being a historian;[31] set himself up as a dictatorial literary critic, with only the most narrowly prejudiced tastes in literature; and, moreover, could only write a constipated sort of English prose to which Macaulay gives the name "Johnsonese." And yet, for all Johnson's worthlessness as a writer and thinker, and Boswell's distasteful personal idiosyncrasies, the book is nevertheless the greatest of biographies, to be classed, in its *genre*, along with the *Iliad* and *King Lear* in theirs.

How does this most startling of journalistic paradoxes come about? Because, Macaulay tells us, it portrays Johnson's peculiar physical habits so vividly:

> His figure,[32] his face, his scrofula, his St. Vitus's Dance, his rolling walk, his blinking eye, the outward signs which too clearly marked his approbation of his dinner, his inexhaustible appetite for fish-sauce and veal-pie with plums, his inextinguishable thirst for tea, his trick of touching the posts as he walked, his mysterious practice of treasuring up orange-peel, his morning slumbers, his midnight disputations, his contortions, his mutterings, his gruntings, his puffings . . .[33]

and so on. The appreciative enjoyment sounds rather like the fun English tourists used to get out of the antics of the unfortunate inmates of Bedlam ("his scrofula, his St. Vitus's dance"). Only Boswell's meticulous record of these bizarre personal traits will preserve Johnson's memory, after his incompetent *Dictionary*, his worthless edition of Shakespeare, his obtuse and narrowly prejudiced literary criticism, blindly bigoted writings on politics, and execrable prose style have long been forgotten. Macaulay sums it up:

> What a singular destiny has been that of this remarkable man! . . . The reputation of those writings which he probably expected to be immortal is every day fading; while those peculiarities of manner and that careless table-talk, the memory of which he probably thought would die with him, are likely to be remembered as long as the English language is spoken in any quarter of the globe.[34]

The prophecy has proved reasonably accurate for most of a century and a half.

## III. TOWARD A SOLUTION?

This then is the formidable obstacle, constructed by the firm of Boswell and Macaulay, that stands in the way of the serious modern biographer of Johnson. It is rather like one of those huge, and, to the minds of many modern critics, tasteless "Scottish baronial" castles erected by well-to-do industrial magnates in the Highlands in the nineteenth century, sometimes built from the stones of a splendid old ruined Gothic abbey. It is difficult to circumvent; it raises its spurious battlements so prominently over the neighboring landscape that it cannot be ignored; picture-postcards of it are wildly popular among casual tourists, simply because its shape now seems so amusingly bizarre. Will it ever be possible to demolish it and reconstruct it in the shape of the original?

Oddly, other seemingly solid Victorian constructs of monumental "official" biographies have later been subjected to radical change through the work of recent biographers possessing many more facts about their subjects, and a wider perspective, than their predecessors, with little resistance on the part of those brought up on the earlier versions. Macaulay himself was the subject of a superb biography published in 1876 by his nephew George Otto Trevelyan; yet John Clive in 1973 found much more to add which makes Macaulay a considerably more human figure, and since then the publication of a full edition of his letters has filled in the outlines even more accurately. The hagiographical first biography of Tennyson by his son, and the reticent life of Thomas Hardy, nominally by his wife but actually by himself, have been superseded, to no one's great regret, by fuller and franker ones. Even Queen Victoria, after the shock of Lytton Strachey's book, came to appear, to Strachey himself, and to later biographers such as Lady Longford, and to their readers, a far more likable, intelligent, and sympathetic person than the marmoreal figure of the nineteenth century.

The Boswell–Macaulay "Doctor Johnson," however, stands firm: the granite is solid and the cement that holds the stones together powerful. How could we possibly get along without it?

Perhaps, as I've suggested, we treasure the grotesque artifact of "the Great Cham" because we can feel superior and mildly patronizing to its oddities; and, of course, since we have Macaulay's assurance that his writings need not be taken seriously, we are spared the trouble of reading and digesting their formidable and weighty bulk. Besides, if we did read them, we might find some of his observations on the human condition profoundly disturbing to our preconceptions; it is much pleasanter, as well as easier, simply to let oneself be amused.

Moreover, there are many friends of the designers of our baronial castle who maintain that, as it stands, it is a great work of art, and should be preserved intact, at whatever cost to authenticity. The discovery a few decades ago of Boswell's great cache of manuscript journals has given rise to a flourishing Boswell industry, dedicated, naturally enough, to exalting the reputation of its hero.[35] There was once even a time when devoted Boswellians insisted that discrepancies between his original report of a conversation and what seems like a doctored version of it—the pun is unavoidable—in the printed *Life* are to be explained by the fact that Boswell had "total recall," and his additions to a dialogue a decade or two after it originally took place are the result of his truly phenomenal memory.[36]

More recent Boswellians seem to have abandoned this line of defence, and, confronted with overwhelming evidence of editing and suppression by Boswell, have retreated to the position, "Yes, much of Boswell's Johnson is fiction. But what stunning fiction, what a work of art it is!" One student has put it thus: "Of all the subjects of all biographies, Johnson virtually alone lives for us in a way comparable not to Napoleon or Lincoln or Frederick the Great, but to Hamlet or Sherlock Holmes."[37] Another has argued, "no matter how many new facts are brought to light, Samuel Johnson will always be somebody's hypothesis. And none has pleased so many, or is likely to please so long, as Boswell's."[38] One might also argue along these lines that, although historians have discovered many more facts about Richard III than Shakespeare knew (or, for artistic reasons, cared to make use of), no hypothesis about Richard has pleased so many, or is likely to please so long, as Shakespeare's. Does this fact justify us in substituting Shakespeare's Richard for the historian's? The question is of profound importance for the work of the biographer. Is it the biographer's duty merely to construct a pleasing and memorable work of art? Or does his duty also partake of that of the historian, to try to search out the truth and plead for its acceptance, however artistically or psychologically attractive falsehood is to his audience?

Johnson wrote much on the duty of the writer to tell the truth. Of his many such remarks that are recorded, perhaps the one most relevant here is his comment on Vergil's First and Tenth Eclogues, based, he thinks, on Vergil's own experience: "It may be observed that these two poems were produced by events that really happened; and may, therefore, be of use to prove that we can always feel more than we can imagine, and that the most artful fiction must give way to truth."[39] That judgment should be kept in mind if there is to be a contest between two schools of biographers, those whose chief aim is to construct a compelling work of art—but in that case, should they not frankly call their products novels, as with Irving Stone's *The Agony and the Ecstasy: The Life of Michelangelo*, which has certainly pleased many and, as best-sellers go, pleased long?—and those who consider themselves, like Johnson, when defending himself against the charge of saying things better left unsaid about Lyttelton and others in his *Lives of the Poets*, "as entrusted with a portion of the truth."[40] It might just be that the Samuel Johnson of reality, in so far as we can reconstruct him from the evidence at our disposal—actually a very large amount of evidence, much of it either unavailable to Boswell and Macaulay or ignored by them—could turn out to be a more rewarding work of art than Sherlock Holmes or the "Dr. Johnson" of the Boswell–Macaulay workshop.

Yet there has been, ever since Johnson's lifetime, though sometimes leading a furtive underground existence, another tradition of Johnsonian biography. Probably its most important element is the recognition that Johnson's chief claim to immortality is not his tics, his consumption of tea, his sometimes caustic put-downs of bores (in particular, of Boswell), but as one of the greatest of English writers and thinkers. This is not the place to go into detail on this matter. But every serious student familiar with recent English literary scholarship can pose against Macaulay's denigration such judgments as Yvor Winters's "A great critic is the rarest of all literary geniuses; perhaps the only critic in English who deserves that epithet is Samuel Johnson";[41] F. R. Leavis's "Johnson's criticism . . . is alive and life-giving. . . . When we read him we know, beyond question, that we have here a powerful and distinguished mind operating at first hand upon literature. This, we can say with emphatic conviction (the emphasis registering the rarity), really *is* criticism";[42] Edmund Wilson's "The *Lives of the Poets* and the preface and commentary on Shakespeare are among the most brilliant and most acute documents in the whole range of English criticism, and the products of a mind which, so far from being parochially local and hopelessly cramped by the taste of its age, saw literature in a long perspective and could respond to the humanity of Shakespeare as well as to the wit of Pope."[43] His *Dictionary* has been shown to be a great pioneering work of modern lexicography. The Shakespeare edition, especially in its copious and acute annotation, has at last been given the recognition and praise it deserves. His many political writings have been shown to be far from the "knee jerk" responses of a bigoted "Tory." Of his poetry, T. S. Eliot has written, "[*The Vanity of Human Wishes* and *London*] seem to me to be among the greatest verse Satires of the English or any other language. . . . I do not think that Juvenal, his model, is any better."[44] So much has been done, especially in recent decades, on the rehabilitation of Johnson "the great highbrow" that anyone ignorant of the thorough documentation of that process convicts himself of a failure to keep up with modern Johnson scholarship and disqualifies himself from passing any judgments on the question. And yet the process of demolition of the Macaulayan myth of Johnson's negligibility as a writer, even among academics familiar with the problem, goes on at an agonizingly slow pace.[45]

The second aspect of the "alternative tradition" is that serious attention has begun to be paid to the very many sources for biographical knowledge of Johnson about which Boswell and Macaulay were uninformed or misinformed. Of the bare facts of Johnson's outward life, we know, or are prepared to disclose, far more than Boswell did of the first fifty-four years of Johnson's life; indeed, we know more than Boswell tells us about the twenty-two years after he had met him. Many biographical works were written about Johnson before Boswell's *Life* appeared in 1791. An excellently edited collection of fourteen of these recently appeared;[46] some are brief and contain errors, as early accounts of writers just achieving fame tend to be, but the conscientious biographer cannot ignore them.

Besides these, there are two substantial volumes: one, Sir John Hawkins's *Life*, 1787, by someone who had known and worked with Johnson as a young man before Boswell was born, and, like Johnson, but unlike Boswell, resided in London; the other, Hester Thrale Piozzi's *Anecdotes of Johnson*, 1786 (chiefly deriving from her voluminous manuscript *Thraliana*, which first saw print in 1942). Mrs. Thrale spent many more days and hours in Johnson's company than did Boswell. For many years Johnson made the Thrales his second home; she was also his most frequent correspondent, and published the first substantial collection of his letters in 1788. The press campaign by Boswell and his friends Malone, Steevens, and Murphy to discredit the Hawkins and Piozzi volumes and so prepare the way for the reception of *the* Biography was one of the most determined and successful feats of "public relations" in the history of book publishing,[47] and its effects persisted, largely through Macaulay, until the middle of the twentieth century.

There was also astute little Fanny Burney, with whom and whose family Johnson had been as intimate as with the Thrales. Boswell approached her with a request that he might use the many Johnsonian entries in her diaries; Fanny mercilessly snubbed him and sent him away empty-handed. Not only does the modern biographer have the versions of these that were published in the mid-nineteenth century and later, but he can now see them in their original form before, in good nineteenth-century fashion, they were drastically edited and bowdlerized.[48] And, as Johnson became a "celebrity" after the much-publicized award of his government pension in 1762, dozens of others noted in their diaries or letters encounters and conversations with him. Boswell printed in full or substantial part in his *Life* some 200 of Johnson's letters from his last twenty-two years, and short excerpts from 75 others. We now have, from this period, around 1,300 of them.[49] Careful biographies of many of Johnson's most intimate acquaintances, Hawkesworth, Hawkins, Percy, Fanny and Charles Burney, Thomas Birch, have recently appeared or are on the point of appearing.

When Croker came in 1831 to edit Boswell's *Life*, he had what might seem to us the excellent idea of trying to incorporate in it excerpts from much of this non-Boswellian information, so as to produce something like a continuous narrative of Johnson's doings during at least the later part of his life. As we have seen, Macaulay tore it to pieces; having affirmed that Boswell was the first of biographers as decidedly as Shakespeare was the first of dramatists, he objected to having the pure text of the Master diluted by such inferior productions as those of Hawkins and Piozzi. So the Croker edition fell into immediate disrepute, in spite of the fact that Croker, in his useful annotations, had corrected such errors by Boswell as his statement—based on hearsay rather than the inspection of college records carried out by Croker—that Johnson had attended Oxford University for three years, from 1728 to 1731. He actually attended for thirteen months, leaving in December 1729—a not insignificant difference in the life of a young man, one might think. But such is Boswell's authority that, a century and a half after Croker corrected it, the mistaken "1731" still appears in encyclopedia entries about Johnson and even anthologies of Johnson's writings.

Perhaps it was Macaulay's merciless lashing of Croker that discouraged serious new work on Johnsonian biography for many decades.[50] Most of the short "lives" of Johnson published in the late nineteenth and early twentieth centuries—Leslie Stephen's, for instance—frankly profess to be little if anything more than abridgments of Boswell. To be sure, in 1887 G. B. Hill published his magnificent six-volume edition of the *Life* (together with Boswell's Hebrides *Journal* and Johnson's diary—unknown to Boswell—of his trip to Wales with the Thrales in 1774, an expedition as long as that to Scotland in the previous year). Hill sought, somewhat in the spirit of Croker, to make his a kind of encyclopedia of Johnsonian biography by incorporating in his many footnotes much of the material from Hawkins, Piozzi, Burney, and others, to help fill up the conspicuous gaps in Boswell's narrative. Hill's edition was given a superb revision, in the 1930's, by L. F. Powell, who added a very great deal of valuable information that had come to light since Hill's time. This edition of the *Life* is still the standard one for scholars. But the inconvenience of having to hunt for its valuable store of non-Boswellian material in the form of footnotes and appendices hitched, sometimes tenuously, to passages in the Boswellian text is frustrating to the reader and the researcher.

Meanwhile, work has begun in earnest in trying to fill the gaps and correct the errors in the early part of Boswell's *Life*. One of that rare and precious breed, the English amateur scholar, Aleyn Lyell Reade began to devote his weekends and vacations from his regular employment to his hobby of genealogical research. Beginning, as so many amateur genealogists do, with his own

family's "roots," he discovered connections between it and
Johnson's family. Thereupon he spent the next fifty years of his
life in the same way, rummaging tirelessly through church
registers, wills, and other archival material in the Midlands,
collecting "hard" information about Johnson's family and his
activities during the first forty years of his life. From time to time,
when he had collected enough material to fill a volume, he would
publish one—eventually there were twelve in all—at his own
expense;[51] publishers eager to profit from popular new recensions
of the "Dr Johnson" legend were not interested in such "primary
research," some of which might indeed have inflicted dents on the
cherished old image. So might some of the revelations in materials
about Johnson's early life in Boswell's possession, but omitted
from the *Life*—that about his projected second marriage, for
instance, or reports of his occasional use of profanity, or of a
spectacular drinking bout at Birmingham when he was a young
man. Such materials gradually surfaced during the 1940's and
beyond, and with the researches of Reade and other local
historians of the Midlands made it possible for James L. Clifford
to write the definitive biography of Johnson's earlier years, *Young
Sam Johnson*, 1955, which takes him up to the age of forty, in 1749.
For another twenty years Clifford worked at assembling material
for the biography of Johnson's "middle years," spent chiefly in
London between 1749 and 1762. Clifford often complained that
there had been no Reades to have spent a lifetime doing the minute
documentary research for this period, when Johnson was establishing himself as the best known English writer of his time. So
*Dictionary Johnson*, 1979, has fewer surprises than *Young Sam*.
Nevertheless, it contains new biographical information that the
next writer of a "popular" biography of Johnson is going to have
to incorporate.

I was invited to contribute this essay to a volume on the
problems of the modern literary biographer because I have
undertaken to write a third volume of Johnsonian biography, to
supplement Clifford's earlier two, dealing with his life between
1763 and his death in 1784. These are, of course, the "Boswell
years" in Johnson's life, and I have sometimes been reproached
for my temerity in entering into competition with the greatest of
biographers. But, for reasons described above, I don't feel as
overwhelmed by the thought as perhaps I should. The bulk of
Boswell's account of these twenty-two years, as we have seen,

consists of edited versions of his diary entries for the three hundred or so days he and Johnson were in each other's company in England (plus another hundred which they spent together in Scotland). My main job, then, simply described, will be to find out as much as I can of significance that happened to Johnson on the remaining 7,500 or so days during those years, and try to weave it into a connected narrative of the later years of Johnson's life—something, astonishingly perhaps, that has never been attempted before. One of my problems of course will be to keep Boswell in his place, which, on a mathematical basis, should be something like 400/8,000 or 5 percent—20 pages—of a 400-page book. I anticipate no great problem in filling the remaining 380 pages. Unlike Clifford in *Dictionary Johnson*, I shall have a wealth of material to draw on, from Fanny Burney, Mrs. Thrale, and dozens of other memoirists of the period, now that Johnson has become a celebrity. We have far more letters of and to Johnson than Boswell was aware existed. We know of the existence of far more of Johnson's writings than Boswell or Macaulay did, and we have excellent editions and critical studies of the most important of them.[52] In short, my problem will be not so much one of collection of material as selection.

It will be, I think, a sober and unexciting volume. In Clifford's earlier ones, the reader's attention was held by the suspense of the ups and downs in Johnson's career as he slowly and painfully made his way up from the status of obscure hack-writer to that of the most celebrated English literary figure of his time. After 1762 he had "made it," and the biographer will inevitably have to struggle against a certain sense of anticlimax. Startling new discoveries are unlikely to be forthcoming—probably no illegitimate daughter, as in the case of Wordsworth, though of course one never knows. Yet there will be matters Boswell knew nothing about. Even on the days in which he recorded his meetings with Johnson, Boswell was not omniscient about Johnson's activities. In 1768, for instance, Boswell, having come down from Edinburgh to London, learned that Johnson was not there but in Oxford. So Boswell pursued him there, and recorded a reasonably pleasant week-end; though it was then that Johnson snubbed him with "You *have* Lord Kames; keep him," and, when Boswell remarked fatuously, "When we see a very sensible dog, we know not what to think of him," retorted with "No, Sir; and when we see a very foolish fellow, we don't know what to think of *him*." Boswell found Johnson lodged at New Inn Hall, where he was the guest of Robert Chambers, "a lively, easy, agreeable Newcastle man," as Boswell somewhat condescendingly describes him, who had recently been appointed principal of the Hall, and, as well, Vinerian Professor of English Law, in succession to the famous Blackstone. Boswell supped with Johnson and Chambers on three evenings and took tea with them one morning, and reported the conversation on those occasions.[53] But what Johnson and Chambers were doing during the rest of the day, Boswell seems not to have known. We now know (as Mrs. Thrale did) that on this and many other occasions over several years Johnson was clandestinely helping Chambers to compose his course of Vinerian lectures, the successors to Blackstone's *Commentaries*. They are a significant contribution to the history of English legal education, and are in process of being edited for the first time by Thomas Curley, who has also investigated the long-lasting and important relationship between Johnson and Chambers, of which Boswell was ignorant.

If there were, as there has been for a number of recent writers of one-volume accounts of Johnson, little more than Boswell and a few well-known supplementary sources to draw on, it might be necessary for me to pad out my pages with speculative analyses of Johnson's psychological make-up—to "get *into* Johnson," as the phrase has it.[54] "A book that does not tell you *about* Johnson, but causes you *to become* Johnson," gushes Jessamyn West in the dust-cover blurb of a recent popular account. The experience of "becoming" Johnson, as depicted in some of these recent works, cannot, however, be a particularly pleasant one: in them we seem to be getting not so much either "the great Clubman" or "the great highbrow" as "Johnson, the great neurotic." He was neurotic, of course: but as Freud might have retorted, aren't we all? Perhaps, as our uneasy awareness of our own intellectual and aesthetic limitations has been assuaged by Macaulay's lurid account of Johnson's, so our own neuroses seem easier to bear when we are told of Johnson's massive ones. As Swift said, we

> hug ourselves, and reason thus,
> It is not yet so bad with us.[55]

Certainly, if one reads Johnson's annual New Year's Day reflections on his sins of omission of the previous year—a regular

exercise recommended for practising Christians over the centuries—one emerges with a very gloomy picture indeed of
Johnson's "inner life." And yet, if one takes the trouble to look at
the letters he sends to friends in the next few days, sometimes
describing a gay round of social events, or exchanging private
jokes with Mrs. Thrale or his old schoolfellow John Taylor, the
picture becomes more complex. At any rate, I think there is still
an important job for the biographer to do in gathering and
assembling the facts *about* Johnson's later life before we plunge
head-first into a full-dress psychoanalysis of him.

At the very least, the book will put "You *have* Lord Kames; keep
him" into its factual context, and that will be one small stone
dislodged from the Boswell–Macaulay citadel.

CHAPTER TWO

# John Butler Yeats

## WILLIAM M. MURPHY

*Prodigal Father: The Life of John Butler Yeats (1839–1922)* was published in June 1978. Two months earlier I had held in my hand the first copy off the press. That was twelve years and one month after I had set off for Dublin to begin full-time work on the book. When it began I was in my late forties; when the book appeared I was in my early sixties. The entire decade of my fifties was spent full time, except for teaching, in working on the book.

How the book came to be written may be a salutary story for my colleagues at colleges and universities throughout the country and to graduate students contemplating careers as scholars. Like many toilers in the academic vineyards I had from an early age hoped that I might some day produce a work worthy of the profession, that I might even, if I were lucky, "so leave something to aftertimes as they should not willingly let it die," to use Milton's phrase—a phrase he wrote twenty years before *Paradise Lost*, a work he embarked on "after long choosing and beginning late."

Every graduate student knows the history of Milton's most well-known work. I find that people think *Prodigal Father* was also the culmination of a life-long ambition, the bringing to fruition of a seedling planted in my salad days. The fact is much less grand than the assumption. Fate had far more to do with it than Intention, and Irony provided a stronger element than Resolution in its creation and completion. For when I began my professional career as a teacher and scholar, the name of William Butler Yeats was not one I thought I would ever be associated with. I had at that time only the sophomore's compelled knowledge of his work gained from the survey course in English literature. Like virtually every reader, I suppose, I admired "The Lake Isle of Innisfree," "The Second Coming," the "Byzantium" poems, and these were the works which, when it came my turn, I assigned to my students. But of Yeats's family, of his father, I knew little except that he had a father of great influence on him. While I dwelt in the cocoon of my ignorance, all over the world the study of William Butler Yeats was developing into an industry, one so extensive that today two thick volumes are required merely to list all the articles written by and about him, and every year the bulging file grows thicker. Among the army of bookworms moving across this vast and fruitful plain there was a hunger for new subjects relating to the great man, and one such subject was obviously John Butler Yeats. Scores of my colleagues would have sold their wives and children into slavery for a chance to work on him. I, who cared nothing about him at all, wound up as the executor of the project. This article is the story of how that came about.

While I don't wish to talk about *Prodigal Father* the book, anyone reading these lines ought to be told at least what it is about. John Butler Yeats was not only the father of the poet, but of the painter Jack Yeats and of two talented daughters, Elizabeth Corbet Yeats (known in the family as "Lollie," famous as the publisher of the Dun Emer and Cuala Presses), and Susan Mary Yeats (known as "Lily"). The four were often referred to as "Willie and Lily and Lollie and Jack," a grouping G. K. Chesterton called "a litany of Irish names endlessly repeated in a kind of Celtic magic." John Butler Yeats (or "JBY") was the son and grandson of clergymen in the Church of Ireland and heir to a small estate in County Kildare. He studied at Trinity College, Dublin, and at the King's Inns and was admitted to the Bar in Ireland in 1864. At the age of 24 he married Susan Pollexfen of Sligo and began the practice of law in Dublin.

JBY was a most unusual person, a Darwinist ahead of his time, a follower of Auguste Comte, a rationalist, but also a lover of literature and art and the possessor of a formidable talent as a painter. Unwilling to accept the principle of "getting on" pursued by most members of his society, believing only in the power and validity of Art, he abruptly gave up the practice of law at the beginning of a promising career, took himself and his family to London to try his hand as a painter, and so embarked on a lifetime career of conspicuous failure. He was a man of charm and brilliance, one of the world's great conversationalists and letter-writers, but he was utterly hopeless as a businessman, "head-strong but no manager," as Lily said of him. He found it difficult to finish a painting, always trying to improve on what he had done, scraping off his canvas work that other artists would have sold for hard cash, and then charging almost nothing when his conscience finally allowed him to let a painting escape from his hands. He was forced to mortgage his properties to keep body and soul—and his family—alive, but his impecuniousness did not prevent him from trying to fashion his oldest child, William Butler Yeats, into the perfect artist and thinker. Of course the son rebelled. The father eventually lost all his money, failing in both London and Dublin.

Then, aged and almost defeated but with the old spark still flickering, he journeyed to New York City at 68 to begin a new life. He came for a six-week visit and never went home. By the time he died, fourteen years later, he had left an indelible mark on a generation of American artists and writers and gained for himself an international reputation in two specialties, conversation and letter-writing, which he regarded as hardly avocations. He died as he had lived, poor and feckless. Although he painted hundreds of portraits, none of his works was exhibited after his death in any museum outside Dublin. His elder son's success as a poet and his younger son's as a painter buried the father's reputation, and he remained for most people a classic example of a "failure." It was the story of this life that I tried to tell in *Prodigal Father*.

But how did I, not a member of the Yeats establishment and having no desire to be one, come to be the biographer of the Ur-Yeats? If I indulge in some autobiography, be assured that everything I write will have a direct bearing on the history of *Prodigal Father*.

When I entered Harvard as a freshman many years ago, the first teacher I met, in my first class, was David Worcester, who, with a shiny new Ph.D., was teaching his first class, the required course in Freshman English, from which I had not been exempted. He was a magnificent writer of English prose and a formidably charming person as well. He liked the first paper I wrote for him and took me under his wing. It was he who instilled in me the notion that the production of at least one good book was necessary to the making of the compleat man. He himself wrote one slight but splendid book, *The Art of Satire*, in my judgment still the finest essay on the subject yet produced. In sophomore year he became my tutor. When I graduated from college it was through his influence that I got my first job, at the age of 22, teaching at

Harvard the same course in Freshman English that he had taught
me. Meanwhile he had become a good personal friend. When my
future wife and I met, she had to pass his inspection; when we
married we followed David's advice in the choice of an apartment;
when our first child was born we named him David. When David
Worcester joined the Navy to work in Anti-Submarine Warfare he
asked that I be commissioned in the Navy to assist him, and there
we produced together an anonymous book called *Aircraft Rockets in
Anti-Submarine Warfare*.

When the war ended he was called to Hamilton College as its
12th President. In the following year I was being considered for an
Assistant Professorship at Union College in Schenectady, New
York, and it was his letter of recommendation that got me the job.
Less than a year later he died of a brain tumor at the age of 39. The
loss to me was devastating, but it was also significant in a way I
could never have imagined at the time. David's friends established the David Worcester Memorial Library at Hamilton, and
the Trustees asked me to write a memorial essay to be placed with
the collection. I did so, and had my first experience in attempting
biography. I discovered that outside the many letters he and I
exchanged I could find little additional material, and what I
produced was not really a biography at all but a personal
recollection of his remarkable self disguised as an objective critical
review. At the suggestion of Professor Hyder Rollins, his teacher
and mine, I had the essay published privately for distribution to
his students and to those who had contributed to Hamilton
College in his memory.

In Schenectady, meanwhile, settling in as a young Assistant
Professor, I became active in local community affairs. Like David
Worcester and many others of that generation, Rooseveltian New
Dealers all, I had become interested in politics and hoped to join
in the founding of the Brave New World. In 1948 I was asked by
the local Democratic Party to run for Congress, not because I was
a potential winner but because the district was so heavily
Republican—only one Democrat had been elected since the Civil
War, and he for a single term—that none of the old-line
Democrats wanted to run. The idea appealed to me and I
accepted. Just as the fall campaign was beginning, a young fellow
just my age, newly appointed to the Union College faculty, asked
if he could manage my campaign, and I quickly said yes, having
myself no knowledge of campaigning. He, however, did. His name

was Sam Stratton. He had managed a congressional campaign before and was a gifted politician. I lost the election but ran ahead of the ticket. (Ten years later I managed Sam Stratton's campaign for the same office; he won and has been in Congress ever since.)

Despite my loss that year the Democrats picked up strength generally, and in the following year, led by Sam Stratton, they won a majority on the City Council, the first time that had happened in many decades. Naturally, many jobs became available to the winners—who soon discovered, in the bitter phrase of the politicians, that there are always more victors than there are spoils. Some of these, though carrying responsibility, had no salary attached. The local public housing authority had five members who served without pay but had full legal responsibility for managing, directing, and financing a number of housing projects with a budget of several million dollars a year. When one of its members died in 1951 I, as a member of the victorious group within the party, was appointed to take his place. My tenure there was brief, for in the next election the Republicans were swept back into power and I was replaced.

But while there I met the person who more than any other was responsible for the later course of my career. This was Jeanne Robert Foster, a woman then in her early seventies, though she pretended to be only sixty. She was in charge of tenant selection, probably chosen for the job because of her dignity, diplomacy, and sense of fairness. I discovered that she was eager to meet me; at every opportunity she would discuss the affairs of the authority with me and then veer off to other matters. Gradually the secret of her interest was unfolded. She had been born in a small upstate New York village in 1879 and grown into an astonishingly beautiful young lady, so beautiful that she attracted the attention of a man older than her father, who married her at 16 and carried her off to the big city. Jeanne Foster was as intelligent and sensitive as she was beautiful, and to her the first two qualities were more important than the third. After a brief career as an actress and a model in New York City, she extracted permission from her husband to continue an education scarcely begun in the Adirondacks, though she had become a schoolteacher there in her teens. Leaving him in New York, she took off for Boston and there spent the most impressionable years of her life studying in the extension divisions of the universities there.

The one institution that captured her soul was Harvard, where she studied and met and befriended many students, among them Frank Wilson Cheney Hersey, who later became an Instructor in Composition at his alma mater. Jeanne Foster never recovered from her sense of wonder and delight at her association with Harvard, and she developed an automatic attachment for anyone associated with it. Now, in the twilight of her life, to find as one of her employers an authentic Harvard man, one furthermore who had majored in English, had taken his doctorate there and had taught there, was to her a miraculous touch of Heaven. More and more she sought me out, and more and more, but slowly and carefully, she told me of the circumstances of her life, and particularly of her association with two people of whom up to that time I knew virtually nothing.

One was John Quinn, New York lawyer and art collector, the other John Butler Yeats, father of the poet, whom she had known during the last decade of his life. She had fallen in love with Quinn, and he with her, and she and he had taken care of the impecunious painter in his last illness. They had been the last people to see him the night before he died. When the Yeats family proved unable to have the body returned to Ireland for burial, she donated a grave from the Foster family plot in the Chestertown Rural Cemetery in the town where she grew up. There John Butler Yeats was buried in 1922 and lies buried today. Two years later John Quinn died, in his early fifties, but not before he and Jeanne Foster had travelled together to Europe many times, where she met his friends Augustus John, James Joyce, Ezra Pound, Ford Madox Ford, and many others. She herself published three volumes of poetry, served for many years as literary editor of the *Review of Reviews*, and was chosen by Ford as the American editor of the *Transatlantic Review*. After Quinn's death she gave up her life in New York and, quite broken by events, returned to the home in Schenectady which she had bought to house her impoverished family: father, mother, brother, and sisters—and husband, who had been an invalid for almost twenty years. She outlived them all.

Gradually she let me know these details of her life and told me of her own hopes and plans. She had for years been working on John Butler Yeats's letters to her and thought that some day she might write his biography. She had been given by Quinn during his lifetime hundreds of interesting letters, manuscripts, and miscellaneous documents of Irish people—Lady Gregory, W. B. Yeats,

Jack Yeats, George Russell (AE), Douglas Hyde, and others. Her home was a miniature museum. Hanging on the wall behind the antique piano was a portrait of herself by André Derain, on the opposite wall another by the Rumanian painter Costin Petrasco. In a dark corner hung a beautiful oil portrait of William Butler Yeats by his father, and near it an oil self-portrait by JBY, as well as half a dozen of his pencil sketches. In a bookcase were a dozen or so books published by the Dun Emer and Cuala Presses. Upstairs, I was told, was a file cabinet crammed with interesting stuff. At the end of my first visit Mrs. Foster presented me with a manila envelope. When I opened it at home I found an original handwritten letter of Lady Gregory's to William Butler Yeats. After that, whenever I visited her she insisted on presenting me with "a little gift," so that it became embarrassing for me to call on her and I made my visits as infrequent as possible.

As a modest and inadequate recompense for her generosity I gave her a copy of my monograph on David Worcester, but this only excited her further, for it spoke of Harvard, and when I happened to mention that I had taken a course in composition with her old friend Frank Hersey her ecstasy grew. Over the years, but very slowly, our relationship developed, but at no time during the first seven or eight years of our acquaintanceship did it occur to me, even remotely, that I might some day be involved with John Butler Yeats or with Anglo-Irish literature at all.

For all this time I was still involved in politics, helping Sam Stratton to be elected Mayor of Schenectady, serving on his unofficial cabinet after he took office, and later joining in his campaign for Congress. In 1956 I sought election again myself, this time to the State Senate, and in 1959 to the State Assembly. Both times I lost, and as a devout believer in democracy I felt that the voice of the people had spoken loud and clear. Gradually, after 1959, I began disentangling myself from politics, something not easy to do, for the associations made at party meetings, at clambakes, oxroasts, cornboils, and covered dish suppers are hard to break, and many of my liberal friends tried to make me feel that by removing myself from the infighting of elective politics I was somehow a traitor to the cause. It was not till about 1965 that I was able finally to clear myself of the last entanglement with politics.

During all these years, of course, I was still a college professor interested in scholarship. For many years I had thought it would be fascinating to trace the history of the anti-Stratfordian movement and to seek to discover the hidden sources of the dark underground stream from which it flowed. I began a study of what some call the "Anti-Stratfordian heresy"—the theory that William Shakespeare of Stratford-on-Avon did not write the plays attributed to him—and within a few years had completed a good deal of work on it when, one Sunday morning, settling in over the *New York Times Book Review*, I read a review there of the book I was planning to write.[1] Since the point the author made was the one I had reached myself—that anti-Stratfordianism is essentially a subject for specialists in mental disorders rather than for those in literature or history—I gave up my work on it.[2]

I then turned to a study of Delia Bacon, the New Haven spinster who was one of the first to suggest non-Shakespearean authorship. Miss Bacon had led an unhappy life, having been seduced by a young clergyman from the Yale Divinity School and then involved in a notorious ecclesiastical hearing into the young man's dereliction of ministerial behavior. The history of the seduction and trial is unbelievably gripping and is also thoroughly if not always openly documented. I found myself for the second time involved in the writing of a biography, but this time with far more information at my disposal than I had had with David Worcester's essay. I proceeded in a leisurely fashion, feeling no pressure to publish. I had always felt, and still feel, that one should not rush into print without having something to say. In the academic world such an attitude can be fatal. I had finished about 150 pages of typescript on the story of Delia Bacon and Alexander MacWhorter when, settling in one Sunday morning with the *New York Times*, I read a review of "my book," again, unhappily, written by someone else. That book,[3] like the one on the anti-Stratfordians, was so good that I felt it would be foolish to continue my work on the subject. By the time of this second frustration I was in my mid-forties and had achieved little —perhaps "nothing" is a better word—in either scholarship or politics.

All the time I had been seeing Mrs. Foster regularly if infrequently, and all the time she had been feeding me letters, documents, and books. She was a theosophist with a belief in the ultimate power of some mighty purpose at work in the universe. She placed great significance on matters, strange and unlikely, which I thought mere coincidences. While I regarded my essay on

David Worcester as an act of simple fealty to an old friend, she saw it as a thick thread in a patterned fabric. She liked the way the book was written and told me I should write more. One day I mentioned that I had to leave early to celebrate my older son's birthday. It was June 13, William Butler Yeats's birthday, and Mrs. Foster found the coincidence significant. Some time later she learned that my younger son had been born on the anniversary of William Butler Yeats's death. All these things together: Harvard, the book on David Worcester, the coincidence of the birthdays, convinced her that I was the one who should be writing the biography of John Butler Yeats. By the end of 1962 she had turned over to me more than one hundred original letters from John Butler Yeats to herself and John Quinn and a vast assortment of other Anglo-Irish material, and over the years, especially in the last year of her life, almost the entire bulk of her collection.

I was by no means prepared to work on John Butler Yeats; after looking carefully at his letters I was not sure I ever wanted to get involved. His handwriting, like that of his son the poet—fourteen of whose letters she had also given me—was virtually illegible. While one could, with difficulty, decipher it, it was not easy to make use of the original letters themselves because by the time one got to the end of a letter one had forgotten what came at the beginning. I did, however, make a faint stab at doing something. When I learned that JBY had known Van Wyck Brooks during his New York days I asked Brooks for his help and was rewarded with an invitation to lunch with him and his wife at his home in Connecticut. Like most of the distinguished people I was to consult later—including Padraic Colum, Conrad Aiken, and Ezra Pound—Brooks was extraordinarily kind and generous and even lent me for transcription the letters which John Butler Yeats had written to him.

I also wrote to Mrs. William Butler Yeats, who I knew was the owner of her husband's copyrights, asking if she could help me with my work on her father-in-law, but received no reply. I knew that without her help, which would require my visiting Ireland, the project would be impossible. Yet I was not eager to assume such a burden then as our children were in college or secondary school, and my wife and I felt we should be on hand to lend them support and not go haring off after doubtful quarry overseas.

What with one thing and another it was not until March of 1966, with our youngest child safely in college, that my wife and I took off from Logan Airport for Dublin and its uncertain treasures. We had no high hopes. We knew Yeats scholarship was a crowded arena. The lack of a response from Mrs. Yeats was not encouraging.

The day after we arrived in Dublin I sent a letter to Michael Yeats, the poet's son, whose address I got from the phone book, with no expectation that anything would come of it. To our surprise Mrs. Michael Yeats responded by telephone and invited us to lunch. I was to learn later that the Yeatses, despite the demands made on them, are extraordinarily patient and thoughtful and will do anything within reason to help Yeats scholars. We had a delightful time at lunch and—again the forces of Fate at work—my wife and Mrs. Yeats got along extremely well. My wife was a public-school teacher and administrator, Grainne Yeats a professional player of the Irish harp. Strong-willed and able, each found a kindred spirit in the other, and before long they were deep in discussions of the difficulties of women trying to make headway in a world of male folly.

Michael and I moved into the drawing room, beneath the enormous unfinished self-portrait in oils of JBY (which appears as the frontispiece in *Prodigal Father*), with the portrait of WBY by Mancini on the opposite wall and the original piece of lapis lazuli, on which WBY wrote his poem, on the mantelpiece. Briefly I told Michael who I was and what I wanted to do and presented him with a copy of the little book on David Worcester, my only passport to the nation of writers. I suggested that without access to family manuscripts my project wouldn't progress very far. He nodded but said little. We fell to talking about other things, and eventually the conversation turned to politics, which happened to be one of Michael Yeats's great interests. He was at the time a member of the Senate of the Republic of Ireland and would soon be President of that body. Later still he became the representative of his nation to the European Parliament. (Today he is Deputy Director of one of the main agencies of the Parliament.) He proved as interested in American politics as Irish. Before long John Butler Yeats was forgotten as we talked of the Fíanna Fáil and the Democrats, of taxes and campaigns. When, later in the afternoon, I suggested it was time we leave, the Yeatses proposed that we have tea instead, later that they give us a guided tour of the countryside around Dalkey. At seven o'clock I tried once again to engineer a departure; instead we were urged to stay for dinner. It was not until late that night that we returned to our hotel. From that long visit dates a friendship that continues to this day.

Next morning Michael telephoned his mother sometime between five minutes to eleven and eleven, the only time of day when she would receive calls, knowing one of her children would be on the other end. By that time in her life the poet's widow had become exhausted answering inquiries and had developed two ways of handling them. The first was to put a letter aside for three months and consider it answered. The second was even easier: she would simply not open the mail. When Michael presented his request she was aroused to interest because it was uncommon. Most people asked for material about William Butler Yeats; those interested in the father seldom bothered to find out whether she had documents that might relate to him. She would not go out of her way to look for material, she told Michael, but if she happened to run across something she would let him have it. Within a few days I was sitting in Michael's living room with a biscuit tin of about two hundred letters written from JBY to his son. We soon met Anne Yeats, Michael's sister, and she generously turned over to me for xeroxing all the letters in her possession from JBY to his brother Isaac and his son Jack. In the library of Trinity College, Dublin, I found the originals of JBY's letters to Clare Marsh and devoted about three weeks to transcribing them. When we returned to America in June we brought with us material amounting to about 100,000 words.

Among the most interesting of the manuscripts, on which I worked first, were the unpublished memoirs of John Butler Yeats, written in his crabbed, difficult handwriting in two notebooks. In letters to other people JBY had to write with some care, though they were still almost illegible; in the memoirs, which were for himself, he was responsible to nobody. For me the result was agony. It was a good day when I could transcribe more than a page or two, but eventually the secrets were revealed, and within a few months I felt that I had mastered the knack. The moment of revelation came when, after days of puzzling over a baffling passage, I saw at last that the words I was reading were: "surefooted as a chamois." After that, I thought, nothing could defeat me. Yet even now, seventeen years later, there are words here and there that I have not deciphered. Typing the pages out myself proved too slow. I developed a system of reading the material into a recording device and letting a stenographer do the typing from the playback.

Before many months had passed I realized that I had taken on a project that might be endless. Working in every spare minute every day I still after two years had barely made a dent in the vast body of material brought from Ireland. I knew that there were other collections of JBY's letters at Leeds, Reading, Northwestern, Yale and Princeton, and many letters in private hands as well, and that these would have to be consulted too. By the time I returned to Dublin in 1968 for a six-month stay I had accumulated enough material on the family of John Butler Yeats's wife, the Pollexfens, to be able to write an essay on them which I presented as a lecture at the Yeats International Summer School in Sligo. When we had arrived at the Dublin airport some weeks earlier Michael and Grainne Yeats were there to meet us, and we had hardly settled into their car when Michael handed me two thick manila envelopes extracted from his mother's supply. It was clear that no biography could be written until I was able to consult all the material in Mrs. Yeats's house on Palmerston Road. It was also clear that she would not yield to any kind of pressure to allow me to go scouring through the desks and closets and locked rooms of the house.

So it was arranged in a kind of conspiracy that after I had given my talk in Sligo, Michael would invite his mother to dinner some Sunday, as he did periodically, and that the Murphys would just happen to be there as guests. If all went well, perhaps I would be able to persuade her to dig out all the remaining JBY material and let me use it. But what if all didn't go well? What if she didn't take to me? What if we simply rubbed each other the wrong way—or, more to the point, what if I rubbed her the wrong way? What if the flow of material, instead of increasing, should be stopped? What would happen to the biography begun so uncertainly and so late? I worried through many a sleepless night.

My wife and I lived in a flat in Dublin, near Donnybrook, within walking distance of Trinity College. Every day when I wasn't working on the Pollexfen lecture I looked up material at the library there or at the King's Inns, where many legal records are kept and where, to my surprise, I learned much about the Pollexfen family that nobody had ever bothered looking into before. That led me to a conclusion about the Yeats industry: so many people were concerned with WBY's writings directly, with critical analyses of his poetry and prose, that factual information about him and his family had been systematically disregarded. Obvious sources of information, like the records in the King's Inns, had never been consulted by anyone. When I read my monograph that August, entitled simply "The Pollexfens," I discovered that nobody at the school devoted to W. B. Yeats had ever discussed the family of his mother. One student even went so far as to ask me before the lecture, "What *is* a Pollexfen?" as if it were a geological specimen or Celtic artifact. One effect of the lecture was that other Yeats scholars became aware of the work I was doing and offered assistance. The lecture was later published as *The Yeats Family and the Pollexfens of Sligo*;[4] and by the time the big book came out I had published several scholarly articles and edited one slim volume of JBY's letters, becoming quite without intention another member of that vast community of Yeats scholars.

Then, just a week after I had given the Sligo talk, while plans for the conspiratorial Sunday dinner were still going forward, Mrs. William Butler Yeats died, suddenly and unexpectedly. All had instantly changed, changed utterly. After her burial in Sligo, which my wife and I attended with the Yeats family, Michael and Anne began the melancholy and difficult task of cleaning out their mother's house. In one room which had been closed to them for years were all the trappings of W. B. Yeats's occult interests, the wand, the tables, the Tarot cards. In a pantry, stuck between two sheets of newspaper, was the famous painting by Jack Yeats, long believed lost, called "Memory Harbour." In the hallways were stacks of books, still in their postal wrappings, inscribed by their authors to Mrs. Yeats, who had never bothered to open them. There too were hundreds of unopened letters, some of them containing royalty checks from sales of WBY's books. There too, in rooms and closets and on shelves here and there, were the things I had been looking for—letters of JBY to his two daughters, their letters to him, early letters of WBY, Lily's and Lollie's diaries, a scrapbook kept by Lily in which was a treasury of information about the family. Almost every morning there would be a knock on the window of our ground-floor apartment on Appian Way, and there would be Michael and Anne with packages of goodies for us. For the rest of our stay in Ireland that fall we spent almost every day xeroxing the material that had suddenly descended on us like manna from heaven. For the first time I felt that there might be sufficient material for a biography.

Home again in Schenectady I worked at the lonely and demanding task, familiar to all biographers, of transcribing, typing, annotating, organizing and arranging. The long days stretch into weeks, depression settles in, one feels the task will never, *can* never, be finished. While working away at the letters the following spring I received a note from Michael Yeats informing me that a solicitor in Dublin had found in the basement of his office building—an eighteenth-century structure about to be torn down to make way for urban renewal—several boxes of legal documents bearing the name "J.B. Yeats." Did Michael want them, the solicitor asked, or should he destroy them? Needless to say, within a month all the boxes, with hundreds of original legal documents, some dating to the 1750's, were at my home in Schenectady. One of the Yeats daughters was visiting us at the time, and she and I spent several weeks xeroxing copies so the originals could be returned to Dublin. In those papers was the complete history of the estate which John Butler Yeats had inherited from his father. Seen by no one in seventy years, they proved of great value in the working out of many of the details of JBY's life. Yet if it had not been for "urban renewal," if the solicitor had not been a man with a sense of history, if Michael had been abroad and unable to give a timely response to the solicitor's request, the whole batch might have been thrown out. Of the whims of chance that colored the project throughout, this was certainly one of the happiest.

Some letters of JBY's had already been published, but these had been badly transcribed, and much of the interesting biographical material in them had been removed, so I was compelled to read every transcript carefully. In another way I was most fortunate: two American scholars, Glenn O'Malley and Donald Torchiana, were planning to edit the letters of John Butler Yeats to his American friends—those letters that were in American libraries and not in my possession or the Yeatses'—and asked whether they might see JBY's letters to Jeanne Foster. We struck a bargain. They agreed not to attempt a biography of JBY, I not to edit the letters to the American correspondents; they could have my letters for transcription and would in return send me typescripts of all the letters they were dealing with. That was for me a happy arrangement, for by the time they were finished they had transcribed four thick volumes, a total of about 250,000 words, about ten percent of my final total wordage. Also in 1968 the biography of John Quinn by Ben Reid was published. Quinn's relationship with JBY was explored in that book through the material available to Reid, and I was able to make good use of it. Without the work of those three scholars my book might have been many more years in the making.

At last the time had come for writing. Even though I knew revisions, corrections, and additions would have to be made continuously, by the fall of 1969 I felt I had to get down to the most difficult task of all. On October 22, 1969, three years and seven months after taking off from Boston for Dublin, I slipped a sheet of paper into the typewriter and took off. I did not plan to write anything like a finished copy, simply sentences and paragraphs that I hoped would provide some continuity, inserting in them the facts, the quotations, the conclusions that flowed from the material. The going was slow, for every time I gave a fact or quoted a passage I stopped in mid-sentence and, within brackets, gave the precise source. Although this tarnished the elegance of the prose in the first draft, it also meant that in later drafts I did not have to repeat the notes but could assign them numbers, which could be carried from draft to draft. Every day I tried to type at least a few pages. My record shows that I often typed only one, while on one day I did 23, a number not only never equalled but also never approached. Very often I wasn't able to get to the typewriter at all.

By the fall of 1971 I had enough of the first draft finished to ask for and receive a contract from a distinguished publishing house. It called for a manuscript of 200,000 words to be delivered by the end of 1972. So I was able to work without the nagging worry, so destructive to the writer's will, that his creation might lie *in utero* forever. Every day I continued transcribing letters and documents, a chore that altogether lasted five years, and reading and annotating them. At the end I had 40 volumes of 250 typewritten pages each, well over two million words. As I came upon pieces of information that belonged in the chapters I had already written I would add them to the original typescript. By the time I had finished the original draft it looked like a field of hen scratches. At last, at midnight on August 9, 1972, in my study at our summer home in Nova Scotia, the last words of the first draft were typed. It filled more than 2,800 pages and came to more than 700,000 words.

In the kitchen at the other end of the house sat the members of the family gathered for my daughter's wedding, to take place three days later. All seemed bright and shining that night. The end looked near. I had no way of knowing that the younger of my daughter's two sons would be three years old before the book finally appeared.

How does one go about writing a biography, even when one has all the facts, or thinks he has? That is a complex subject which I will touch on only briefly here. First, I felt that I had one distinct advantage in working on this particular subject. Not being a charter member of the League of Yeatsian Scholars, I could approach the subject freshly, with an open mind, with no axe to grind. I had no obligation to massage the egos of those who transferred their worship of W. B. Yeats's magnificent poetry to his not always magnificent personality or, conversely, to join the army of his haters. In a sense, the chains of ignorance had set me free.

And what of method? Once committed, I refrained from reading other biographies so that I would not be unduly influenced, so that the form of the book would shape itself, would flow out of the material. If I had to consult a book like Richard Ellmann's *James Joyce*, for example, I confined myself to pages the index told me might be fruitful. What resulted was not at all unorthodox, in fact a book written in straight chronological form. The most serious problem was that of inclusion. Should I do strictly the life of the painter and conversationalist and neglect the world around him? In the course of my work I had come upon material, all somehow related to JBY, that I knew would be of enormous value to other students of Anglo-Irish literature and was fairly sure would never be known if I didn't reveal it—material on Edward Dowden, Edwin Ellis, J. T. Nettleship, John Todhunter; on John Sloan, Van Wyck Brooks, Conrad Aiken, Rockwell Kent, and John Quinn; on the history of the Dun Emer and Cuala Presses; on the Contemporary Club and the Abbey Theatre; on the family history of the Yeatses and the Pollexfens; on the Kildare properties, on the tensions in the Yeats household between the half of the family that was genial and the half that was crusty, on the pathetic and almost tragic relationship between the two daughters, Lily and Lollie, almost a separate story in itself.

I held in my control a rich mine of information about the early boyhood of William Butler Yeats, about how he was viewed by

outsiders and members of his family, about his role in the Abbey
Theatre and his relationships with Lady Gregory and Annie
Horniman. I had material showing a consistent Anglo-Irish
Protestant (or at the very least a non-Catholic) attitude toward
Irish nationalism. I felt that it would be a dereliction of my
scholarly duty not to make use of this material, all connected in
some way with John Butler Yeats, and so provide my colleagues
with a kind of source-book, bristling with useful footnotes. That,
rather than a simple biography, is what it finally became,
although the central pillar of the book was indeed the story of a
man's life.

And how should one handle such a life, how even justify a
biography at all? Here was a man who could not make money or
hold on to it, could not sell his paintings and seldom was able to
exhibit them, never worked from nine to five, troubled his family,
died broke. How can such a life, or the consideration of it, have
value? Marxists would deplore it, Ronald Reagan would frown
upon it, and yet it was appealing, at least to me. The theme I
found in it is expressed in the very first sentence I wrote, in 1969
on a bus from Dublin to Dalkey, a sentence that appears as the
very last one in the main text of the book: "How many 'successful'
men have left a legacy as great?" JBY's life, especially in his New
York years, was lived on the assumption that, although virtually
penniless, he had all the money he needed and could do as he
pleased. I admired a man who knew how to create for himself an
imaginary but perfect world and have the determination and
courage to take himself there, even if with many falterings and
uncertainties along the way.

I also, and perhaps principally, wanted to write a book that
could be easily read, no matter whether it was classified as
biography, history or criticism. I tried to follow the advice I had
been drilling into my students for almost forty years—with no
noticeable success—that the job of a writer is to make the work of
the reader easy. I wanted to write with accuracy, clarity, and
grace, and particularly to avoid the pretentious jargon of the
critical journals, which I loathe. On the whole I hoped, again in
Milton's phrase, that I might "fit audience find, though few." My
son Christopher, who is studying to be a wit, has remarked that no
matter what might be said of the first half of that aspiration I had
certainly achieved the second.

The comfort of having a contract was mitigated by its terms, which called for a maximum of 200,000 words, though I believed there was a verbal understanding that footnotes were not included in the total. The second draft, finished a year after the first, still came to more than 425,000 words, though I had never intended it to be final. I am not comfortable with a typewriter. Like David Worcester, I was born into a world in which most self-respecting writers used pen and ink. I took the second draft and, trying to polish the sentences one by one, wrote out a complete third draft in ink on sheets of yellow lined paper. It came to about 350,000 words. By the end of May 1975, I had reduced the text to 275,000 words, plus notes, had it typed, and hopefully shipped it off to my publisher.

After a summer of waiting I discovered that he was now my former publisher. The book was far too long, he said, and could never be reduced to an acceptable length. I protested, offering to cut drastically, even sinfully. I had learned from my earlier career an old saw of the politicians: "To survive, there are times when you must rise above principle." All was in vain, and I was left, after almost ten years' work, with a completed but rejected manuscript. The rejection was bad enough. Worse was my suspicion that the manuscript was no good, that the publishers had discovered the secret I had been trying to conceal for years, that I really did not know how to write.

Fortunately, the Cornell University Press came to the rescue, and although there was another delay of more than a year, the book, trimmed to the 225,000 words I had originally assumed as an irreducible minimum, with the added hundred pages of notes (2,522 of them) was published in June of 1978. The next year a second printing was run off and a paperback edition printed. Cornell did a splendid job with the book, even allowing me all the illustrations I asked for, placed precisely where I wanted them throughout the book, and agreeing to a color frontispiece of the JBY unfinished self-portrait. It now appears that the first publisher's rejection was one of the luckiest things that ever happened to me.

That brings us to the question of how the book came to be done anyhow—what the real reasons were as opposed to the apparent ones I have mentioned. J. Paul Getty had a simple prescription for success: "Rise early, work late, strike oil." I have often felt that my relationship with *Prodigal Father* is fully explained by his epigram. As I reflect on the past I see so many examples of apparently haphazard events developing into parts of a fixed plan that I begin to wonder whether Jeanne Foster was right when she thought I was fated to write the life of JBY.

In Dublin in 1966 I met a number of people directly or indirectly, who were of enormous importance to me, through the kindness of a Dublin novelist and journalist, Terence De Vere White. And how did I meet him? Through an introduction provided by David Worcester's widow. In Dublin that year an American professor, a woman, was visiting an old friend of hers in the hotel in which we were staying. Happening somehow to hear that my wife had gone to Wellesley, the professor, also a Wellesley graduate, asked to meet her. When we joined her in the lobby she introduced us to her friend, Olive Purser, niece of the Irish painter Sarah Purser and the young English teacher who had taken Edward Dowden's place at Trinity College in 1913 when he became ill. When Miss Purser discovered what I was doing she told me she had something that might be of value to me. The next evening she presented me with a copy of a letter which Lily Yeats had sent to Olive's uncle, Louis Purser. That letter contained the key that unlocked Lollie Yeats's private life. Without it the book would have been quite different. It was a most important document, yet I could not have searched for it.

When working on the New York letters I came across the name of Maunsell Crosby, with whom and with whose wife JBY had had some dealings. I wanted to know more about him but could learn little. One summer in Nova Scotia I had promised my daughter that I would go bird-watching with her on Labor Day on Seal Island, a lonely place about fifteen miles off the coast. When the day came I tried to beg off, explaining that I was far behind schedule. My daughter insisted that I keep my promise, so reluctantly I did. On the boat I met a bird-watcher named, appropriately, David Finch, who was revising *The Birds of Dutchess County*, which had been edited in the early 1920's by Maunsell Crosby, about whose life he told me.

After leaving Dublin in 1966 my wife and I headed for Italy to see Ezra Pound, who had known John Butler Yeats in New York in 1910 and had edited a selection of his letters. Jeanne Foster, a friend of Pound's, had written to introduce me. When we arrived in Rapallo we found that Pound was not at home, and there seemed to be a conspiracy of silence among the villagers, who would tell us nothing about him. We took a room at the Albergo

Rapallo, where we knew the Pounds had once stayed, and hoped something would happen. Next door to us was an old lady in frail health. We got to know her and learned she had difficulties with such chores as shopping and doing her laundry, so while we were there we did these things for her. Just as we were about to leave Rapallo, defeated, she invited us to a little gathering on her piazza to meet some friends of hers, one of whom was a woman physician, Dr. Bacigalupi, who thanked us for the care we had taken of her friend and then just happened to ask us what we were doing in Rapallo. "Trying to meet Ezra Pound," I told her, "but not having much luck." "But I know Mr. Pound well," she replied, "and because you were so good to my friend I will tell you how to find him." Pound had gone to Venice unexpectedly a few days before to see his dentist and was still there. Forty-eight hours later we were talking to Pound in the living room of his house in Venice.

Was it all planned by some mysterious force in which I do not believe? When Mrs. Foster died in September 1970, I was named executor of her Estate and was in charge of the funeral arrangements. She died at ten minutes after eleven on a Tuesday night. The burial was to be at the Chestertown Rural Cemetery next to the grave of John Butler Yeats—which, incidentally, she had also deeded to me some years before, so I can claim what may be the unique distinction of being the only biographer who owns the corpse of his subject. I set the time at eleven o'clock Saturday morning. I asked Ben Reid, Quinn's biographer, to be a pallbearer, and even though he lived a couple of hundred miles away he agreed. On the Saturday morning we were all gathered at the graveside, the friends, the funeral directors, who had driven the hearse eighty miles from Schenectady, the pallbearers—all but Ben Reid. At eleven the mortuary scientists looked at me anxiously. "Could we wait a few minutes?" I asked. At five minutes after they began glancing at their watches. At last I said, "O.K., let's proceed. It looks as if Professor Reid isn't coming." The five remaining pallbearers moved to the hearse and began carrying the coffin to the grave. There was a squeal of brakes, and into the cemetery drove Ben Reid, just in time to take his handle on the coffin. We laid Jeanne Foster to rest at ten minutes after eleven.

A few weeks later, going through her effects, I found the handbook of the Theosophical Society. In that book I came upon something that sent a chill down my spine. According to the rules laid down there, a body must not be buried until at least 84 hours after death, for it takes that long for the soul to escape the body fully. Jeanne Foster had died at 11:10 Tuesday night; 11:10 Saturday morning was exactly 84 hours later. If Ben Reid had arrived on time her soul might still be in the coffin rather than wherever it is now. Ben later explained that a big tractor-trailer must have blocked his view of the exit sign at Chestertown, and he had driven about twenty miles too far before turning back, arriving just properly late. I have friends who believe somebody put the truck there.

Perhaps the oddest coincidence is that Jeanne Foster should have been so fond of Harvard and Harvard men. When I drifted into her life I just happened to have the qualifications she was looking for—augmented by my sons' birthdays and the book on David Worcester. All these things might have been explained as part of a predictable pattern if I had come upon my Harvard connections legitimately, as a Cabot or a Lowell or a Conant. I must inform those not familiar with the élite Eastern Establishment that Harvard has not historically been the Murphy family college. At that time the Murphys had no family college at all. I attended a public high school in Queens, a borough of New York City. Although my parents were determined that I should some day go to college, they knew little about higher education, as no other member of my family had ever graduated even from high school. When the time came for me to go to college the country was in the depths of the depression. My parents could not afford to send me away, so, like many another ambitious New Yorker, I applied for and was accepted by the College of the City of New York, and was fully prepared to go there.

At the eleventh hour, my mother remembered reading in the newspaper a few months before I was born that a man named Murphy had left a sizeable bequest to Harvard for the education of men named Murphy. I thought my mother was crazy and told her so. She persisted, and her nagging so annoyed me that I wrote, in my 17-year-old sophistication, to "The University of Harvard, Harvard, Massachusetts." A few days later I received a reply: yes, there was a Murphy scholarship, an application was enclosed, and if I filled it out it would be considered. Five months later I met David Worcester, and altogether, counting the three years that I spent in the Navy, it was twelve years before I left Harvard, having been student, teacher, and administrator, and having received there three degrees. CCNY was then, and for all I know still is, just as good a college as Harvard, and I am sure the education I would have received there would have qualified me just as well to write the biography of John Butler Yeats. But somehow I do not think CCNY would have rung quite the same bells in Jeanne Foster.

Did the book come to be written by accident, as I maintain, or was it the mysterious working of some Higher Force? When one thinks of the obstacles that stood in the path of its completion, the mind boggles. What if I had been elected to Congress and had never had to take the position with the Housing Authority? What if my sons had not had significant birthdays? What if David Worcester had not died and I had not written a book about him? What if Mrs. William Butler Yeats had lived to have Sunday dinner with me and had not liked me? What if the generous Mr. Murphy had misdirected his bounty and I had been forced to go to Yale? John Butler Yeats believed that the stars directed everything that happened, and so did Jeanne Foster. If they were right, why did JBY's biography fall on the shoulders of a skeptic like me? I leave the resolution of such philosophical questions to my betters. I know only that I am grateful to those perceptive citizens of upstate New York who chose to exclude me from their halls of government. The years of late nights working over illegible manuscripts, the frustrations and headaches from misplaced footnotes, the long years of wondering whether anyone would finally read what I had written—all these may have been unpleasant, but they ended in something which, I hope, aftertimes will not willingly let die—and they sure beat the daylights out of clambakes, oxroasts, and covered dish suppers.

CHAPTER THREE

# Wilfrid Scawen Blunt

## ELIZABETH LONGFORD

A literary biography may be either commissioned or spontaneous. This distinction of course applies to all biographies—indeed to all non-fiction—though it is liable to have special force in regard to literary biography. Writers are articulate and tend to leave eloquent source material which the biographer will be eager to use. If the book is commissioned he can almost certainly get hold of it.

No doubt many biographers are lucky enough to acquire all the vital material from the family, as I was with *Queen Victoria* and *Wellington*, without being actually commissioned. But in the case of Wilfrid Scawen Blunt no uncommissioned biography could have been of value, at least in the 1970's. The reason was simple. In 1972, fifty years after Blunt's death, his "Secret Diaries" were scheduled to be opened. Until that date they had been hidden in tin boxes at the Fitzwilliam Museum, Cambridge, under the guardianship of an academic syndicate. It was known that they contained a juicy collection of skeletons and scandals. Therefore it would have seemed hardly worth memorialising Blunt until after "Open Day"; and in fact only three writers tackled Blunt's life before that date, apart from Desmond MacCarthy's brilliant chapter in his literary *Portraits* (I) and Shane Leslie's stimulating if inaccurate sketch in his *Long Shadows*. The first was Blunt himself, who had published *My Diaries* before his death. The second was Edith Finch, fourth wife of Earl (Bertrand) Russell, who brought out a straightforward life of Blunt in 1950 based on his poetry and politics but perforce ignoring his private affairs. Third came a memoir in 1961 by his grandson Anthony 4th Earl of Lytton, which was richer in personal content than anything before but dependent on family memories and letters rather than on the documents still locked up at Cambridge.

As a result of the fifty-year ban on Blunt's "Secret Diaries", Blunt himself became a shadowy figure. His *Poetical Works* and *My Diaries* were out of print and by the seventies he was known mainly to the verse anthologists or to historians in search of pungent quotation against the British Empire.

At last came 1972. The generation of academics who now *reopened* the tin boxes were a great deal less shockable than those who had taken a glance at their contents in 1952 and hastily sealed them up again. (Blunt had hesitated between a thirty-year and fifty-year ban on his explosive legacy. The syndicate chose fifty years.) Nevertheless there were enough devastating rumours going around—was Lady Churchill, for instance, Blunt's natural daughter?—to make the syndicate cautious. Their official biographer must be both experienced and discreet. I do not know how much to feel complimented by their choice falling on me. But I am infinitely thankful.

I well remember the day on which the commission was offered. The advisory board of the Victoria and Albert Museum, of which I was a member, had met at lunch in the Garrick Club to thank our retiring Director Sir John Pope-Hennessy for his dazzling services. After the lunch, Professor Michael Jaffé, a fellow-member of the board and director of the Fitzwilliam Museum whom I greatly liked and admired, said to me, "What would you think of writing the official biography of Wilfrid Scawen Blunt?"

My first reaction was simmering excitement. I already knew something of Blunt's character from having read Lord Lytton's *Memoir* at the time of publication. I was also well-up in the Byron story—Blunt had married Lord Byron's granddaughter Lady Annabella King-Noel—from having written a short life of the poet in a series on Great Men, initiated in the United States by Little Brown. Most important, I had studied Blunt's *My Diaries* when writing on Queen Victoria in the early 1960's. At that time Blunt had stood out for me as a refreshing "baddie" among so many "goodies" like the Queen herself and her Consort. The passages in *My Diaries* that I particularly remembered were those pouring scorn on Queen Victoria's imperial ambitions.

My first move was to consult my own family. Hitherto I had always written on "great" men or women—Victoria, Wellington, Churchill, Byron. W. S. Blunt was a man of genius without being "great" or indeed known at all to perhaps the majority of potential readers. My family were enthusiastic. "If you want a change, you have reached the stage when you have every right to seize this opportunity." (I was seventy.)

Not so all my good friends in publishing. One of them expected "Wilfrid Blunt" to turn out to be the distinguished contemporary writer and director of the G. F. Watts Museum. When he heard that my Wilfrid Blunt was not at all the same person (though a distant cousin after whom the younger Wilfrid was named) he was horrified. He felt it was not my line. "Leave that subject to an aspiring young don." I pursued it nonetheless and was generously supported not only by my British publisher but also by Knopf in America who, by a most happy coincidence, had published W. S. Blunt's *Poetical Works* and *My Diaries* in the 1920's. I had some delightful letters from Alfred A. Knopf himself, by then in his nineties.

Before exploring the problems and challenges of this literary biography it is necessary to summarise Blunt's unfamiliar life and work.

Wilfrid Scawen Blunt was born into the class of landed gentry in 1840, his father being the squire of Crabbet near Horsham in Sussex. His mother came of the same prosperous class and furthermore was closely related to the notable Sussex family of Wyndham at Petworth House. Wilfrid felt a lifelong pride in his strong, centuries-old Sussex ties.

Misfortune, however, followed swiftly on this auspicious start. His father died of a chill caught out cub-hunting four years after his marriage; Blunt's widowed mother leased Crabbet, travelled abroad and entered the Roman Catholic Church with her three young children; then died of consumption in Wilfrid's presence when he was fourteen. His saintly brother Francis and sister Alice were also to die under Wilfrid's eyes of the same horrible disease, while he himself lost a lung. These experiences helped to undermine his faith, which his early years in the Diplomatic Service among clever European sceptics did nothing to sustain. One of his finest sonnets questioned Death and Time but found no answer, certainly not a Christian one. He called it "The Two Highwaymen" and in it he asked:

What have we done to thee, thou monstrous Time?
What have we done to Death that we must die?

Meanwhile his friends and relatives had resolved to deflect his increasingly reckless hedonism from a maze of *liaisons dangereuses* into an advantageous marriage. Blunt's union with Annabella, daughter of Ada Countess of Lovelace, Byron's only child, he called "a practical romance". This was a euphemism for a marriage of convenience; and after the manner of such marriages it ended in tragedy. But not before Wilfrid and his wife Anne, as he always called Annabella, had achieved much through their partnership.

Primarily it produced a period of important travel and exploration in Arabia, followed by the founding of the Crabbet Arabian Stud in Sussex. Anne's money enabled Wilfrid to resign from the Diplomatic Service and his own magnificent skills turned him into a striking sportsman. Having no profession and plenty of spare time, he could not only become a full-time writer and poet but also, thanks to his dark poetic beauty, a notorious lover.

In 1872 Anne gave birth to their only surviving child, Judith, who married Neville Lytton. Judith resembled her father in many things: beauty, the writing of poetry, excesses of temperament, a failed marriage. But she never lost her Catholic faith. Nor did she share her father's political ideals and ambitions.

Through his Middle-Eastern travels, Wilfrid came to espouse Egyptian nationalism as a total and fierce commitment. But after being banned by the British government from his stud and estate outside Cairo, he transferred his support to nationalist India (mainly the Islamic peoples) and then to Ireland. Standing twice for Parliament, in 1885 as a "Tory Democrat" and in 1887 as "Anti-Coercion", he lost both contests but by only a few hundred votes. He was proud to be the first Englishman to suffer imprisonment for Ireland. He had called a political meeting to oppose Irish evictions in defiance of a government ban.

His second failure to enter Parliament may have rightly convinced him that he was too much of an individualist to work through any institution. But being again without disciplined occupation, he allowed his passions to run riot, seducing not only his beautiful cousin Lady Elcho (née Wyndham) but also the wife of his most revered friend, William Morris the socialist poet, and attempting to seduce the daughter of his earliest and best friend, Lord Lytton.

The family indignation over the Elcho affair contributed to the break-up of his élitist tennis-cum-poetry houseparties in Sussex, known as the Crabbet Club. They had been graced in the early nineties by members of the "Souls" coterie as well as by Oscar Wilde and Lord Alfred ("Bosie") Douglas. Blunt eventually gave Crabbet to his daughter Judith.

All this notwithstanding, he became a famous guru when disabled and Sussex-bound from 1910 onwards by prostate trouble. Rather than suffer the surgeon's knife (influenced by and influencing Bernard Shaw's *The Doctor's Dilemma*) he endured twelve years of intermittent agony. Among his famous visitors and admirers were the poets Yeats and Pound, the statesman Winston Churchill, the Irish patriots Lady Gregory and Sir Roger Casement and, after the Great War had been fought and won, contrary to Blunt's hopes, the Arabists T. E. Lawrence and St. John Philby. To Blunt it was something of a consolation that the Great War would probably end the British Empire. The Boer War had been of interest to him only in so far as it might benefit the blacks. (In fact it led to the further erosion of their status in South Africa.)

Having been divorced by Anne and denounced by Judith he died peacefully in 1922 at Newbuildings, his equally loved secondary Sussex home. A pretty and adoring young "niece", Dorothy Carleton, had looked after him since 1906, his mistress until his health failed. He was received back into the Catholic Church in his last year when "The Two Highwaymen", Death and Time, could no longer be resisted. It might be truer to say, however, that Blunt himself had been the highwayman and now was to live his last months within the law.

His renewed Catholicism did not prevent him from being buried in his own woods instead of a church. His body was wrapped in the blue and white oriental carpet upon which he had made love to Mary Elcho, and his tomb was blessed by Father Vincent McNabb, a Dominican. Truly his life had been "a checker-work of good and bad", as he himself wrote. Perhaps after all he preferred things checkered to those of one colour, however lovely. On his tombstone was graven the sestet from one of his own sonnets:

> Dear checker-work of woods, the Sussex Weald!
> If a name thrills me yet of things of earth,
> That name is thine. How often have I fled
> To thy deep hedgerows and embraced each field,

Each lag, each pasture,—fields which gave me birth
And saw my youth, and which must hold me dead.


To be invited to write a literary biography such as Blunt's was a
windfall indeed. I had all the advantages of being commissioned
plus others that were unexpected. I saw the empty tin boxes at the
Fitzwilliam Museum—suitably 'checkered", one being black and
the other white—and all the various versions of the "Secret
Diaries" and letters that had for so long lain inside them and were
now still being catalogued. I discussed Blunt's life closely at every
stage with Paul Woudhuysen the archivist, and was allowed to
take bundles of "secrets" from Cambridge to my home in Sussex
for study and transcription, an inestimable boon without which I
could not have accomplished the research.

My uncovenanted advantages were the result of the generosity
of Blunt's descendants. It turned out that Blunt's grandson,
Anthony Lytton, possessed a large collection of correspondence
that had already been sorted and filed by Peggy Aldridge, a family
friend and connection of the Lovelaces. Not only these letters but
Anthony's personal recollections were at my disposal. Blunt's
three grandchildren by Judith and Neville Lytton—Anthony,
Anne and Winifred—were all prepared to share with me vivid
memories of the sage of Newbuildings. Anthony, who lived with
his family at Keeper Knights Cottage on the far side of the lake
from Crabbet, produced, for instance, letters and documents from
India all proving how much W.S.B. had meant to the national
movement. Lady Anne Lytton was occupying Newbuildings itself
(bequeathed to her by the "niece" Dorothy Carleton) and she not
only told me how much she missed her grandfather during
divisive family rows, but also invited me to stay at Newbuildings.

I have always found it vital to see with my own eyes the homes
and places visited by my subjects—especially if they are writers or
poets. It goes without saying that it was extremely stimulating to
work at Apsley House and Stratfield Saye (Wellington's town and
country houses) when researching his life. But to stay at Stratfield
Saye in particular, though highly enjoyable, was not absolutely
essential. Wellington was not "visual" in the sense of liking to
write descriptive passages about people and places. He was
"cerebral"—though none had a better eye for a battlefield.

Both Byron and Blunt his grandson-in-law, on the contrary,

saw with their pens. It was vital for me to have seen Byron's Greece, his Turkey, Belgium and Rhineland, his Nottingham, Newstead Abbey, Trinity College, apartment in Albany—all of which I eventually covered. Thanks to the Lyttons at home and advice during travels abroad, there was little of Blunt's life that was not in the end "visible" to me.

At Newbuildings I met the descendants of Blunt's pure-bred Arab horses and saw at once why their beauty had had to be celebrated so often in his verse. I slept in the narrow Spanish double bed that Blunt had bought in Madeira and in which his son Berkeley Sumner had been conceived—not to mention other natural children who did not survive. Because of the doings in that bed over the years, Judith refused to sleep in it, saying that it was haunted. But as an objective biographer I dared not harbour such perceptions and in fact slept in it very well.

William Morris's refectory table in the hall and Burne-Jones's tapestries on the wall showed me how close Blunt was to the Pre-Raphaelites. (The women he loved most profoundly all had a Pre-Raphaelite cast of countenance.) The innumerable oriental trophies everywhere told me of his determined effort to bring the East—its customs and beliefs as well as artefacts—home to Sussex. I could see him in his flowing white Arab robes madly driving his Arab four-in-hand along the narrow Sussex lanes, to the imminent danger of other road-users, especially the rare unwelcome motorcar. I saw at Newbuildings his self-portrait painted when he was fourteen, and the recumbent statue of his dead brother Francis in nearby Crawley Monastery, carved by him at thirty-one. W.S.B., I saw, was indeed a man for all activities.

I saw something of Blunt's India, realising how innocent was his wife Anne in not recognising the innumerable Hindu *lingams* for the phallic symbols they were. But Blunt was no sightseer, as I also realised when I saw the Monkey Temple of Benares and Humayum's tomb, and noted that Blunt, unlike Anne, had not found them diary-worthy. For he was deeply absorbed in his political period, enunciating such slogans for the Indian national- ists as, "*All* nations are fit for self-government and few more so than the Indians." Or being ready with prompt retorts to British imperialists, as when the white Vice-Chancellor of Bombay University regretted that the Muslims' "religious fanaticism" would always fatally impede their worldly progress—"You might as well run a race with a knapsack on your back", concluded the Vice-Chancellor. To which Blunt replied: "Perhaps if the race was a long one and the knapsack full of bread you might not find it an encumbrance."

But the "visual" aspect of Blunt's life which I felt it most necessary of all to discover was his beloved Egyptian estate called after the Islamic saint, Sheykh Obeyd. Without Anthony Lytton's directions I could never have found it, and even so it was touch and go, Cairo having grown far into Blunt's beloved desert. No taxi-driver seemed to have heard of it, and I was about to return dispirited to Cairo when I saw a large board advertising "Property Development" above a long stone wall. In the wall I recognised an ornate gateway—the gate of Sheykh Obeyd.

Blunt's delightful house had been swept away, his lovely fruit trees cut down and the bare dusty earth prepared for modern buildings. Beyond the wall, instead of desert, rows of apartment houses were already crowding in. But the Muslims' "religious fanaticism" had preserved the actual shrine of the saint, the well and the gemeyseh trees to which Mary Elcho had been led on her first day. The small dome, the huge stone sarcophagus and the saint's little blue-green turban were still just as Blunt had described them eighty years ago. When I came to write my chapter entitled "Grande Passion 1895–1896" it was easy to understand how Wilfrid had bombarded Mary with poetry and prayer until the fortress fell.

I have not yet mentioned one major advantage of writing an official biography: you can rest assured that no one else is working on "the papers" at the same time, and will perhaps pre-empt you with a slightly earlier publication. You may have your suspicions when the books you need from the library are always out. (This was not, however, the case with me when I was researching Byron and found all the books on Albania unavailable at the London Library; they had been stolen.) There is nothing you can do about it. The best you can hope for is that there will be room for two new books on your subject, and that you will bear with patience the annoyance of always being reviewed in tandem with your rival. I once suggested to a publishers' association that authors should register on a special list the titles on which they were working. The publishers laughed sardonically. Such a scheme had been tried and abandoned, since the list was simply used by other authors in search of a subject as a source for good ideas.

None of these traumas afflict commissioned authors. Yet such authors have one unavoidable disadvantage. They cannot know accurately what they are in for. If they have selected the subject themselves they must know that their subject's published work, say, will compensate for any distasteful aspects of the life. Commissioned authors have no such safeguards. They may be taken by surprise. I know one commissioned biographer of a famous cleric who gave up three-quarters of the way through. Another author, commissioned to write on a national hero, found himself fluctuating from pro to con from page to page.

No such extremes afflicted me during the writing of Blunt's life. But I have to admit to a moment about halfway through when I felt he was prostituting his poetry to an unworthy mode of life. He felt it too; which was one reason why my loyalty and affection returned to him long before the end.

"All this I am afraid is very *fin de siècle* and immoral", he wrote in 1891 when he found himself sending copies of precisely the same passionate verses to three different ladies on the same day. "But what can one do?" he continued. "Love is no respecter of time and place." (One might reply, what did he mean by this kind of "Love"?) With a final burst of ingenuousness, he concluded this unattractive passage by asserting the odious Victorian "double-standard" in sex with apparent sincerity. He expected no trouble, he wrote, from the three recipients of his love-verse even if they found out. "Women are not jealous in this way as men are", he assured his Victorian self, "for it is in the order of nature that a man's love should be divided."

After reading this poppycock in his "Secret Diaries", I turned to the entries dealing with the light verse presented at the Crabbet Club in 1893. True, Oscar Wilde was to watch the young Apollos dancing naked on the lawn after singing drunken operatic choruses in a shallow pond—no women allowed—but at least Wilfrid did not suggest that it was "in the order of nature" for these Apollos to dominate the rest of the world. He read a satirical poem addressed to three of them, George Curzon, George Wyndham and George Leveson-Gower, whose careers were to bring "civilisation" to "savages":

Teach them your virtues, your plain ways, law courts and
    parliaments.

> Build them South Kensington Art schools, sky signs,
>     gasometers. . . .
> Take control of their home life. Show them how royalty
> Does it at Osborne and Windsor, you of the Bedchamber!
> Go to them, Lords of the Household! Teach them your
>     thirstiness,
> How to behave on occasion, drunk but decorously. . . .
> Go—only leave me protesting, pleased and polygamous.

For the purposes of this essay I decided to count up the number of women with whom Blunt had made love; not always managing to sleep with them—bedroom doors tended to be locked when Blunt was around—and very occasionally refraining for reasons he considered valid; but rather more often accepting surrender for reasons he considered even more valid. And capitulation was often swift, for he specialised in frustrated, titled or at any rate aristocratic women—Talbots, Grosvenors, "Souls", who had to pretend to be above all that.

The total number of his "loves", from the year 1862 to about 1910 when he was no longer "capable", amounted to 38. These all made it into his "Secret Diaries"; but no doubt there were others too ephemeral to win even a paragraph. In roughly chronological order they were: *Lola*, *Skittles*, Lady Feodore Wellesley, *Zizi*, *Cora Pearl*, *Mrs. Ella Baird*, *Anita*, Lady Anne King-Noel whom he married, *Mrs. Georgie Sumner*, *Mrs. Thurlow*, Rosalind Howard Lady Carlisle, *Mrs. Minnie Pollen*, *Mrs. Madeline Wyndham*, Pansy Pollen, *Lady ("Doll") Zouche*, *Mrs. Mabel Batten*, *Mrs. "Angelina" Singleton*, *Lady (Augusta) Gregory*, *Princess Berthe Wagram*, Mrs. Waldo Storey, *Lady (Mary) Elcho*, *Lady Blanche Hozier*, *Mrs. Jane Morris*, Mrs. Marie Stillman, *Mrs. Margaret Talbot*, Lady Edmund Talbot, Sibell Grosvenor, Queenie Grosvenor, Princess Hélène of Orleans, *Margot Tennant*, Lady Helena Carnegie, *Lady Galloway*, Lady Emily Lytton, Lady (Gay) Windsor, Lady Margaret Sackville, *Dorothy Carleton*, *Lady (Adeline) Russell*, Nellie Hozier. (The names in italics are those of his mistresses.)

Here was a real problem posed for the biographer. Not of discretion exactly; this could be achieved, especially when there were natural children, by withholding married names as in the case of Blunt's lovely natural daughter Mary Charteris. (Berkeley Sumner's son changed his name.) No, the problem was to prevent the beauty of Blunt's best poetry, the virility of his prose, and the courage and effectiveness of his political career from being damaged by the monotony of his lusts. When for the fifth or sixth or seventh time Blunt wrote of having found the real thing, "the ideal love" at last—"We are to live together for the rest of our lives"—his biographer may be forgiven for saying, *"Not again . . ."*

Personally I did not find him a "cad", though some readers have found him so, and with them I feel that to a certain extent I failed in my delineation of this "Renaissance man". One reviewer implied that being a Catholic myself I was too prejudiced to appreciate Blunt at his true worth. So with her I evidently failed in an opposite sense, giving her the impression that I thought him a cad when I did not.

Now that my biography has been out for over four years I think I can sum up the worst and best of his amorousness in a few lines. The case of young Doll Fraser who was married to Lord Zouche while still in her teens was the worst: Blunt seduced her, as he later confessed, for a mere "buccaneering whim" but with the result that her marriage broke up and eventually the family (Anne's cousins) died out. Blunt escaped divorce proceedings only because the generous courtesan Skittles persuaded her lover the Prince of Wales to intervene on Blunt's behalf. Anne and Wilfrid could no longer face a censorious society and so they escaped into their first Middle-Eastern adventure. It was typical of Blunt that even this disgraceful affair should have its silver lining. But the majority of his "loves" remained his friends for life, even after all passion was spent. Indeed he admitted to finding it impossible to become friends with a women with whom he had *not* slept—or had not wanted to sleep.

While still in his twenties Blunt drew a sharp distinction between the highest kind of love and all of the rest. The highest involved a sense of tragedy: "without tragedy love is hardly love". In his early thirties he was to enlarge upon this distinction, so familiar to the Romantic poets of the past. A love affair with his beautiful first cousin Mrs. Madeline Wyndham (mother of Mary Elcho) satisfied his "paganly aesthetic" needs but was not "a full devotion of the soul", not "heroic". Some lines in his *Love Sonnets of Proteus* explained a little more of what he meant:

> You ask my love. What shall my love then be? . . .
> The sweetest love of all were love in pain
> And that I will not give.

Putting together his use of the words "paganly" and "soul" above, and applying that contrast to the lines just quoted, it seems that "love in pain"—the highest love—was love with a sense of guilt. Hence his affairs with Mrs. Baird and Mrs. Pollen seemed to him the very highest love of all, since both women were exceptionally good (Minnie Pollen was a Catholic like himself) and they were risking their eternal souls. Not only did these affairs show him that the world was well lost for love, but heaven too.

Blunt's interweaving of religion and love was not always on this high romantic level. Very often he was attracted by the sheer excitement of doing the forbidden thing, especially in the case of the unfortunate Lady Zouche. All his life he was attracted by danger—"the footsteps in the next room"—and loved the idea of nets, which he often put into his poetry. One imagines him very happily playing the part of Vulcan trapped with Venus under the net.

Blunt's growing knowledge of the East and Islam was also to affect his idea of love. If tragic love was the highest, "love within the clan" was to him the happiest. Hence his many affairs with blood relations or connections, sanctioned as he believed by Arab customs of polygamy. Apart from the Wyndham cousinship (which included Dorothy Carleton) there was Margaret Talbot, sister of Ralph Lovelace's wife; Minnie Pollen he was pleased to call more his sister than ever Augusta Leigh was Byron's. Thus this man of many and apparently disparate parts—sportsman, artist, political agitator, poet, amorist—turned towards the East and saw there the justification and harmonising of all his instincts.

I must not end without emphasising two literary factors, one of which greatly affected Blunt's work while the other enormously assisted his biographer. The Byronic influence on Blunt was substantial in a variety of ways. Because his wife Anne, Byron's granddaughter, was so unlike the author of *Childe Harold* and *Don Juan*, Wilfrid virtually took it upon himself, consciously or no, to make manifest the Byron inheritance in his own poetry and life. (Anne was not allowed even to *read* poetry as a girl for fear of becoming like Byron. She could, however, write most moving prose, as her diary in the British Library shows.) There are many Byronic echoes in Blunt's verse, for instance the famous phrase, "in my hot youth"; and Blunt's resolve to oppose British, French, and Turkish tyranny in Egypt was strengthened by Byron's fight against Turkish tyranny in Greece.

If ever a biographer received a narrative gift from the gods, it was in the form of a visit to Blunt by the group of "modern" poets in 1914, and the entertainment he provided them with at his celebrated "Peacock Dinner". I described it at some length in my book since it raised some interesting questions. Was Wilfrid Scawen Blunt a genuine poet? His poetry reflected real life, said the visiting poets. Otherwise W. B. Yeats, Ezra Pound, Richard Aldington and others would not have written laudatory verses in Blunt's honour and brought their scripts to Newbuildings. Moreover, their party dish of home-grown roast peacock had a pleasant *double entendre*—always a welcome grace-note in biography. Yeats, like many of Blunt's close friends, believed that the peacock was not only on Blunt's table but also in his character. Pound denied it. The symbolic gift was both a tribute to and a criticism of his personality.

Another rewarding aspect of this particular biography was the opportunity to correct the errors or myths of misunderstanding. For instance, Blunt's famous affair with Skittles, the last of the great *poules de luxe*, has often before been represented in print and on television but always inaccurately. I have been able to put the record straight. Again, Judith's diary and memoirs *Myself and Others* (not available except to her father's biographer for another four years) gave immense new substance to Blunt's extraordinary character though introducing many errors of her own which I did my best to put right.

Love affairs undreamt of were brought to light such as that with Janey Morris, William's wife, and Lady Gregory (a committed political partnership with a froth of passion); but any idea that his affair with Lady Blanche Hozier resulted in his sireing her daughters Clementine Churchill and Nellie Romilly is out: *les dates ne correspondent pas*.

There are two problems of the literary biographer which I have certainly not solved to my complete satisfaction: quotations and literary criticism. One might argue that a biography of Blunt should carry far more quotations than one of Byron, the former's poetry being so much less well known. On the other hand there seems something perverse about loading a book with quotations from a minor poet while using the work of a major one more sparingly. As for literary criticism, I felt it my clear duty to distinguish between a work of literary criticism and a literary biography. In so doing I reduced my own literary criticism to the minimum but quoted the largest possible number of contemporary opinions.

Perhaps the chief bonus resulting from a literary biography of this sort is the collection of information and anecdotes about other literary figures that accrues. Some have already been mentioned such as Yeats and Pound. I would add Swinburne (details supplied by Skittles to whom he tried in vain, because of his drunkenness, to make love); Dante Gabriel Rossetti; various members of the Souls including the philosopher Arthur James Balfour, later Prime Minister; Cardinal Newman; Hilaire Belloc; Wilfrid and Alice Meynell; and the poet Francis Thompson.

In the end it is a toss-up between Blunt the freedom fighter and Blunt the diarist as to which will bring him the surest immortality. *My Diaries* should never have gone out of print. Who but Blunt could have responded during a poets' symposium on heaven with such literary elegance matched so perfectly to pleasurable thought? When asked what was his idea of heaven he replied:

> To be laid out to sleep in a garden, with running water near, and so to sleep for a hundred thousand years, then to be woke by a bird singing, and to call out to the person one loved best, "Are you there?" and for her to answer, "Yes, are you?" and so turn round and go to sleep again for another hundred thousand years.

Surely a poet's dream; broken only by one awkward fact which the reviewer Terence de Vere White pointed out. The trouble in Blunt's case would be that to his question, "Are you there?" "the volley of replies would shatter the peace of the garden." But Blunt would cope.

CHAPTER FOUR

# Joseph Conrad

## FREDERICK R. KARL

We start with a very simple premise. The biographer of a literary subject must relate the latter's life and work to each other meaningfully and profoundly. If he cannot achieve that end, the biography, whatever its other illuminations, fails. Yet this apparently simple statement harbors, possibly, the most difficult part of all biography, since it involves the writer in several areas both practical and theoretical. He must be, in this enterprise, aesthetician, novelist, linguist, philosopher, literary critic, historian, psychologist; minimally, the final three.

Further, literary subjects differ considerably: from those, like Proust, Gide, Kafka, Beckett, whose work is so supercharged with their lives that a line of demarcation is difficult to draw; to others, such as Conrad, Lawrence, Joyce, Eliot, Pound, Mann, for whom there are visible seams between life and work, however finely stitched the seam is. To each of these groups, there accrues a particular problem, in strategy, tools, taste. Yet for each, writing *is* the life: his exaltation and thralldom.

If we assume this is correct, we claim for literary biography unique qualities. Biography, then, is as much a "creation" as are novels, poems, and dramas. Such views invalidate several biographies: for example, Baker's *Hemingway*, Blotner's *Faulkner*, and Bell's *Woolf*, all of them able pieces of research which neglect or ignore questions raised by their subjects' fiction. By eschewing psychology, they have turned a creative figure into an historical one. In another category—to keep our model to modern biography—we have Jean Strouse's excellent *Alice James*; yet this is not literary biography, but, in reality, social history, where a different theory of biography obtains.

In the latter, with the figure caught in social history, or a military or political personage, the life is so compelling that

69

the subject exists apart from what he has accomplished. A Napoleon, Gandhi, MacArthur, or Bismarck take on qualities which in our collective memories have moved beyond whatever they have done; and we may, in fact, be quite ignorant of their actual achievements. We know of them quite differently from, say, Dickens or Pound. They exist in some towering sense beyond even the history they were involved in, where their performance initially made them worthy of biography. It would appear we need another biographical theory for them, where de-mythicizing them takes priority over blending man and work.

But even here, we could claim that while they transcend individual works in our memory of them, they are revealed most tellingly in a work—whether military or political campaigns, forms of strategy or maneuver, areas of compromise, acts of defiance. Each one of the latter is a "work" which, while embedded in history, goes beyond it; in the way we say a literary work is located in history and transcends it. In this area, Alice James is significant as a life which has compelling social and cultural meaning.

Nevertheless, we must not muddle the difference between a literary subject and an historical/political/military one. We start from different premises. With the literary subject, we are thrown immediately into psychological analyses and interpretations, for the chief consideration if we attempt to blend subject and work is internal, analytical.[1] With the non-literary figure, the historical–political–social axes are so compelling that backgrounds, cultural developments, cause and effect help pre-empt stress on individual psychological development: not eliminate it, but dilute its ultimate significance. Roosevelt's achievement with the New Deal, for example, was in some profound way connected to his earlier polio, but inevitably the New Deal is more significant than what polio meant to Roosevelt's internal life. A corollary of this is that while psychoanalytic interpretations of a literary subject are often reductive, when psychoanalysis is brought to bear upon a non-literary subject there is less dimunition—since blending of subject and work is less loaded with metaphorical freight, closer to conscious rather than unconscious drives; i.e. less complicatedly imaginative. The linguistic model for a writer is always more complex than a military or political campaign for a non-literary subject.

What I am claiming, then, for literary biography are readings in depth of the subject in conjunction with his work; but, further, such readings of subject/work should not be psychoanalytic, although they may be informed by psychoanalytic theories. The latter as pure method tends to observe both life and work as illness and/or neurotic drives, repetitive patterns, fetishes, compulsions, obsessions, clinical evidence. Psychoanalytic interpretation seeks the etiology of particular behavioral patterns, defines how the subject fits into clinical evidence, and then uses the work as a way of justifying that definition. This is inflexible: the work should be used only sparingly to understand the subject and the subject only tentatively to understand the work. The nature of reciprocity makes anything else sophistry.

Psychoanalytic theories by attempting clinical definition become guilty of reductiveness. Norman Holland, for example, in discussing the psychoanalytic potential of *The Secret Agent*, makes some perceptive points about Conrad's use of geometric forms, light and dark imagery, even fisheries. He remarks that from this "fantasy content" and "defensive management" we can infer Conrad's myth: "the wish to bring to light a 'distinct significant fact' and hang onto it lest one sink into engulfing depths."[2] That "myth" may well suffice for an interpretation of one novel, but biographically we have innumerable contexts—national politics, social and familial forces, definition of adult inner will, uses of language, among others—for which that myth is distinctly limiting or inapplicable. Nevertheless, psychoanalytic interpretations *are* indispensable if they do not delimit the work by making it the primary data of the subject's life. Conversely, such analyses should not restrict the life by making it solely what nourishes the work.

Both psychology and psychoanalysis are concerned with knowing the mind, but we make distinctions as each applies to literary subjects; in the first, the method assays the mind without any restrictions on what is knowable; in the second, psychoanalysis, the method, starting with certain clinical positions, seeks in the individual those elements which demand clinical diagnosis. In *Out of My System: Psychoanalysis, Ideology, and Critical Method*, Frederick Crews fudges the difference, saying that " 'psychology' will here be contracted to mean psychoanalysis. . . . Psychoanalysis is the only psychology to have seriously altered our way of reading literature."[3] Crews uses "psychology" to mean learning theory, physiological psychology, perception and cognitive psychology, Gestalt psychology: all physiological, laboratory methods. My sense of psychology, as contrasted with psychoanalysis, is different. I use psychology as a method by which we can bring together the man and his work, as against psychoanalysis, which attempts to find out what kind of man wrote those particular works. George Painter's *Proust* is a model of this kind of psychological insight, in which childhood, illnesses, eccentricities of behavior and motivation are not used clinically, but aesthetically; in which Proust's life is not a scenario of sickness, overcompensation, mother deprivation, or fetishism, but the unfolding of a man using his qualities to achieve his artistic life, a life indistinguishable from its vision.

Crews' first essay "Can Literature Be Psychoanalyzed?" supports psychoanalytic interpretations of literature, as I do; but biography differs from a literary text, and what applies in the latter does not obtain in the former. When we use psychoanalysis to open up a text, we derive latent and manifest meaning, seek out forms of language which reveal subtexts, examine dream, reverie, stress, analyze particular images for their definable content; but we rarely try to form a model of the author's mind. We may move closer to it, but we emphasize the work. In biography, we must edge up to that meeting point between mind and work, to areas where the figure who has created something must be related to the work he has created; so that we have a model of his mind. Ultimately, we are concerned not with literary values alone, but with crossings, junctures, intersections, reciprocating ideas, assimilated influences. The arena is very different and, in fact, far more complex, because biography is at all times the reconstruction of a human model who seems suitable for the work created. Our goal is to understand the transformations that occur when life becomes work, when work pre-empts life.

The biographer of a literary subject whose achievement is considerable—a minor or neglected historical figure requires a different dimension of analysis—must, as Conrad himself put it early in his career, "make you *see*." By "seeing," Conrad suggested a dimension beyond understanding with one's reason or logic; he meant comprehension based on total response of viewer and viewed. To make you see in Conrad's words is a willed quality, a corollary of his artistic achievements, and it does not lend itself to a psychoanalytic viewpoint. This willed quality is a crucial aspect of the mature Conrad—described when he was nearly forty—and it has no ostensible reference to loss of mother at seven, death of father at eleven, or to his being thrust from one guardian to another, as it would in psychoanalytic practice; nor does it relate even in an extended sense to his childhood, and certainly not to those childhood episodes which analysts see as recurring beyond his willed desire to change or refocus them.

Conrad's desire to make the reader *see* is, in fact, profoundly connected to the willed part of his life associated with the sea. "Seeing" is a dominant part of a maritime life, whether one is staring at water, waves, and sky for some message or meaning; or whether one is staring at water in order to detect wreckage which may mean disaster for one's ship. The seaman stands daily watches, and his orders are "to see"; or else he seeks significance in the immensity of things as part of going to sea. In writing of wind and wave in *The Mirror of the Sea*, Conrad stressed: "To see! to see!—this is the craving of the sailor, as of the rest of blind humanity."[4] As a ship's officer from the 1880's on, Conrad needed not only to see objects external to the ship, he had to see into the crew for signs of laxity, rebellion, malingering, as we find in *The Nigger of the "Narcissus,"* his first sea novel.

This need "to see" nourished a different kind of temporal and spatial order in Conrad the seaman, and it inevitably carried over into his way of seeing when he turned to writing. His introduction of Marlow early on in his fiction was only one way of organizing the power of seeing, and his use after that of tellers, intermediaries, letters, diaries, and other narrative strategies was connected to his peculiar sense of temporal/spatial relationships. A psychoanalytic interpretation can illuminate little of this, although a psychological view—while speculative and tentative—might help, in that it explains how Conrad carried over from one willed situation to another in a very different medium.

A further key example, Conrad's shift of languages from the Polish and French of his childhood to the English of his adulthood, cannot be explained by psychoanalytic interpretations. An analyst may say that Conrad was, in some tortuous way, imitating his father, since Apollo Korzeniowski translated several English classics into Polish. Following this argument, Conrad's three languages were, also, Apollo's, and we find here the son replicating the father despite his extreme ambivalence toward Apollo's life and career. Yet the son's decision to write in English—however that decision was ultimately reached—is of a completely different order of being from translating English into Polish. Conrad went the opposite direction, in a sense, translating from Polish into English, sometimes literally in his early works when his English was still uncertain. If we wished, we could scramble the point and see this as rejection of the father; the analytic point could, willy-nilly, face in either direction.

Rather than seeking psychoanalytic interpretations of Conrad's use of English for his fiction, we should discover, psychologically, what it was in Conrad that made him dare fate when he willed himself into a writer of English. He was, after all, not young: he started *Almayer* when he was close to thirty-two and finished it five years later. He had run through nearly all of his inherited stipend; he was thinking of marriage—the women in his life begin to pile up, Marguerite Poradowska, Emilie Briquel, finally Jessie George; his health was uncertain, and, although not actually disabled, he had gone to Champel in Switzerland three times for hydro-therapic treatment for nerves; he was, at the time he chose to write in English, halfway through his life span, an old man in his thirties. Further, and this is psychologically significant, he was starting up a new career, having ten years earlier willed himself into a sea captaincy, and this new career meant all the dangers inherent in, what was then, a midlife shift; so that he transferred his life from the dangers of the sheet of water to the sheet of white paper. We are confronted with a decision of momentous import in the subject's life, coupled with his plans for marriage, and when we try to discover why he did this or that, we find little basis in childhood experience, relationship to dead mother or sick father, any of the usual analytic diagnoses.

We must, instead, seek a willed existence in several other factors: in social and political contexts; in the way Conrad, as he matured, began to organize and see his own life—what we call the willed element; in how that willed part is connected to his early development. Psychoanalytic theories stressing his childhood development before and after his parents' deaths, especially the tender years when he shared his parents' exile in Russia, are of great significance. But their overall importance, ultimately, derives from their connection to what was willed; and that segment of his life, which incorporates the years when he wrote his fiction, becomes what the biographer must elucidate and illuminate. What, psychologically, can we discover?

We discover patterns of behavior which seem to refute the

childhood experiences; for instance, when Conrad decided to write and settled into a series of houses in and around Kent. Thus, psychoanalytically one might claim he was responding to child-hood chaos by choosing absolute stasis—the writer at a desk overlooking a meadow, establishing a daily routine for his final thirty years. But this interpretation has it both ways: if he had continued to move on as a middle-aged man, the theorist could point to his consistency; but since he chose to refute his early exile and wandering with a settled existence, theory stresses the significance of his negation of those early years. Psychologically, however, we can posit not the significance of moving on or settling down, nor the way in which he duplicated his father's literary career, but the ways in which he redefined his life after thirty-two to achieve consistency with his own willed sense of himself. Here, he would do whatever was necessary in the present to make his craft possible.

Put another way: psychoanalysis depends on seeking confirma-tion in the individual life for universal laws. Freud stated this purpose in the opening lines of his portrait of Leonardo da Vinci,[5] and it has become a commonplace of later psychobiographies. Psychological interpretations, without discounting psychoanaly-tic tools, allow the biographer to break from general rules, so that will and inner direction count significantly. Put still another way: the psychoanalyst is seeking ways in which the subject can be more mature, healthier, more balanced, and the ways in which he has failed because of pathology. The psychologist is far more interested in how illness or pathology, if present, feeds the imagination of his subject, how that subject uses all means to achieve his art.

From early childhood, Conrad suffered from one illness or another, to the extent his Uncle Tadeusz Bobrowski suspected epilepsy. Although epilepsy seems an exaggeration, we can assume illnesses were sufficiently frequent and severe to elicit that kind of response. Real sickness persisted, not just temporary indisposition, and intensified during troubled times (his wife's ailments and pregnancies, for example) when he took to his bed, as if in some kind of sympathetic magic. For the biographer, illness is a feast. It can also be a trap. One can, like Dr. Bernard Meyer in his sensitive psychoanalytic biography of Conrad,[6] argue that such illnesses were signs of his infantilism; that faced by situations he could not control, the middle-aged and then older

Conrad regressed into illness so that he had to be nursed by a wife-mother. Such a man, accordingly, required the reappearance of the mother lost at seven, and established adult patterns whereby his wife, friends, even children were forced to serve and mother him, as though in a Dickensian drama where parents and children reverse roles.

The case for this is persuasive. Yet there are alternate views if we see Conrad in a larger context, not only as a frail human being but as *the* person who will develop into the novelist. Pathology can illuminate many functions. In this larger context, illness served him as a writer, for it allowed him time, periods of observation and perspective. It was, of course, self-serving, but it nourished his function as a writer while perhaps reflecting poorly on him as a man. The psychoanalytic view perceives him as a weak, infantile male; the psychological view perceives him as a man ready to sacrifice everything in order to achieve his larger sense of himself as a writer.

Conrad used illness as much as, or more than, illness used him. Pathological symptoms are such a constant in his letters and life we recognize them as part of his willed character, not simply as determinants from childhood situations. He may have developed his illnesses as ways of dealing with childhood situations that were beyond conscious control—here psychoanalysis is helpful—but once those illnesses extended into the life of a man who produced thirty volumes, we must cite them as productive, intrinsic to the way his life and art meet. We can say in certain respects his imagination depended on his pathological symptoms; that while they rarely brought him so low he could not function at all—a 1910 nervous collapse did just that, however—they performed a useful function. Just how they performed this service, or how they nourished his art, or how he absorbed illness into artistic imagination are areas of speculation. But we can be certain he needed illness as a way of spurring him, although how it spurred, what shape it took, and how Conrad decided to respond are outside verifiable contexts.

In a related area, psychoanalytic interpretations atomize rather than unify. Withal their clinical theories, analysts cannot tell us why that particular author wrote those particular books. Even with Conrad, who consistently stressed certain motifs and character types, there is no analytical view that accounts for the twists and turns of his career.[7] Connected to what we are saying is the methodology of psychoanalytic interpretation, which isolates elements, discards many others, discounts exceptions, moves to extremes so as to establish clinical patterns in which individual accomplishment confirms general clinical observations. Even Erikson, who invented the term and discipline "psychohistory," in which psychoanalysis is blended with historical analysis, at his best in *Luther* and *Gandhi* severely isolated elements in order to permit clinical diagnosis. And in Luther's case, Erikson's translation of a particular passage, on which much of his study depends, is debatable.

Further, psychoanalytic interpretations have not found firm ways to deal with the subject's language, unless usage involves slips and comparable accidentals in which the unconscious surfaces. In painting, psychoanalysis cannot tell us why Matisse painted his trees purple; in music, why Wagner chose that particular form of musical language, not some other; in literature, such analyses cannot tell us even why Conrad turned to English, no less why he wrote that peculiar brand. If we want to understand his usage, we must study the derivation of his language in French and Polish; we must comprehend the myriad influences on him from various literary sources, in Polish, French, and English; we must try to unravel his coloring, textures, images, repetitions, his selection of rhetorical devices and figures of speech. We must get at his "purple trees," as it were.

In none of these activities is psychoanalytic method of more than passing use. Lacan's approach, perceiving in the language of the unconscious a true language, has potentiality, once Lacan's method can be translated into (1) understandable language which the biographer can adapt to his own use; (2) a means which can be modified and extended toward a language theory bridging unconscious and conscious: that is, linking imagination, dreams, nightmares, fantasy, and the actual work done by a major writer.[8] The difficult area here, as in any method, is to trace what occurs between the imagining mind and what actually appears on the page. As of now, aesthetic theory and literary history seem more adaptable, whereas psychoanalytic method promises a great deal it cannot deliver.

As already suggested, psychoanalysis does not in a writer like Conrad afford even the basic linguistic model, since it cannot trace how profoundly anchored in Polish and French Conrad's English actually is: so that slips, traces, and intimations which seem clinically useful are connected to childhood through linguistic models, not behaviorial patterns. These linguistic models are not clinically meaningful in themselves. They are unique phenomena, only manifest to the extent Conrad in his willed way created an English which no other writer had ever tried before, and because he, unlike any other writer, was equipped to do so. Here, even Saussure's distinctions between *langue* (system of language) and *parole* (spoken words) are inadequate for what has occurred biographically in the writer's mind and for how that occurrence is linked to the work. True, *langue* is a hoard of forms from which a writer selects the *parole* to use; but the theory does not explain why that writer has chosen such *parole* and not others. As Saussure recognized and as Chomsky repeats, possibilities are infinite; yet the biographer is interested not in infinitude but in the finite: this writer and no other, that usage and none other.

While psychoanalytic method offers an unconscious language from which the conscious language derives, so Saussure and his successors offer a *langue* (unconscious) from which *parole* (conscious usage) derives. Yet even as we say this, we recognize unconscious and conscious languages are disconnected in the very act of expression, and so *langue* and *parole* are, also, disconnected when the general matrix of language becomes the specific utterance. Here, deep in linguistic theory, we find the same schisms which occur in psychoanalysis; and even more than most authors, Conrad poses problems that multiply the difficulties of any theoretical system because of his immersion in three languages, two of which (Polish as against French and English) are grammatically and syntactically very different from each other.

The remainder of this essay will grapple with an extremely difficult biographical area, connected to the above remarks on that split between imagination and performance in a literary subject and the problem this creates for the biographer. Although the reader's sense of Conrad is that of a writer concerned with action, the biographer comes to understand Conrad as a novelist of inertness, passivity, languor, inactivity.[9] Action is, in fact, not only the enemy of many of his protagonists, it is also Conrad's enemy in terms of his descriptive powers. This inertness, if we agree that it dominates, would of course be of interest to the psychoanalytic interpreter, since it can be connected to every aspect of Conrad's childhood and to the shaping influences upon him. But the inertness he adopts in his major work is associated, I think, not so much with those early aspects of his life as with literary theories and practices *joined with* perceptions from his sea years. Thus, while not denying that childhood and other early influences account for some of the inactivity, I would argue that Conrad's years at sea, and his reading, created that "other" time and space which nourish his sense of passivity and languor.

The 1897 Preface was, after all, appended to *The Nigger of the "Narcissus,"* a novel based on the languor of James Wait and the effects of such role-playing on the crew. And if we backtrack, we can see Conrad's two earliest novels, also, deeply, indebted to a *fin de siècle* mode and vocabulary of inertness, inaction, passivity, in which jungle backgrounds, as in Gauguin's Tahiti scenes, serve as backdrop for Almayer's and then Willems' surrender to deep languor.

The question specifically is, if we reject a purely psychoanalytic explanation of Conrad's emphasis on languor and inertness, how do we interpret it? Without ignoring the childhood etiology of his desire for inertness, I would seek richer explanations in several other areas: in his willed desire to create another career for himself within certain literary perimeters, in his adult experiences of going to sea, standing watches, waiting for sail to respond to wind and wave, and in his exploration of literary modes which were becoming common in the 1890's, in typical *fin de siècle* writers, as well as in Gide, Pater, Yeats, and others less typical.

We start in the period just after Conrad completed *The Nigger*, appended to it his Preface, and began work which, deeply personal, drew, respectively, on his trip to the Congo, his disablement and stay in Singapore, brief glimpses of the South American coast; more generally, on his concern with exotic places and how they affected the lives of his reclusive, isolated protagonists. We have, in this, the making of the typical Conradian paradigm, and his fiction in these respects is deeply intertwined with many strands of his life. The biographer must unravel, then, not only the chronology of what was occurring in Conrad's life as he wrote these books, but the ways in which these novels reflected earlier aspects of his life when the experiences occurred that he was now mirroring in his fiction. Further, the biographer must deal with how the writing and publication of these books—and all the difficulties inherent therein—weighed upon his subject's life, changing it in large or small ways even as the latter pushes ahead with subsequent work. Time is both collapsed for the biographer and projected. Past burdens present, but future is there even as present and past are sorted out. And when the life seems all action, the fictional motifs are languor, passivity, even anomie.

To illustrate my method, I will respond to a particular passage in one of Conrad's letters; a passage which, while not lending itself to psychoanalytic interpretation, in its definition of literary practices and imagination behind them has profound psychological implications for Conrad, and of course for his biographer. The passage[10] comes in a letter Conrad sent to James Brand Pinker, his literary agent, on January 5, 1903, when he was immersed simultaneously in writing *Nostromo* and *The Rescue*. The latter, however, would continue for another sixteen years. He wrote:

1. I've been turning around *Rescue* to do away with retrospect. A most bothersome task. A most bothersome task. You shall have the amended copy soon.
2. Since Xmas day I've for relief been writing a story called (provisionally) *Nostromo* which will do for the Kensal [he means Kendal] people. Half or so of the MS. you shall have by the *15th inst* and the balance end of the month. About 35000.

This seemingly careless passage is supercharged with meaning for Conrad as a man and writer, and the biographer must disentangle what doing away with retrospect in one book while doing, really, the opposite in *Nostromo* means biographically. We can see how in his major work Conrad found inertness more congenial than action. We can explore how biography and literary analysis blend in a seamless web once we draw out every dimension of meaning above and its significance for Conrad's life and work.

If we agree that use of language is crucial in understanding Conrad's development, then verbs, so different in English and Polish, establish his sense of both time and space. His use of verbs is connected to his way of "seeing," which reflects his years at sea and his sense of what art should and can do. As his most ambitious work, *Nostromo* would prove almost entirely retrospective: the past tense of narrative creating an historical dimension without which the novel cannot be understood; the novel as history co-equal with the novel as fiction. *The Rescue*, however, which Conrad hoped would be his masterpiece, proved intractable for a variety of reasons; one of them being that with its composition coming at nearly every point in Conrad's career, from 1896 to 1919, it was subject to his shifts in style and technique. In their respective ways, *Nostromo* and *The Rescue* become the obverse of each other. The fact of two major novels being written at the same time, but pointing in opposite directions, helps us see the tensions in Conrad's life as manifest in his mature work.

*Nostromo* gains its thickening sense of a cultural tidal wave as a consequence of Conrad's daring in narrating it as retrospect; that is, through a network of mediators who serve as middle men between fiction and history, between certain events and their historical significance and inevitability. Action or event is transformed into retrospective narrative, i.e. into passivity. In *The Rescue*, Conrad moved toward a present tense narrative, that kind of story-telling associated with action/adventure novels, the popular form of Stevenson, Hope, Haggard, and others. Even as he worked on *The Rescue* and shifted it forward, its "presentness" was a narrative method he had forsaken with *Heart of Darkness* and, especially, *Lord Jim*. Thus, while *The Rescue* pointed back toward what he had already renounced, *Nostromo* was a natural development for him, its narrative technique already implicit on a smaller scale in *Lord Jim*. In that respect, *Nostromo* became an opening up, even as its narrative included historical pastness.

Unlike the presentness of *The Rescue*, the retrospection of *Nostromo* as narrative technique suggests different imaginative modes; certainly, greater complication in narrative means, but, also, far greater engagement of the writer's creative processes. Conrad became a juggler of time, and space, as the result of his decision, since he would be molding pastness to presentness. He would, eventually, have to meet the present, but method forced him to come upon it not suddenly but in serpentine fashion. Retrospection is rarely simply past versus present, or historical process versus contemporary event. Conrad found himself, once he chose pastness, moving among several dimensions of the past, each with its own etiology, its own processes, its own consequences. He was, in effect, travelling his own inner world, which was one of constant dredging up. Conrad became, here, a novelist of memory, a writer in whom time past or past recaptured was almost as significant as in Proust, whose work, later on, he greatly respected. Conrad's talent matured, then, when he grappled with verbs, that is, with narrative modes which permitted memory to become a weight on everything present; when stasis overbalanced event.

We must inquire how elements of time in two different novels can become of biographical significance. In a sense, the tensions of Conrad's mental state are laid bare. The retrospection of *Nostromo*'s narrative reflects Conrad as "removed," as isolated and reclusive; it is character trait as much as imagination. Information buried deep in the past and then coming to the reader from depths is information which no longer has the reality of immediacy. It is material which has become meaningful because it has been transformed through its removal in time; information which must be retrieved through the agony of a creative process.

If we recognize that the Costaguana of *Nostromo* has the sense of historical process associated with Poland, and particularly with the doomed Poland of Conrad's and his father's youth, then we note how Conrad perceived his developmental years in a land which desperately sought identity even while partitioned into three. Conrad's need to transform the immediate reality of Costaguana, its presentness, into a land with some historical identity is an effort at psychological retrieval. The form this took for Conrad could not be easy, and his numerous letters to Pinker, Galsworthy, and others about his difficulties with the novel testify to the psychological burden that writing it put upon him. The act of writing nearly "wasted" him, bringing him down almost as much as *Under Western Eyes* did, when, after its completion, he suffered a severe nervous collapse. *Under Western Eyes*, also, was an act of historical retrieval, less about pastness than *Nostromo*, but nevertheless about the past, with Razumov's nemesis, Haldin, patterned in part on Conrad's father, Apollo Korzeniowski, and his political activities against Czarist Russia.

Delving into the past was for Conrad like digging in a graveyard: not only for the particulars of his own situation, but in a more general sense for the history of the land called Poland. In the decade of his major achievement, from *Heart of Darkness* and *Lord Jim* through *Under Western Eyes*, Conrad was recreating his past in the form of various roles his protagonists played. Each novel involves creativity grappling with memory, memory turning event into stasis, nearly all attached to the retrospective-historical method. The nervous collapse at the end of this period of intense creativity was the consequence of profound involvement in personal history; but, as we can see, the collapse was also connected to matters of imagination, to the way Conrad's creative sense made him transform his material—some of it psychologically based, some of it his willed desire to move along where literary currents were carrying him and his major contemporaries. For the methods Conrad employed in *Nostromo* were not unique: not the results of a singular writer, but practices of a generation, Gide and Proust in France, Musil in Austria, Joyce in Ireland; what we associate with the Modern movement.

Thus, if Conrad's practices had only psychoanalytic roots—connected to his confrontation with deepest mental recesses and his ambivalence about meeting such matters and also avoiding them—then we agree such tensions could lead to the nervous collapse, a condition near death. These practices, however, were not only Conrad's but a generation's, and, therefore, we explore a far more complex problem: not only difficulties he found in his own exploration of pastness and past history so as to create his works, but in a developed, willed sense this was the sole way he could write if he hoped to be a serious novelist. The simple remarks on retrospection in *Nostromo* carry us this far.

Not only does the psychoanalytic interpretation[11] avoid other considerable pressures on Conrad—financial worries, slowness of production faced with the strain of earning more money, familial discords because of Jessie's physical deterioration, his older son's seeming lack of direction, Conrad's own ailments—its chief omission is its neglect of imaginative processes. As we have seen, Conrad was part of that generation leaning heavily on pastness, memory, aspects of the unconscious. He was employing Polish memories—memories which occurred in another language, country, culture, as well as "another life"—in order to nourish English fictions. Not only was he moving from past to present, from event to inertness, he was moving laterally across cultures and languages so as to retrieve those memories and historical moments. The process was tortuous and for Conrad increasingly difficult since it meant reliving a disastrous family situation in order to nourish a literary imagination.

Unlike the psychoanalytic interpreters, we *must* assume imagination and creativity are biographical matters, more significant than dating, external events, even childhood developments. From Freud himself and thereafter, psychoanalysts have found difficulty in relating life and art,[12] and very possibly Jung proves the better guide. Jung speaks of a condition in which the artist is "nothing but his work, and not a human being." In this view, the writer's artistic drives have consumed him, so that while he functions as a human being, his conscious self has been subsumed in his work: words, paint, musical composition. Words, then, would have become the reality for Conrad, and he would lie exposed wherever language and memory took him. We can extend this idea to say that just as Conrad was transforming pastness and memory into present creation, so he was himself undergoing a transformation from a conscious, acting person to a man who was "receiving" messages from the unconscious which he could not ignore. Retrieval meant transformation.

If we grant this, then we can describe Conrad as a "visionary artist," to use Jung's term in "Psychology and Literature." Unlike the "personalistic" or "psychological artist," who presents human destiny in nominally straightforward terms, the visionary artist must confront intense and troubling anarchic elements in himself; so that the very act of confrontation is shattering. He becomes two people: the conscious person functioning in his routine world, even condemning chaos and anarchy; but, alongside that, the almost demonic creature flirting with anarchy, even celebrating it. In announcing he was turning *Nostromo* into retrospect, Conrad was taking that chance, descending into himself—a term he begins to explore in the Preface to *The Nigger*—and experiencing transformation into a prophet or visionary. Once this occurs, psychoanalytic interpretations, even Jung's perception of the artist redefining himself through his work, lose their effectiveness.

We must seek literary and mythical analogues for this transformation. However imperfect they may be for biographical purposes, they provide a context for that meeting between life and art. We can assume a contrast between the Promethean artist, concerned with a present-tense, straightforward narrative, associated with an active, doing life, stressing externals and now; and the Orphic artist, our hero of internal change and transformation, moving into historical processes, the protagonist of past tense and passivity. If Promethean narrative is all outwardness, then Orphic narrative is inwardness, embedded in personal and world historical process. Although Conrad was unconscious of Promethean–Orphic contrasts, his mature work in the 1899–1909 decade demonstrates that, like Proust, Mann, Musil, he had cast his lot with Orphic descent and become a novelist of history, memory, pastness, inertness.

Commenting on Orphic themes in a different context, Walter Strauss reaches conclusions that illuminate Conrad biography:

> The Orphic poet is ... at the beginning of a journey, confronted with the task of sacralizing time, space, and language before the Orphic spell can take place. His task is to face the Nothingness, to overcome (abolish) it in order to make poetry once more possible ... the Orphic poet seeks to regenerate himself particularly through remembrance and its mandatory self-transformation, followed by return to the world that will become the ground of a vast metamorphosis." [13]

Journeys into pastness and memory, sacralization of time, space, and language, confrontation with Nothingness (that sheet of wind, wave, and sky, that need for personal transformation), use of fifteen or more names from Konrad Korzeniowski to Joseph Conrad: all such elements implicit in the Orphic experience are significant in Conrad's major phase. These elements demonstrate that Conrad's life as it is subsumed in his work can be analyzed and interpreted at levels of myth, literary forms, recurring patterns in human history. The Orphic descent is an archetypal pattern, and in plumbing this aspect of his experience, Conrad relived, in some respects, his earlier life. Although he chose an existence very different from his father's, certainly one less self-destructive, nevertheless he challenged his past with something of the abandon we find also in Apollo Korzeniowski. The sea and then writing career have such strong Orphic overtones we can assume that without history, memory, pastness, Conrad would have ended up as a minor adventure writer, if a writer at all.

The Orphic vision entails sensory derangement, disruption of spatial and temporal elements: the archetypal nineteenth-century Orphic writer was Rimbaud, or Baudelaire. Orpheus can exist only through descent, an uncontrollable or open process in Modern literature; not the orderly procession the classical writers provided for Aeneas or Odysseus, but a derangement of events which approximates a living hell. Orpheus nourishes himself on recesses, his sense of space and time emanating from self, not from clock or calendar.

While sacralizing routine spatial and temporal processes,

Orphic visions encourage myths of silver, treasure, caverns, secretive places. They encapsulate memory and stress innerness. But they also promise liberation, associated with art's freeing powers even as Orpheus moves us closer to death images and death itself. This paradoxical nature of the myth is one reason it so appealed to Conrad's creative powers: for while it investigates death, it also contains powers of freedom, this tension between death and freedom a paradigm of Conrad's own life. We recall his attempt at suicide just short of his twenty-first birthday. That retrieval of self which occurred afterward was an Orphic act; not less than a facing of Nothingness, followed by a transformation in which he overcomes Nil by changing it into treasure by way of a "magic language," English. In the process, he discovers regeneration, directing energies into positive elements and returning to the world from underworlds of destructiveness.

As early as the Preface to *The Nigger*, Conrad explored art's powers to provide salvation from stale routine; but in that novel, he was still the Promethean artist, not quite Orphic. By *Heart of Darkness* and *Lord Jim*, he entered the Orphic phase, descending to his own pastness, transforming memory into art, history into fiction, event into passivity. Paradoxically, inner space and time of the Orphic descent are greater than the vastnesses of the Promethean vision, although the latter seems to sweep sky and mountain. What Orpheus uncovers is the larger hoard, the vaster cavern of potential. In *Nostromo*, Conrad's great Orphic novel, we sense that a few bars of silver, the visible hoard, are emblems of a great ancestral treasure, the Gould hoard, which would transform not only Sulaco and Costaguana but the world, if only it could be got at. Like memory, that inner world is depthless, immeasurable, whereas the Promethean world is a region our senses can delimit.

*Nostromo* becomes the repository of Conrad's life up to that point, in his late forties; and his effort to turn its narrative into retrospection indicates he was bringing to bear on it his entire sense of himself. In *Eros and Civilization*, Herbert Marcuse yokes Orpheus and Narcissus: the first, part of the inner world of regeneration; the latter, the inward-turning youth full of self-love. That juxtaposition is not inappropriate for Conrad, whose concern in his mature narratives was not so much what his narrators experience as how they respond to those experiences. His reliance on central narrators as surrogates for self or as projections of self exploits a full awareness of the Orphic–Narcissus concept. Self-absorption negates an active role. Whether Marlow, Captain Mitchell, Decoud in his long letter, or Razumov in his diary, Conrad's narrators sidestep activity in favor of talking or writing about it: a perfect manifestation of languor, exhaustion, and Orphic–Narcissus descent.

By *Nostromo*, Conrad was indistinguishable from the books he was writing, what we can claim for only a very few Modernists, Proust and Kafka coming immediately to mind. In this arena of tensions and tentative solutions, in his efforts to find narrative equivalents of his own life, its pastness, memories, and staring, we have his *real* biography. By eschewing the Promethean and embracing the Orphic, Conrad had transformed himself into a particular kind of author, probing a different order of reality from that of his English contemporaries, whether Stevenson or Wells. He excelled in the passive strain because he had willed himself into an Orpheus searching the underworld for what would, finally, elude him; but in the process, he used his art to transmute his memories while allowing his work to change him.

No psychoanalytic tools exist to interpret this kind of reciprocal process in which biographical data are buried within the work and the work curves around to transform biographical data. While childhood, relationship to Apollo, longing for the dead mother, illnesses are extremely valuable as ways of defining Conrad's early development, of greater importance for a major literary figure are those willed experiences of his adulthood. However childhood influenced his adult experiences, we cannot account by means of those early experiences for decisions he made in his art. We must, mainly, perceive him as a man undergoing descents into memory and history; the seamless web that results is the true matter for the biographer.

The moral authority we feel in Conrad derives from the fact he lived in the world he created; his moral/ethical system is a closed circuit in which life and work join, from which there is no escape. Such a moral philosophy was a growing development in Conrad, part of the artistic process as it blossomed with *Heart of Darkness*, *Lord Jim*, *Nostromo*, and continued through *Under Western Eyes* and *Victory*; and it is effective only to the extent Conrad could blend his life as he had lived it with the willed authority of aesthetic achievement. He equated the mirror of the sea to the narcissistic mirror of one's own self, outward and inward, to create moral purpose in an artistic frame of reference. For the biographer, the challenge lies here: *not* to reduce the man to childhood, backgrounds, early development, relationships to parents, but to use these elements psychologically so that they blend with what, really, cannot be traced except through historical contexts, myth, aesthetics, and, most importantly, the individual will.

CHAPTER FIVE

# Norman Douglas

## MARK HOLLOWAY

I

In 1948 Secker & Warburg, after reading a manuscript I had sent them, and deciding that they could not publish it, asked me if there was anything else I would like to write that might interest them. Yes, I replied, I would like to write a biography of Norman Douglas, about half of whose work they had published. Alas, they said, they had just commissioned such a book from John Davenport.

Douglas was still alive then, but died in 1952. Two years later two books about him were published—*Grand Man*, by Nancy Cunard, and *Pinorman*, by Richard Aldington. These did not in any way pre-empt a full biography, and in fact increased the need for one, but by the time John Davenport died, in 1966, none had appeared. I then wrote to David Farrer, at Secker, reminding him of my interview with him years earlier, and saying that I would still like to write Douglas's biography. I enquired if Secker knew of anyone else with that intention, and whether they were proposing to publish anything to commemorate the centenary of Douglas's birth in 1868. My letter was written in September 1966, and it was obvious, as I mentioned in it, that I could not get a biography researched, written and published in that space of time. I said also that I could not undertake the work unless I had a commission from a publisher or a grant from a foundation: I had just enough money to live on, but none to spare.

When we met, Farrer said that there did not appear to be anyone else in the field. He had read my book, *Heavens on Earth*, and was satisfied that I could write the sort of book we both wanted. We agreed that the biographer of Douglas, whose life had been the subject of much gossip and speculation, especially with

regard to his liking for boys, would have to deal frankly and fairly
with this matter as with everything else. The question of access to
letters and other documents would be of paramount importance
in any attempt to discover and tell the truth. He gave me the name
of Douglas's friend, benefactor, and literary executor, Kenneth
Macpherson.

Macpherson lived in Cetona, a small country town between
Florence and Rome. My letter reached him through the floods
which devastated the former city that autumn (1966). He was
busy with flood relief, but was also about to go on a world tour
lasting several months. His welcoming letter gave me some idea of
his own collection of Douglas letters and manuscripts, and
mentioned others at Yale and UCLA. He was tired, fussed, and
busy. He had to visit Rome for half a dozen injections against
tropical diseases, and the injections might make him ill. I had
better come to see him in the spring.

I passed this letter to Farrer, and wrote back to Macpherson
asking if he could provide me with assurances I could send on to
Secker so that I might get a commission from them which would
enable me to make a start. These he provided amply and
emphatically. I would have access to everything in his collection;
use of it in print could be negotiated later, but he did not foresee
any insuperable difficulties. He added that he had "always
wanted a responsible and good biography of Douglas . . . I am
only sorry that this is quite the worst time fate could have chosen.
I am rushing about like a carrier-pigeon with amnesia!"

On the strength of these assurances, Secker wrote that they
would be prepared to commission a life of Douglas "subject to
your satisfying us, before any monies are paid, that you can finally
get enough material . . . to make it possible for you to write a full
scale book". Details of the proposed contract followed, and I now
began to feel I could make preparations. While waiting to see
Macpherson in the spring I would complete a skeleton life of
Douglas from sources already available. I would write to
American university and other libraries asking for permission to
examine their collections and enquiring what might be allowed in
the way of xeroxed copies or microfilm. I would write to the
oldest friends of Douglas in Britain, and try to see and talk to them
as soon as possible. Secker approved a letter I sent to the *TLS*
asking for information, naming them as actively interested
sponsors who would commission the book if enough material were

forthcoming. And I obtained the services of A. M. Heath, the literary agents, whose primary function was to try to find a publisher in the USA so that my visit to that country could be financed, or partly financed, by an advance payment. Secker proposed an advance of £500: £250 to start with and the rest on completion. They said a little later that if I failed to find an American publisher, they would advance the whole £500 at once. This was generous, but I knew I would have to visit Austria and Italy as well as the USA and had better try for as much advance money as possible. Such was the situation at the end of 1966.

## II

I had met Douglas during the war, while he was exiled in England, but catch me, as he would have said, telling him that I wanted (even then) to write about him. His magisterial head with its crown of silvery white hair looked very much as it does in Howard Coster's photograph on the back of Douglas's Penguin editions. This was how I envisaged him while working on my book, wondering sometimes with slight dread, what he would think of me if he could see me prying into every detail I could get hold of, of his past life. It was some consolation to know that he had told Constantine FitzGibbon, who had intended to write his biography: "You can write anything you like about me so long as it's true." Truth was what I wished to tell—truth disentangled from rumour and legend. All the same, I had no illusions as to what Douglas would have thought of my intention to put the whole of his life under a magnifying glass, including those parts of it normally considered private. He regarded the privacy of the individual as sacrosanct, and I wondered, as I found out more about him, whether this might be because he had much to hide that would have endangered his liberty if it had been known. He teased the reader with a combination of frankness that was sometimes almost exhibitionistic, and quite abnormal reticence. This was a practice that stimulated an appetite for fuller biographical information. I wanted to find answers to a hundred questions suggested by reading his books, and in particular by the omissions, hints, and evasions in his cleverly contrived auto-biography *Looking Back*.

Why, for instance, had he had to leave Russia in 1896? And

England (so it was rumoured) in 1917? And Italy in 1937? Why, when he wrote freely about his grandparents and father, did he never mention his mother? What was the truth about his quarrel (in print) with D. H. Lawrence; or about Harold Trower, Consular Agent on Capri, caricatured in *South Wind* as the seedy and ridiculous Freddie Parker? What was his married life like, and why was he so bitter about his wife decades after their divorce? Why, having been heterosexual until that event, did he become more and more, and perhaps exclusively, homosexual? Who were his intimate and preferred companions, and what was the nature of his charm and brilliance that captivated so many well-known people?

I had greatly enjoyed his work, and I thought I admired much of his attitude to life, but it was sometimes difficult to be sure whether his particular combination of exaggeration, high spirits, and an apparent ruthlessness of a truly radical kind were part of his everyday life or a persona, a mask to be worn in public. Was his life, which appeared to be both wise and zestful, a happy one?

In spite of wanting to know the answers to such questions I had actually felt relief as well as disappointment after my original interview with Secker in 1948. It cannot ever be easy to write the life of a living person, and were it easy I would still find it uncongenial to try to describe a life that was not yet complete. Also, nothing like the whole story could have been told while Douglas was alive; but at that time, for my own interest, I had bought a large notebook in which I entered most of the events in his life that were described and dated in his books. I gave him a page per year of adult life (half a page before that), writing very small, six months either side of a central vertical line. I had added more material as it appeared, and from Cecil Woolf's bibliography I entered (in a different coloured ink) publication dates of Douglas's books and other writings.

Now, in 1966, I set about revising and checking this outline and seeing how much more I could add to it. I had at least one copy of most of Douglas's books, and now sought for the one or two I did not possess as well as for cheap reading copies that could be broken up and pasted on paper. Anticipating the growth of material which must occur if I were to collect enough for my purpose, I began a chronological archive in ring binders, starting with two. In another series of files I began to collect copies of all his fugitive writings, of the major reviews of his work, and of articles about him; also a biographical dictionary of his friends, correspondents and other associates. I lived in a remote hamlet in the west of England, and to save time and expense it was important to me to get every scrap of information back to my cottage quickly, so that I would have it permanently for reference and could go through it at leisure whenever I needed to. I had known for years how I would organise these matters, and derived much pleasure and satisfaction from actually doing it. As to the rest: I would collect all the information I could get and then go carefully through it making a chronological narrative.

It did not occur to me at this time that I had been lucky, only that I was faced with a rather daunting task. Nor did I know how large a part luck was to play in the entire undertaking. My first luck had been that both FitzGibbon and Davenport had failed (for personal reasons) to write intended biographies, and that their intentions had obliged me to wait more than a decade after Douglas's death. By that time more material was available both in print and in collections of letters and manuscripts in libraries. Also, copying machines, rare before I started, were becoming more and more generally available, and I cannot believe now that I could have done the job without them. Also, Douglas himself helped: he had a neat and easily legible hand, was a meticulous dater of letters, and had gone through all his books making comments on them and correcting misprints as well as any information they contained which he had subsequently discovered to be incorrect or misleading.

## III

Macpherson had said he would return to Italy from his world tour in March 1967. Early in April I wrote to tell him how I was getting on and to remind him that I felt I could not properly start on my task until I had seen him and his collection. I told him I had talked to old friends of Douglas's such as Martin Secker, and had heard helpfully from others such as Rebecca West. I was in touch with libraries in the USA; I was shortly going to London for another interviewing session; and I had nearly brought my skeleton life of Douglas up to date. Meanwhile, the *TLS* letter had brought in several useful replies which took me to Scotland, Douglas's ancestral homeland, where his nephew was laird of the family estate. Above all, Secker had signed my contract, which, although seven months had passed since my initial letter to Farrer, was nonetheless pleasing, and a good morale booster for whatever might lie ahead.

Early in June, before going to Scotland, I wrote to Macpherson asking if he had received my letter of early April. His reply awaited me on my return from Scotland two weeks later. Yes, he had had my April letter, but in India, alas, his world tour had come to an end. He had had a heart attack. After two months in hospital he had been flown home. He had had to go slow for a long time, and would have to continue to do so. Everything had been postponed. July, which I had suggested for a visit, would be impossible; September would be all right. He was extremely sorry. It was a friendly well-wishing letter but nevertheless dispiriting. Eight months had elapsed since I had first written to him, and still I had not arrived at what I was sure would be the fountain-head of the information I required.

I wrote back suggesting September 1 or as soon as possible after. This letter received no answer, and I began to fear the worst, but waited several weeks before writing again. His reply told me that he had been having "a long siege of falling apart, with rest and medication . . . I HOPE I will be well enough in September; at the moment I'm not up to much". I could send him a list of questions, if I liked, "just in case I am not available in September". With mixed feelings of sympathy and frustration I went ahead and made my other arrangements in Italy for September, and luckily, or generously he let me come to see him then.

His collection was large, and rich in quality and interest. Leaving aside the collection of Douglas's published work in almost every edition and the score or more of manuscripts, corrected proofs, and typescripts, with many pages variously inscribed and annotated by the author, at least ten days would have been needed merely to read through and list everything else: stacks of letters, several long family journals, and many other documents. So when I was told after four days that my room was needed for a weekend guest I was in despair. When I tried to convey my state of mind to Macpherson, pointing out how I had sat closeted in my room every day and all day except for meals and had sat up half the night as well in an attempt to copy only the most important letters, he began to understand, and with impulsive largesse solved my problem by agreeing to let me take away dozens of letters to Rome, my next destination. No limit was put on what I could take, nor any inventory required. Such trust dispelled any hard feelings I had begun to have about the sudden termination of my visit. I stuffed my spare collapsible bag until I could hardly close it, slightly horrified at the thought of being responsible for its contents. These were restored to their owner in London a few weeks later.

Up to this point I doubt if Macpherson had understood that my system of getting the record down accurately and in detail before being able to select from it what might eventually prove to be relevant, was essential to success. Although I had tried to explain this, he probably still thought, as many people do, that what is significant is immediately apparent, and that it alone needs to be recorded. Also, as it was part of my plan to let Douglas speak for himself as much as possible in actual phrases from his letters, accurate transcription was extremely important.

This only proves that it is not always easy to make even the most intelligent and cooperative owner of documents understand the importance of something that seems to him unimportant. Thus it was with Douglas's pocket diaries, mentioned by Macpherson in his first letter to me as being "of no interest except in mentioning names of people he had written to, or places at which he arrived and the hotel name. Nothing else". That was in November 1966. There were forty-five of these little books, I gathered, and I used to think of them standing in a row perhaps fifteen or eighteen inches long, hiding from me a complete record of his whereabouts at any given time, not to mention a parallel record of his correspondents. In vain did I point out at one time or another how valuable these diaries would be to me. In July 1967 he wrote again that "the diaries tell nothing. They record only letters or cards he has written and where he stayed on his travels." Three months later, when I stayed in his house I was given completely free access to the whole Douglas collection, stored in a cupboard; but was only allowed to glimpse the outside of the diaries, ranged along a shelf in Macpherson's own room. After I had returned to England, he said he would have the diaries copied by his secretary; then his secretary "failed" him. By January 1968 I was no nearer the diaries. In February he said I must try to forgive him, and he sent me a specimen typed page—was that the sort of thing I wanted? Yes, I replied, it was vital information, groundwork for the whole book. He did not want to let them out of the house, he said, and I had better, as I had suggested, come out to Italy again and copy them there. He added, tantalisingly, that he was flying to London in a week or two, but the diaries were "too heavy to bring by air". I did not see them, in the end, until June 1969 when I went to Florence. He then sent them to me in my pension by hand, and I spent a solid fortnight copying, copying, copying, from 9 am until 4. But never was a fortnight more profitably spent. I was overwhelmingly grateful. He could simply have refused; but I think he was probably too conscientious on Douglas's behalf to risk obstructing what might be vital information for the success of the book, or both too weak and too kindhearted to resist any longer. In any case I had discovered that tactful but unrelenting patience and persistence were necessary items of the biographer's equipment. During the course of research and writing there were at least three other mini-campaigns or sagas of this kind continuing over a considerable period of time, with other people.

## IV

Six months after my initiation in Italy into what might be called far-afield research, I set out to do the same in the USA during a visit of three months to libraries at Yale, Berkeley, UCLA, Texas, Dartmouth College, New York Public Library, and elsewhere. Except when travelling I worked eight to ten hours every day, and was still at it until two or three hours before boarding the *Queen Elizabeth* to come home. I travelled seven thousand miles by Greyhound, and returned with suitcases bulging with material enough to keep me busy for months, later to be augmented by reels of microfilm sent after me by those kind, hospitable, and efficient institutions. (Research abroad continued into the following year with a second visit to Italy, mainly for the diaries, and visits to Bavaria and Austria.)

By the time I came back from the USA in 1968 I had reached a stage at which Macpherson had had time and opportunity to make judgements about my character and ability. Apart from trusting me, he was also prepared to protect my interest against competitors. When I had begun there did not appear to be any, but they revealed themselves one by one as time went on. In the end there were six rivals, only two of whom were potentially dangerous. Their aim, as one of them put it, was to "get in first", with publication. My aim all along had been to write as definitive a biography as possible and take as long as was necessary in doing it. Secker approved of this, and so did Macpherson, who was ready to bar access to anything over which he had control or influence to all other contenders. Anyone prepared to publish without such access could not hope to produce a book of much substance. My two dangerous rivals faded away, probably for this reason.

The actual research in libraries in the USA was fairly straightforward, information tending to lead from one source to another, librarians often having some knowledge of each others' holdings, especially in the case of substantial collections. Small collections were not always easy to locate, but by writing to likely librarians quite a lot were found. Writers engaged in editing or writing biographies of people with whom Douglas corresponded suggested likely locations or remembered making incidental discoveries in this or that library, and one of the gratifying pleasures in the hunt was the ability to add to this free exchange of special knowledge by swapping information with another researcher whose subject overlapped one's own. It was always worth spending an extra day or more going through any card-indexed catalogue of holdings which might even remotely have any bearing on one's subject, especially if it was cross-referenced. One or two nuggets were dug up in this manner.

In England, copies of wills, births and deaths not only helped to trim and light the family trees, but also led on occasion to the discovery of people still living whom it would have been impossible otherwise to find. No amount of looking up people under former addresses in telephone books or town guides, or even resorting to electoral rolls, however long it took, was wasted once a few identifications had been made and the knowledge of even one such person had been assimilated. All results thus obtained, whether positive or negative, settled a doubt, and made the rest of the enquiry easier by reducing the quantity of information still to be gathered. Research in the Public Record Office, and application to the Foreign Office, however, failed to produce any confidential report on Douglas's career as a diplomat. According to an ex-diplomat I consulted, such a report might not have been helpful. A friend of his had once by chance seen his own report—an impressive folder containing a summarised curriculum vitae and one other sheet of paper on which two sentences had been noted in a cramped hand: "Has pimples. Will be rich".

## V

Luck continued to pursue me and from time to time catch me up. I advertised in an East African newspaper for anyone related to a certain name, and received an answer almost by return of post which led to much. I had gone to Austria with little knowledge, less German, and only two contacts, but by chance met a keen rich amateur interested in Douglas who spoke English and drove me about the province to meet others who loaded me with treasure. Later, trying to obtain confirmation of an appearance in court and a week in a police cell endured by my subject in his homeland, where his family was held in honour and the affair had been hushed up even to the silencing of press and police, I was eventually led to the one man in the province capable of extracting the truth from a reluctant head of department. Even my footsteps might once or twice have been thought (albeit rather fancifully) to have been guided, as when in search of an evening meal on my first day in Florence I stepped in the dark into the nearest trattoria, only to find, once inside, that it was Douglas's favourite. Or, when landing from the funicular in Capri I booked a room in the Ercolano, which I did not then know was the house in which *South Wind* had been completed. In between good omens of this kind I tried to make sure I was still deserving of Fortune by leaving no clue untried, by continually revising my shopping list of desirables, possibles, and improbables by writing to unknown correspondents in all three categories and arranging meetings; or occasionally, as with two separate people in Paris, stopping off there on impulse and posting notes under their doors, securing to my amazement, an instant helpful interview in one case, and in the other a valuable memory in a letter.

On the whole interviews were successful and enjoyable; but I had two failures. After a fascinating hour and a half with Compton Mackenzie, I reached the point at which it was my custom to ask whether, if the interviewee had any letters from Douglas, he would allow me to see them; Mackenzie stared at me quizzically for what I now think must have been a full fifteen seconds before answering gently: "No. I don't think I shall." He did not believe, he added in merciful explanation, in showing private letters to anyone except members of the family concerned.

The other unsuccess, had a third person been present, must have seemed a matter of extreme comedy or farce. My hostess, a tenuous relation by marriage of Douglas, had accidentally come into possession of a mass of correspondence and other documents relating to the family although it had been lodged by that family in an official archive. I had been told, confidentially, that if I could bring it all back or persuade the lady to return it, I would stand a good chance of being made a Hero of the Vorarlberg or the equivalent, or at least of being warmly thanked. This did not happen. I was received very pleasantly indeed by this youngish attractive woman in her garden, and entertained to a superb tea of delicious freshly picked raspberries, with cream, shortbread, and Earl Grey tea. All about us in their boxes were the family letters I had come to see; and in due course my hostess selected some of these, and after reading extracts from them to show that, in her words, "they could only be of interest to the family, and the family, as you know, is all dead", she tore them up one by one, slowly, into eighths and then into sixteenths, in front of me. In vain did I plead that if she did not want the correspondence and did not wish me to see it, the Archiv would be exceedingly grateful to have it back. "But it is none of their business" she replied with an expostulatory gesture which involved raising her graceful arms and pretty shoulders. What upset me most, I think, was pique: the thought that I had been no more successful in trying to see these papers than the Archiv had been in trying to get them back. It was a blow to pride, a denial of persuasive powers which until then had seemed to be adequate and effective.

As well as the occasional refusal, there was the occasional hazard. One concerned Edward Hutton, who was ninety-one when I first consulted him. He was determined to lend me a bound volume of carbon copies of letters he had written to Douglas, and to this end took me to the shelves in another room, where the volume should have been. It was not there, its place being marked by a gap. "Now who *can* I have lent it to?" he asked himself and me. It was not important to me, because I had already seen the originals in the USA, together with the other half of the correspondence, but one naturally hates that sort of situation, and feels for the sufferer. I commiserated with him on his apparent loss, we resumed our talk, and in due course I returned home to the country. About a month later I had a letter from him saying that he had had the impression when he lent me that volume that I would return it within a couple of weeks. He hoped I would not think him rude if he now asked for it back, as he wanted to lend it to someone else. . . . This is a situation which intending biographers can only be advised to avoid, if they can. I was fortunate; he evidently believed my explanation, or remembered the truth, for he wrote apologising, and also invited me to drop in whenever I was in town and tell him how my book was getting on. This I did, last seeing him about a year before his death at the age of ninety-four.

I found the old endearing: five or six octogenarians, and three in their nineties. All were mentally alert, and with one exception had excellent memories for that sort of age. Or appeared to have. It was always necessary to be sceptical, not only of the old, and never to assume that a statement was true unless, as evidence built up, it seemed characteristic or circumstantially likely, or could be corroborated. People seem to remember, especially about someone who has been dead for a number of years, two or three main characteristics about which their personal memories cluster, or they may repeat, often without questioning them, the stories, anecdotes, misquotations and fudged impressions of others. There also seems to be a general tendency, once these so-called memories have crystallised either through verbal repetition or in print, to repeat them automatically thereafter as though they were proven facts. One has to try to frame questions that will act as filters to the truth, easily and casually in the course of conversation.

It usually seemed sensible to take ample time, to talk generally about the subject as well as specifically, to ask for enlightenment rather than to make any assertions, and to reassure the interviewee. I never used a tape recorder, and made notes only afterwards. I always promised that nothing I was told or shown would be used without permission, and that I would send an extract from the final typescript for approval if asked. And to keep in touch was important, especially with the old, by post or telephone or return visits, asking the occasional new question or for confirmation of statements already made, to encourage afterthoughts and recollection of the apparently trivial detail that is sometimes important, or to hear a story repeated and note whether it had changed in any significant way. If one has interested and helpful people to talk to and one genuinely likes them for themselves—I have made and kept a good many friends from those days—the thing becomes a pleasure rather than a task.

So much, perhaps, is obvious. What is not so obvious is the obsessiveness that gradually takes hold of the investigator, the growing passion for detail, the desire to know how his subject would have behaved in almost any circumstances. As the jig-saw pieces gradually fit together and the portrait begins to emerge, so does confidence increase in one's ability to distinguish between a remark made for effect and one made from conviction, or vice versa, and in similar perceptions relating to the characteristic or uncharacteristic behaviour of the subject. Not to let this apparent diminution of nescience be confused with omniscience is an absolute necessity. This aim will be reinforced so long as one is aware, and knows that it is a good thing to be aware, that there is no natural termination to the enquiry, only an arbitrary end that must be called sooner or later to the collection of evidence. Interpretation of that evidence will go on long after one has made one's own version.


# VI


After I had returned from Austria in July 1969, I knew I had completed all the essential research abroad. My chronological archive had expanded from two to twenty ring binders; I had ten special files, eight reels of microfilm, notebooks, and a box of photographs. I began slowly to write the earliest years of his life and immediate forebears, and nine months later reached the middle of the book. I hoped I would be able to finish the rough draft by the end of March 1971. Secker had asked for not less than 80,000 words; it looked as though they were going to get more than 200,000.

I had discovered far more than I could have imagined existed, and contrary to expectation had been provided with all the evidence I needed to supplement the carefully controlled information given by Douglas himself. The difficult period of his marriage which he had done his best to make inaccessible by destroying any evidence he could lay his hands on, was illuminated by two vital documents—his wife's diary, carefully preserved by her sister, and a German novel written by a friend of his wife, in which their married life at the time of their decision to divorce is described in detail. If these years confirmed the depth of his bitterness towards his wife, which all who knew him well had heard him express, and showed how he had cheated her of their children, other documents proved what he had never revealed in his writing or been credited with by those who had written about him, namely, a consistent and admirable sense of parental responsibility towards his two sons. To the eldest, Archie, there is a series of letters covering thirty years at an average rate of forty letters a year, which proves by quantity alone that Douglas was a loving and conscientious father. However much he may have liked to encourage his readers and some of his acquaintances to think of him as an amoralist whose worst enemies were a sense of duty or concern for others—these letters reveal the much more serious and devoted side of his character (which was the greater part of it) as well as the bluff, ruthless, sardonic satyr with the gentlemanly exterior and the shady sexual background, which were the ingredients of his legend that appealed to the more superficial of his admirers. There can be no doubt, either, of his devotion to his young protégés Eric, René, and Emilio, all of whom he had informally adopted in childhood, and loved and educated. They all married and remained close friends of Douglas all their lives. His friendship and loyalty, once given, were lifelong and deep, to both sexes of all ages. The sillier side of Douglas, the schoolboyish pranks, the rather seamy excursions indulged in by himself and his close friend Pino Orioli (the bookseller and publisher) amongst young males, when one would egg the other on to bacchic foolishness, which I had heard about but had no evidence for, is revealed in considerable detail in the diaries which Douglas himself encouraged Orioli to keep.

# VII

The complete rough draft was delivered in December 1971. It was 240,000 words in length, a fact which depressed Secker and appalled Braziller, the prospective American publisher. It had occupied five years of my life and I had planned it with a good deal of care. I was not going to give up the length if I could help it, since

it seemed to me to be justified by the long and interesting life of my
subject, who was eighty-three when he died. There was so much
in his life that was unusual, and controversial, that in order to
maintain balance and proportion, an enlarged scale seemed to me
to be required simply in order to avoid misunderstandings due to
ignorance or prejudice or both. Arguments about length were
exchanged between author, publisher, and agent through the first
half of 1972. David Farrer thought the book should not be more
than 150,000; my agent did what agents do—tried to please both
parties. Meanwhile I had the thing read by Norman Pearson,
Professor of English at Yale, who apart from other qualifications,
had as he said 'shaken hands' with nearly all the characters in the
second half of the book and knew a good deal about Douglas and
his associates; and by Michael Holroyd. They did not find the
book grossly unwieldy; the latter claimed to discern a certain
succinctness in the style of writing and advised me not to cut very
much, merely to prune judiciously, as I had intended to do
anyway. Farrer upped his limit to 175,000, which was encouraging, and said he would shorten the manuscript himself if I would
agree, but could not start for a month or so. Braziller stuck to a
maximum of 150,000. I persuaded my agent and Secker to let me
try for publication at full length elsewhere. Seven excellent
publishers were tried, but all refused. All right, then, Secker, who
had treated me so well, had better cut, especially as David Farrer
was one of the best editors alive, and two-thirds of a book was
probably better than no book at all. I genuinely was not quite
convinced of this, but capitulated, slightly consoled by my agent's
assurance that I would have right of veto on anything I felt
strongly about. (I felt pretty strongly about nearly all of it.) At this
time we were in the middle of 1973. Farrer said he could not start
work on the book for several months, and suggested I should have
a go at it myself. I declined. Since I did not think it too long once
trimmed (as any rough draft would be) of perhaps a tenth of its
length, my interest would be against judicious cutting. Farrer
started in January 1974 and being extremely busy with other
matters all the time, did not finish until the end of June. It was
agreed that if I wished to retain anything he had cut, I must
eliminate something of similar length elsewhere. Farrer thought
he had removed about 80,000 words, but was not quite sure.

I set to work at once and told my agent I thought I might have
the finished typescript ready by the end of October, or it might

stretch to Christmas. Meanwhile I wanted an assurance that there would be no further cuts. Farrer agreed to this and said he hoped to publish in 1975.

I delivered the revised typescript in mid-December. I had reduced its length from 970 quarto pages to 714; but towards the end of January 1975, Farrer asked for his cut version to compare with my final one, because he found my version much longer than he had expected. I replied by phone to tell him that I had cut his version up to form the basis of my final version, and that therefore it no longer existed. Towards the end of February he accepted the new text, but found to his surprise that it amounted to at least 195,000 words. In essence, he wrote, he now found it "a fine biography, unlikely ever to be superseded". At one time, he added, its length would have presented no problems, but production costs had risen by about 40 percent in the last year. As to the Notes for the book, I had been too self-indulgent, and it was a condition of publication that I must accept his cuts in these. They had been reduced from thirty typed pages to nineteen. I was so delighted at having got nearly everything I wanted back into my text, that the sacrifice of the Notes, though contrary to my policy of featherbedding the reader, was made without unduly hard feelings. Farrer had cut extensively, but judiciously.

Secker received the complete new text and Notes in March 1975. They hoped to publish between April and July 1976. In the end it became early December. This made a period of ten years and three months from my original application to Secker about writing the book until its appearance in the shops: a considerable slice of any life.

Farrer wrote that he had confidence in it. I never have confidence in anything I have written, but felt I had done my best. In spite of agonies about cutting and consequent delays in publishing, I had hugely enjoyed the whole enterprise from beginning to end, and had got so much out of it—travel, knowledge of all kinds, and above all, friends I would never otherwise have met or known, that it added richness to my life and took nothing from it. The thing had brought its own rewards as it progressed, and I could face the reception by the critics almost with equanimity.

Douglas, if he was nothing else, was a writer's writer, and certain of them, who had lived through the twenties and thirties and had enjoyed his work and been intrigued by the stories about him, had waited nearly twenty-five years for a biography. They were eager for it; consequently, when it was found to be readable and abundantly informative, they were ready with their praise. David Garnett, Anthony Powell, C. P. Snow, Angus Wilson, Ifor Evans, and Arthur Calder-Marshall all wrote lead reviews praising the book. There was a dream of a review in *The Listener* by Ronald Blythe. Anthony Burgess, in the *TLS*, wrote "This book is so well done that I doubt if it will ever have to be done again." Who could have asked for more, or have expected so much?

As to Douglas himself, I hoped I had done him justice. Whatever his sins, I was convinced in the end that he had done far more good than harm. And I was very grateful to him. He had evidently charmed Fortune, or perhaps the Devil, as he had charmed many men and women, into looking after me carefully throughout the process of research and writing. Even the final year of delay in publishing had been vital: without it, I might never have known the manner of his death, which had been kept a close secret for nearly twenty-five years. Now, more than ever, I bless the timing of the book. It was probably published at about the last possible date at which a book of that kind was economically likely to succeed.

# CHAPTER SIX

# Thomas Mann

## NIGEL HAMILTON

Germans, who love to make a *Wissenschaft* of literature, generally prove hopeless biographers; the French, who worship ideas, find it equally difficult to concentrate upon the man rather than the work. Biography is, it seems to me, a very Anglo-American profession—and it may repay us to consider why. Years ago I saw a performance of a favourite Brecht play, *Der kaukasische Kreidekreis*, in London. Instead of Brecht's impersonal chorus introducing the play like a Greek tragedy, the lights came on and a well-known English entertainer, Michael Flanders, wheeled himself into the centre of the stage. Phrase by phrase he *wooed* the audience, with all the magic of his personality, making theories of *Verfremdungseffekt* seem pompous and ridiculous. The play, *The Chalk Circle*, was a tremendous success.

The point is, the average Anglo-American is suspicious of theory and ideas—the one leading to National Socialism and the other the excesses of the French Revolution. "First show me your man—then let me listen to what he has to say" is our unspoken injunction. As a consequence biography has become an important literary access route for English and American readers, in a manner that is simply not the case in France and Germany.

Writing the life of Thomas Mann was thus a special joy to me. I had learned German at school and had studied briefly at Munich University. Moreover I was married to a German woman, and I have no doubt that in wanting to delineate the career of the Nobel-prizewinning friend of Roosevelt—a "good" German who stood publicly against Hitler—I wanted to tell a good, moral tale, with the aim perhaps of impressing my wife, and possibly by implication rehabilitating her in the eyes of bigoted compatriots who considered most Germans decidedly "bad".

Lest this sounds simplistic, let me declare I am being serious.

My book, *The Brothers Mann*, was the result—still the only full-length biography of either Thomas or Heinrich Mann in English or in German. It is a very sober work, rather too earnest and idealistic in tone (I was 26 when I embarked on it); but it is still in print and read by students of European literature, so perhaps an examination of the subject matter and my approach may be of interest.

Thomas Mann very early began to see himself as a litmus-paper German. His father had been—indeed his forefathers had been—worthy merchants, consuls and senators in the Republic of Lübeck; and although Thomas Mann left school at the age of 17, lived in bohemian Munich and rarely returned to the Hansa city on the Baltic, a spirit of representation waxed as strong in him as in his fathers and forebears. As the years went by, rocketed to precocious literary fame by the success of *Buddenbrooks* (written when he was 24), Thomas Mann concentrated upon his special skill: the deeply autobiographical delineation of the cares and conscience of the cultured German bourgeoisie. His sensitivity to the power of legend and symbol enabled him to weave stories that are often weak in terms of great drama, but are uncannily suggestive. Such a story, for instance, was *Death in Venice*: an almost unaltered autobiographical chronicle of his own holiday spent in Italy in 1911, which was to become one of the most celebrated novellas of twentieth-century world literature. By the 1920's his work had been translated into English; and in 1929 he was awarded the Nobel Prize.

Here was a literary hero indeed. The danger of biography, it seemed to me, was that it was all too easy for the biographer to fall into a fawning sort of hero-worship, disguised as biographical recitation. So in order to write the *true* life of Thomas Mann I felt I needed an antidote—not the objectifying lens of a Marxist or of a Bertolt Brecht, but something *within* the story that would help give it balance and perspective. And this I found in Thomas's brother Heinrich—also a novelist of considerable stature, best known in Britain and America for having written the novel which inspired the famous Marlene Dietrich film *The Blue Angel* ("my head and her legs", Heinrich once remarked pithily).

Here, in the somewhat competitive, even jealous relationship between two great brothers, I began to realize I had found a theme that enabled me to attempt something *more* than pure biography. For while I was (and am) a great admirer of Thomas

Mann's fiction, I felt the story of his *moral* development was equally important in an account of his life—a development that is still largely unknown in the English-speaking world, since none of his more bombastically patriotic, nationalistic World War I writings have been permitted by his family to be translated into English. By using his brother Heinrich—who was a leading pacifist throughout World War I—as a counter-balance I was able to explore the crisis of Thomas Mann's life: which in turn was the crisis, or turning point, of modern German history: republicanism or fascism.

It was fortunate that I chose this theme of two brothers—for without it, I now realize, it would have been impossible to find a publisher for my book. I was an unknown, unpublished "author" in my mid-twenties; a distinguished German writer, Peter de Mendelssohn, was known to be working on the *official* life of Thomas Mann in German—and in America, the translator of Thomas Mann's correspondence, Richard Winston, was also known to be writing a *Life*. Both authors were to die before completing their tasks—but in 1970 this could not be anticipated, and I was lucky to get a commission for my project from both British and American publishers.

Once commissioned (I had drawn up both a brief synopsis and a more extended "treatment") I must admit that I worked feverishly to get the book finished—determined to beat my rivals! Thomas Mann's widow, having authorized Mr. de Mendelssohn to do the job, was in no mind to encourage a young Englishman who wished Thomas Mann to share the honours with his brother Heinrich—she refused to see me. Others were distrustful—would Thomas Mann's reputation suffer by being linked to his passionately Republican, "progressive" brother?

Had I been writing only the life of Thomas Mann, I frankly doubt whether I would have been able to produce enough new evidence to face my competition. But the very novelty of my dual concept puzzled people—and gradually I was able to make considerable and heartening headway. Thomas Mann's old secretary Miss Ida Herz lived in London; his son Golo, a Professor of History, consented to see me; a friend in Berlin (Elizabeth Plessen) turned out to have done some unique recordings with Thomas Mann's widow. Pretty soon, however, I felt a need to know where I stood in relation to such witnesses and to the material available, both in printed books and in archives—otherwise one might spend a lifetime accumulating information.

The answer, I discovered, was simply to start *writing*—in fact to treat the work chronologically, in sections. Thus an overall command of published sources was necessary in order for me to start; thereafter I worked chronologically, researching and then writing up the Manns' childhood; researching and then writing up their youth, their early creative years, and so on. I had read and been told that Thomas Mann was very methodical: that he rose every day at a certain hour, breakfasted, and began work; that at noon he took a walk, followed by lunch, a siesta, then correspondence and reading—but no further writing. In particular no midnight oil. "Genius comes of a good night's sleep," he once remarked—and if I was to tackle two lives encompassing so much modern literary, social and political history (from the 1870's to the 1950's) in only two and a half years (the date set in my contract), it behoved me to find a similar discipline.

To pursue the task full time I had already taken a full-time manager for the bookshop I had established in Greenwich, on the Thames; following the Thomas Mann protocol (which I still use today) I began to write only in the mornings, between breakfast and lunch. I would then go for a walk with my children, and spend the rest of the day reading or in correspondence. By deliberately pacing myself in this way I was never really daunted by the task; each day the manuscript grew, if only by a page. Moreover by handling the research and narration chronologically, I never felt bored or weary of a period—there was always the excitement of further research, discovery and interpretation ahead of me. In this way the "freshness" of the story could be preserved, even over a very considerable span. Naturally this precluded the Olympian stance of the biographer who has the details of the entire life, after years of research, at his fingertips: who can range backwards and forwards in time without accepting the constraints of chronology.

Yet to adopt such an Olympian stance was neither in my character, as a non-academic 26-year-old, nor did I feel it a "safe" approach for a writer. The temptation, after all, is to assemble one's material and then to pass it, in one massive filtering operation, through one's own literary sieve. It is almost impossible to resist the conscious or unconscious temptation, then, to invent a story rather than to follow it: to weave a life rather than to record it as it was lived. Neither Heinrich nor Thomas Mann can have conceived, even in their wildest dreams, the sagas that were in store for them when writing innocently for *Simplicissimus* in the heyday of Imperial Germany in the 1890's. By taking each period of their lives in turn I felt I was resisting the temptation of forward-looking—and that what my story might lack in mature, digested judgement it gained in veracity: in following scrupulously the life as it had been lived by the subjects, not as neat components in the biographer's own conceit. Almost all Thomas Mann's own writings had grown this way—"organic" growth as he termed it; I therefore tried to let the story, as far as possible, tell itself.

Unfortunately Thomas Mann's diaries were not at that time available—he had stipulated that those he had not burned were to be opened only 20 years after his death—i.e. in 1975. It was utterly impossible, therefore, to even aim at being definitive or comprehensive. What was important was to adopt a narrative stance, deciding as one went along what was important and what was not. And in the course of the work I was able to find much unpublished material—particularly letters written by Heinrich Mann—that gave me a feeling of contributing more than a simple "popularisation" of the story of the brothers Mann: the feeling that I was in fact helping to advance knowledge as well as perhaps understanding. In East Berlin I was able to go through the largely unpublished holdings of the Heinrich Mann Archive; even at the Thomas Mann Archive in Zurich I happened to arrive at a time when a cache of Heinrich Mann letters to his brother Thomas had just been discovered—still unsorted, let alone read and reproduced anywhere. In Lübeck there was much material about the Manns' family background—as well as an almost intact nineteenth-century city in which the Manns had grown up. The son of a dear friend of Heinrich Mann had kept many hundreds of unpublished Heinrich Mann letters—he welcomed me to his house at Sèvres like a son. Or at Kilchberg, in Switzerland, when I got off the bus, walked down a dusty road overlooking the vast lake—and saw a polished brass plate by the doorbell of a small, unimposing villa, terraced on the hillside, and still marked, twenty years after the novelist's death: THOMAS MANN.

The problem very quickly became not one of lack of material for a biography, but surfeit. I had contracted to write a book of 250 pages. When I had finished the work after three years, early in 1973, it came to 650. After some argument Secker & Warburg, the English publisher, accepted the manuscript at this length. The American publisher, Holt, Rinehart & Winston, did not. Without simultaneous American publication (and shared setting costs) the English publisher could not publish.

This was an unfortunate impasse—for I refused to cut the book. I reasoned that I had written it at such length because the story was a long one, spanning eight decades of modern history, 1871 to 1955. Moreover I was bolstered by the knowledge—from my work—that Thomas Mann had suffered the same problem when submitting his first novel *Buddenbrooks*—for the publisher, Sammy Fischer, wished to cut it by at least half!

Identification with one's subject is, however, a dangerous, if not psychologically lunatic thing, and I often wondered if I was being obtuse. A distinguished editor from the Oxford University Press, who had edited Richard Ellmann's James Joyce letters, was called in—and using scissors and paste she made a valiant effort to cut my first 100 pages down to 30, as a trial.

I was horrified by the result. It seemed to me that it was in danger of becoming similar to an entry in the *Dictionary of National Biography*, or an obituary notice: namely a threading together of salient facts, like beads on a string. Whereas what I had intended was an extended prelude, relating the Lübeck background to the two writers when children—not only to help explain their fraternal relationship but because the Lübeck background is in fact the key to both *Buddenbrooks* and *The Blue Angel*. Moreover, without that quiet first setting of the scene, I doubted whether I could sustain my *real* ambition—which increasingly became one of epic.

I suppose this may sound inflated, but the point is crucial. My publisher, in reading my synopsis, had been excited by the "human drama" of the potential book. In fact the quarrel between Heinrich and Thomas Mann during World War I had become a *cause célèbre* in Germany, akin in some ways to the Dreyfus affair in France a generation earlier. Heinrich had accused his brother of blind jingoism (by implication, in an essay on Zola); and Thomas Mann responded by spending the next years of his life defending himself against the charge. *His* essay became so long it had to be published as a book, of almost a thousand pages. The two brothers, though living in Munich, refused to see each other or even appear in the same room or concert hall. Only when Heinrich seemed to be dying of peritonitis after an appendix operation did Thomas finally give in. Thereafter both brothers became staunch Republicans in the Weimar years; both opposed the Nazis—and both were among the very first Germans to have to flee Germany after Hitler was appointed Chancellor in January 1933.

The story of their "wanderings" thereafter—to Switzerland and France, and then to America—was, I felt, a moving and *representative* one.[1] Thomas Mann, in particular, was aware that, like one of the biblical fathers, he bore in himself the *true* literary flame of Germany. He had, after all, an international reputation and his books were translated into many foreign languages.

It was impossible, as narrator, not to be aware of the epic nature of this story. It was, as I saw it, an extended moral fable—only true. Moreover it was a fable in which fiction mixed with fact (owing to the autobiographical basis of Thomas Mann's work), in which literature mixed with politics—and with history. The very relationship between art and society—or rather, between the artist and his time—came into the clearest, cruellest focus. Why had Thomas Mann permitted his books to be published inside Germany during the first years of the Third Reich, and sworn to keep silence on the régime? His publishers, the daughter and son-in-law of old Sammy Fischer, had given me much help and encouragement in my research. Was it fair to spotlight the moral dilemma they had caused Thomas in the years when they themselves remained in Germany under Hitler?

Above all, I wanted to allow this epic story, with its roots in those Protestant Hanseatic merchants of the little nineteenth-century Republic of Lübeck, to tell itself. Once I began to judge or polemicize, I felt, the true epic would be lost: the story would become a tract, an argument: an historical essay. Whereas biography, I was convinced, should enable the reader to see an artist in the context of his time, but also enter *into* his life: its colour, its contrasts, its dilemmas, and its *development*. You cannot teach development—for growth comes from the interaction of personality and experience. I wanted my story to unfold, without haste: not to analyse and explain away the development of Thomas Mann, but to follow it, intimately and scrupulously. And though I recognized that my book could benefit from judicious pruning—particularly in long passages of quotation from letters and documents—I did not see how it could be cut to one-third of its length without emasculating it.

Five whole years now went by. No alternative American publisher could be found to help underwrite the immense setting costs of a 650-page book. To make matters worse, my German wife died in 1973, the year I completed the biography, leaving me with two small boys (then six and two) to bring up. Hannelore's death made me doubly determined not to compromise: she had lived beside me throughout its gestation, and I felt it would be a betrayal of *her* if I were to give in.

Of course today, ten years later, I realize not only how stubborn I was, but also that I deceived myself in "owing it" to Hannelore to refuse to condense the manuscript. For Hannelore was herself a highly intellectual doctoral student who—like most Germans—did not believe in biography.

Something of the Manns' resolute stand against fascism nevertheless gave me a strange courage. I knew that the story of their lives was an important one; chronicling it had in many ways altered my life—for in tracing the course of Thomas and Heinrich's childhood and careers I learned much about myself and my three brothers: about fraternal envy, competitiveness, malice and self-deception. The very *morality* of Thomas Mann's achievement—of living out his profoundly autobiographical, egocentric obsession and coming, in the end, to a rapprochement with Heinrich—had a profound impact on me, as a somewhat wayward 26-year-old would-be writer, and upon my marriage, for in chronicling the lives of the Mann brothers I was forced to question the ethics and morality of my own life, and to reconsider both my values and my goals as a writer. I felt therefore indebted to the Manns, for the privilege of having been able to research and chronicle their lives—and therefore less concerned with publication myself.

Publication, indeed, appeared progressively less likely. I wrote several other books and in 1976, three years after Hannelore's death, I remarried and moved to Finland, my young wife's mother country. It was while living there that I was asked to undertake the official biography of Field Marshal Viscount Montgomery of Alamein, who had died in 1976. Almost immediately my English publisher changed his tune. He would now go ahead with publication of *The Brothers Mann*, unilaterally, without waiting for an American publisher. An outside editor was appointed to look at the manuscript; her decision regarding length would be final.

To my unbounded relief (and gratitude) this editor decided in my favour. Of the 650 pages she felt that not one could be cut. Thus in 1978 *The Brothers Mann* was published in England—set in minuscule print to reduce the number of pages, and the author's royalty reduced to 5 per cent. I was too grateful to care—and the reception in England was so favourable that an American publisher now appeared on the scene—Yale University Press. The book was thus published in the United States in 1979. Again, the reception was so encouraging that a second printing was ordered, and in due course the book was issued as a paperback. Letters came to me from all over the world: and in 1980 an American professor decided to publish a book of essays, based on *The Brothers Mann*, but giving the stories behind *other* great literary brotherhoods—from the Joyce brothers to Isaac Bashevis and I. J. Singer.[2]

I felt, yes, that I had been vindicated. I didn't earn very much, since all American monies were paid to my English publisher and I received the money (9 percent royalty) only years afterwards. But then my English publisher *had* taken the risk of "going it alone". Moreover, though asked to, I refused to pay back the advance royalty I had received from the original American publisher—arguing that his refusal to accept the over-long manuscript was *his* fault, not mine!

There were days, however, when I felt bitter about the whole business. Five years I had had to wait. Without an income from my bookshop in Greenwich I could never have undertaken the research and writing of the book (though the German Government did give me a small travelling grant, which was useful); indeed, if one gave way to self-pity, the story was a pretty miserable one, from the death of my first wife onwards.

Fortunately, however, such days were rare—and once I remarried became rarer still. Ironically—or inevitably—the same problems soon befell my biography of Montgomery. Instead of producing the contracted 250-page life, I very quickly recognized the epic nature of the story—and the first volume, totalling some 850 book pages, was rejected out of hand by the first American publishers to see it (Summit Books and Random House). Undeterred I refused to cut it—and on the basis that no cuts would be allowed it was re-offered in a special "auction" arranged by Harold Ober, my New York agents. Soon there were publishers *fighting* for it—and cables began to arrive at my Suffolk home in England (I had returned in 1977) announcing the latest offer![3]

The story thereafter has nothing to do with *The Brothers Mann*. Nevertheless it is to my experience in undertaking that first major biography that I owe the strength (or stubbornness) to believe in myself: to develop my own vision of what I was trying to achieve, and to pursue it uncompromisingly towards its end.


One final word. Since embarking on a major *military* biography I have often reflected on the difference between the biography of a man of action and a man of words. There is of course something incestuous about literary biography: by definition, a writer writing about a writer. Moreover because the subject is, as a writer, by profession articulate, the biographer is denied his usual role: that of making articulate, in print, the life of a man of action. To combat this, many literary biographers see themselves as super-articulators: men or women whose trade it is to interpret further the work of their subject. This is, I am sure, a great mistake—a wilful confusion with the tasks of literary criticism. As I said in starting this essay, the Anglo-Saxon reader's desire is to get to know his man. The reader wants to know: not in order to judge the work of the subject, but in order to preserve the balanced, individual and human "picture" that precludes Anglo-Saxons from being mesmerized into accepting tyranny. For is that not at heart the great virtue of Anglo-American literary biography? French and Germans may become entranced or enmeshed in the great works of their composers, artists, authors. Thousands of books, tracts and monographs have already, for instance, been written by Germans (and Frenchmen) on Thomas Mann—but no biography: no deliberate distancing: no attempt to stand back and chronicle the man's life as a human being, a man of flesh and blood, capable of error and deceit as well as great art. And without that distance, Germans today still fall into the trap that has bedevilled their country's history for so many centuries: namely the failure of educated, thinking people to distinguish between the man and the work. If Americans and Britons have so far avoided the tyranny of a Napoleon or a Hitler, it is largely because we are educated to make that distinction: to be curious about the man as well as his ideas.

It is for this reason that I abhor the "Germanic" temptation for the literary biographer to confuse literary biography with literary criticism. The literary biographer's task, as I see it, is to help the reader separate the subject from the subject's work—and he will not do that successfully if he becomes too concerned with interpreting his work. It is the *reader* that counts in Anglo-American literary biography: not the author. The author is merely performing a service, based on investigative research and upon a kind of representative curiosity. It is not dissimilar to journalism—which presumably is why academic Germans affect to despise it—and indeed it uses many of the techniques of journalism: the oral interview being the most important. Just as in journalism, the right of the reader to know, to be informed, is at the heart of biography. Obviously the literary biographer is intent upon achieving more than mere journalism—but the central stance is common to both, and is ignored—to my mind—at the author's peril. He is, if you will, the conscience of the nation. It was no accident that the essay which produced the great moral and political crisis of Thomas Mann's life—Heinrich Mann's *Zola* in *die weissen Blätter* in November 1915—was a biographical essay; nor was it accidental that the lecture which provoked a public crisis in Munich early in 1933—Thomas Mann's essay *The Sufferings and Greatness of Richard Wagner*—was a biographical one. Thomas Mann was immediately vilified. No less than a hundred dignitaries of Munich and the German musical world—including Richard Strauss and Hans Pfitzner—made a formal, public "protest" to curry favour with the Nazis. Thomas Mann was hounded out of his home and country, not to return until after the holocaust had proved his worst imaginings correct.

Biography, then, is a matter of life and death: the test of a nation's ability to look at itself with honesty and balance. Moreover, literary biography is even more exacting than chronicling the life of a man of action. It demands a sensitivity to literary art in order to do justice to the literary subject's achievement; it demands insight into the creative process as well as deep knowledge of the literary background to achievement: the artist's "time" which influences, inspires, competes with him. But the most challenging demand of all is upon the *character* of the literary biographer. Can he share the same cell as his chosen poet and yet remain objective; can he balance sympathy with profound questioning; can he retain sight of the human perspective, the human inquiring that is at the heart of biography, while remaining appreciative of the great works of literature—works which, like a spider's web, may all too easily ensnare him?

He *must* if he is to further the craft of something I see as quintessentially English and American—a contribution to *belles lettres* that goes far deeper than any German or Frenchman can understand—to the very heart of civilized, free and democratic society.

CHAPTER SEVEN

# Wyndham Lewis*

## JEFFREY MEYERS

### I

Though the life and work of Katherine Mansfield and Wyndham Lewis seem to be totally different, they were contemporaries and had some surprising similarities. Both were born in British colonies, came from wealthy families but were poor all their adult lives, lived a bohemian existence in France, had a cosmopolitan rather than an insular outlook, were strongly influenced by Russian writers, and wrote their first, satiric books about Germans. Lewis decorated the Cave of the Golden Calf, where Mansfield performed as a *commère*. Both shared a hostile attitude toward Bloomsbury, and wrote for the *New Age*. Both were emotionally involved with Beatrice Hastings, were artistic allies of Gaudier, and friends of the Sydney Schiffs and the Raymond Dreys. Both were hostile to doctors and unwilling to face the reality of their diseases.[1]

In September 1922, four months before her death, Mansfield and Lewis had a disastrous meeting at the Schiffs' London house. He was rude, perhaps even brutally cruel to the dying woman during their heated discussions about the limitations of her stories and her fatal infatuation with George Gurdjieff, whom Lewis accurately described as a "Levantine psychic shark."

My experience with Mansfield's biography was excellent preparation for writing the life of Lewis. She died at 34 and wrote relatively little; he died at 74, wrote 50 books and 360 essays, and was also the most important English painter of the twentieth century. Mansfield's character was consistent; her stories, journals and letters were homogeneous and easy to understand. Lewis

* First published in *Biography*, 4 (Winter 1981), 66–81.

passed through a number of distinct physical, temperamental and artistic stages in his life, and his capacity for change and development was one of the most fascinating aspects of his character. Books like *Tarr*, *The Art of Being Ruled*, *Time and Western Man*, *The Apes of God*, *Self Condemned* and *The Human Age* were massive, complex and extremely difficult. Mansfield's work was essentially autobiographical; her letters and journals were truthful and her dominant mode was self-revelation. Lewis was intensely secretive about his private life, covered his tracks and hid behind a series of masks and *personae*. The editor of his *Letters* has observed that "The scholar concerned with the data of Lewis' life has found himself lost in a fog of rumour and half-proved fact, of conflicting statements and pure fantasy."

Mansfield has been dead for fifty years, Lewis for only twenty-six years. My life of Lewis is therefore more extensively based on personal letters and interviews. There are many more people now alive who knew him than knew her, and his surviving friends, unlike hers, are distinguished by their impressive intellect and fierce loyalty to his memory. His scholarly disciples are a close-knit, rather than a diverse group; a few of them even imitate the style, mannerisms and politics of the Master. Almost all Lewis scholars are men; a significant number of Mansfield scholars are women. Some of the feminist reviewers, who resented my invasion of their territory and assumed a man could not really understand their Katherine, launched attacks on my book. One particularly nasty review was written by the close friend of a rival biographer. Though I sympathized with Mansfield, I never felt I was like her in any way. But I found that Lewis and I had (at least) a similar physique, quarrelsome temperament, dislike of publishers, capacity for work and commitment to intellectual life. I had written a good deal about Mansfield's friends and milieu—Lawrence, Bloomsbury and Garsington—before I began her biography. But I had never done scholarly work on Lewis' closest friends—Pound and Eliot—and had to master the more experimental forms of modernism. Fortunately, with Mansfield and with Lewis, I became increasingly attracted to their characters and books as I discovered more about their life and work.

The reputations of Mansfield and Lewis provided another significant contrast. Mansfield's reputation, founded on the cult established by Murry immediately after her death, has steadily increased during the last fifty years. Though she is particularly admired in her native New Zealand and in France, scholars from all over the world have written about her work; her books are still in print and continue to prosper. Lewis, on the contrary, because of his unpopular satires and Right-wing political tracts of the 1930's, has attracted more hostility than appreciation. In North America, his advocates tend to be conservative Catholic scholars, like Marshall McLuhan, Hugh Kenner and Russell Kirk, who publish with Henry Regnery and in the *National Review*; and he has been either ignored or attacked by the liberal New York literary establishment. Irving Howe, their representative spokesman, has exclaimed in the *Partisan Review*: "When a charlatan like Wyndham Lewis is revived and praised for his wisdom, it is done, predictably, by a Hugh Kenner in the *Hudson Review*." Most of Lewis' books are out of print and difficult to find; and he has not enjoyed the academic prestige of his contemporaries—Pound, Eliot and Joyce—who freely acknowledged his genius. One of my ambitions was to attract new readers and restore Lewis' reputation.

The attractive biographical image of Katherine was established in 1931 by the Ruth Mantz–Middleton Murry biography of her early years and reinforced by Antony Alpers' rather sentimental evocation of 1954. But there has been no biography of Lewis. Roy Campbell's book was printed and announced in 1932, but never published,[2] biographies of Lewis were projected and abandoned by Walter Allen, Martin Seymour-Smith and Catherine Dupré; and Victor Cassidy, who began twelve years ago, has not published a word. My biography, which brings the Enemy out of the shadows and shows him to be more sympathetic than menacing, was the first to appear.

## II

A biographer should combine the scholar's passion for learning about his subject and the period in which he lived with the detective's monomaniacal delight in facts for their own sake. He should be an exceptionally organized person who enjoys gossip and likes to ferret out secrets. When he has finished his research, contemplated his discoveries, and understood the intellectual and emotional life of his subject, he must be able to fit everything he has learned into a meaningful pattern and to satisfy his readers' natural curiosity about the life of an extraordinary person.

Though I followed the same procedure for both biographies, Lewis' longevity, secrecy, complex books and varied careers as a vital and versatile painter, novelist, philosopher, poet, critic and editor made the research for his life much more difficult than for Mansfield's. While I slowly acquired Lewis' valuable books (and sometimes borrowed them from Hugh Porteus and Walter Allen), I compiled a 900-item bibliography of criticism about him and a detailed 14-page chronology of his life. I wrote and received several hundred letters about Lewis, including vivid accounts from Lord David Cecil, Lord Clark, Alistair Cooke, Admiral Sir Caspar John, Archibald MacLeish, Henry Miller, Sir Oswald Mosley, Anthony Powell, Laura Riding, Sir Sacheverell Sitwell, Allen Tate and Sir William Walton.

In May–June 1978 I spent five weeks reading 8000 Lewis documents at Cornell University. Fortunately, the librarians allowed me complete access to their superb collection of Lewis letters and manuscripts and guided me through the complex task of studying them. Since only one other person had read everything at Cornell (and he moved to Ithaca and took a year and a half to do it), it seemed as if the long shelves of papers existed solely for my benefit. The considerable strain of reading manuscripts for eight hours a day and typing the notes all evening was alleviated by the exhilaration of continuous discoveries. I left Cornell with Lewis' stern warning echoing in my throbbing head: "When a person who, like myself, has played a prominent part in the intellectual life of his country, in his time, comes to die, the circumstances of his life are liable, by way of biography, to be distorted and arranged according to the fancy of the biographer."

W. K. Rose, the superb editor of Lewis' *Letters*, who died of a brain tumor in 1968, left all his papers to Vassar College. Reading his correspondence with people who had died since his edition appeared in 1963 provided much new information; and his earlier letters to people I had written to allowed me to check the accuracy of their memories and confirm their stories. I also read Lewis' correspondence at Yale, the New York Public Library, the Morgan Library, the Museum of Modern Art, the British Library, London University Library, the Tate Gallery and the Imperial War Museum. I gratefully received copies of letters from eight other libraries; and from his publishers New Directions, Henry Regnery, Ryerson Press and Chatto & Windus—though his correspondence with most English publishers was destroyed, with their offices, in the Blitz. Dora Stone and Romilly John sent me *original* letters to copy; a number of other people allowed me to read Lewis letters in their possession; Sam Hynes provided a copy of a precious unpublished memoir by Kate Lechmere; and William Wees gave me a revealing tape-recorded interview with Helen Rowe, a model who had known Lewis before the Great War. I traced, with great difficulty and the help of a friend familiar with the Civil Service bureaucracy, Lewis' furious correspondence with the London County Council, which was trying to demolish his Notting Hill Gate flat at the end of his life, and was grieved to find that the file had been destroyed. When I first asked an Indian clerk if they kept correspondence from the 1950's, he said he could not tell me because he was not born then.

Though I succeeded in tracing hundreds of unpublished letters, I had severe problems with two libraries. Boston University, which owns important papers by the mother of two of Lewis' children sent the least helpful letter I have ever received: "Our Iris Barry materials are restricted by the donor [Edmund Schiddel], and relative to his instructions we may not make this correspondence available for research, nor reply to queries concerning the contents of the materials." This seemed particularly absurd in view of the fact that the contents were described in the very useful National Union Catalogue of Manuscripts, the American equivalent of the National Register of Archives in London. Though the total and indefinite embargo of scholarly materials was (fortunately) unique in my experience, I did not—despite help from friends on the Boston University faculty—succeed in penetrating this sanctum.[3]

With SUNY Buffalo, the second most important collection of Lewis papers and a lamentable contrast to Cornell, I had an infinitely more torturous experience. I first wrote to Buffalo asking to read their Lewis letters in September 1977, the month after my extremely pleasant and informative six-hour interview with the still-beautiful Mrs. Lewis. I took her out for lunch and a drive around Torquay, and she frankly answered all my questions, promised to send me her notes on Lewis' life and inscribed my copy of *Rotting Hill*: "To Jeffrey Meyers from G. A. Wyndham Lewis, Thanking you for a very enjoyable visit." (She had mellowed considerably since the early 1960's when she nearly drove W. K. Rose mad with her criticisms of his edition.) I looked forward, with craned eyebrows, to meeting her the following year.

Buffalo replied that written permission was needed to read the letters, I duly wrote for this to Mrs. Lewis and, after an alarming delay, was shocked to hear that she had suffered a disabling stroke in October. The Courts, acting on her behalf, would eventually take over the responsibility of the Lewis Estate; until then, no one could supply the requisite permission. In May 1978 I stopped at Buffalo on the way to Cornell and found the Library was closed during the summer, precisely when scholars were able to visit. In July, when I went to London to write the book on a Guggenheim grant, the Library informed me that they would not supply copies of the letters—even if I got the necessary permission. (After Mrs. Lewis' stroke, in the fall of 1978, the last of Lewis' papers—his final keep—were sold to Cornell via Anthony Rota. Though Cornell and Rota were both willing to let me read these papers in London, before they were sent to America, I was prevented from doing so by a legal technicality.)

My hope for the Buffalo papers was briefly renewed in March 1979 when two of the three members of the committee advising the Society of Authors, which the Courts had appointed to administer the Lewis Estate, gave permission to get copies of the letters. In April the Director of the Library retired, they changed their policy and finally agreed to send the xeroxes. But Mrs. Lewis, who was 78 and had been in frail health for some time, died on April 12; and the committee's permission was suspended until the Estate was once again settled. I completed the biography on June 13, and in August finally received permission to get the letters from Mrs. Lewis' two heirs. Both of them have a serious interest in Lewis' work and had looked after her since his death.

In order to do justice to Lewis the artist I saw a great many of his paintings and drawings, which are scattered in museums throughout America, Canada, Britain, Australia and South Africa. I studied his work in Ithaca, Utica, New York City, Cambridge, Mass. and Windsor, Ontario; in seven London and eight provincial museums; in several art galleries (where I found biographical material in exhibition catalogues of Spencer Gore and Jessica Dismorr); and in the major private collections of Omar Pound, Wyndham Vint, Walter Michel, John Cullis, D. G. Bridson and David Drey. I wrote in advance to view paintings that were not on exhibition; and found it especially enjoyable to see the Tate's entire collection of Lewis spread out for my private view in their storage vaults. The British Institute of Recorded Sound and the BBC enabled me to hear readings by Lewis and broadcasts of *The Human Age*; and the Arts Council of Britain showed me a film on *Blast*.

## III

The next stage of research was the personal interviews, which provided an opportunity to meet many friends of Lewis who were invariably hospitable and kind. At the appropriate time I telephoned the people I had already written to, arranged a specific appointment and got directions to their homes. I had typed out a long list of questions, with space in between, took brief notes on the answers during the interview, and wrote out the complete answers from my notes soon after the meeting. I found it was better not to have a tape recorder, which seems awk-ward—especially to older people—is difficult to transcribe, and collects a great deal of useless material.

I mostly interviewed people in their seventies and eighties, and found that they had good memories for the distant, significant past—though they often did not remember what happened yesterday. But they tended to repeat what they had written rather than what had originally happened, as if their memory had obliterated as well as recorded the primary experience. I usually brought photographs which helped to recall obscure incidents. Older people tend to become extremely tired after an hour's conversation, so rapport had to be established almost immediately. I had to convey the impression of being knowledgeable, serious and sympathetic, yet not appear to be prying into secrets they were reluctant to disclose. It was essential to stick strictly to the subject and prevent them from wandering from it, for time was precious. It was best to begin with rather general questions and then, when they felt more at ease, to lead up to more personal ones. It was important to remember that people born in the nineteenth century have a very different idea of sexual morality than now exists, and can be easily shocked. At the end of the interview I always asked to see their books and letters by Lewis; and if they had written a book I brought a copy (preferably a first edition) and asked them to inscribe it. Though many people claimed, in their letters or on the telephone, that they had nothing valuable to say and scarcely knew Lewis, I never believed this and always insisted on the promised interview. Every conversation revealed something of value and allowed me to corroborate other written and spoken evidence. Personal interviews gave me the most vivid sense of what Lewis was really like.

The most interesting aspect of the research was undoubtedly the seventy interviews conducted, though I had to be careful not to encourage informants to say what I wanted to hear. Those interviewed included three originals for *The Apes of God*. The blind poet, Edgell Rickword, who thought Lewis carried on a one-sided quarrel with him and got his own back in his ironic poem "The Encounter," was indifferent about his role in the satire. Stephen Spender, who wryly agreed that Dan Boleyn, a complete idiot, was based on himself, was amused by his fictional image. And Sacheverell Sitwell, who called Lewis a genius *manqué*, wanted to hear no more about the "malicious, thwarted and dangerous man" and—fifty years later—was still furious about his treachery.

In North America, Russell Kirk asked me to stay in his eclectic Michigan mansion and described his meeting with the blind old man; Father Stanley Murphy, who invited Lewis to teach at Assumption College in the early 1940's, expressed great fondness for Lewis, told me about his effective teaching and identified the originals of *Self Condemned* as we looked across the Detroit River to the big American city. Marshall McLuhan, a loyal friend in the forties and Lewis' leading disciple, described his publicity campaign for Lewis in Missouri, told how the enraged writer tore up a copy of his dangerous *Hitler* book—and how McLuhan got into Woody Allen's film, *Annie Hall*. I helped John Slocum, who lived in regal splendor in Newport, crack open his locked safe. There was no correspondence from Lewis, but we found dozens of forgotten letters from Pound. When my five-year old daughter, accustomed to modest residences without long driveways and caged elevators, boldly inquired: "Hey Slocum, was this place once a palace?" he replied, in a deep and dignified voice: "My dear, it still is."

I smashed up my car on the way to dinner with Dora Stone and never reached Innsbruck; but I saw Roy Campbell's widow, Mary, in their crumbling villa above Sintra, and learned that Lewis' description of their wild wedding in *Blasting and Bombardier-*

*ing* was strictly accurate and that Campbell considered their friendship one of the biggest events of his life. I also found Iris Barry's friend, Pierre Kerroux, in the Alpes Maritimes, heard about her final years and how her papers (including letters from Lewis and drawings by Picasso) had been stolen after her death.

In London, Rebecca West (the only person I met who knew Lewis before the Great War) gave me whiskey with dinner instead of wine, and talked about the days of Vorticism and *Blast* while sitting before her striking portrait that reveals a troubled intelligence in her strained expression and features. Paul Martin, the Canadian High Commissioner in London, made me aware of the damaging rumors that surrounded Lewis in wartime Canada: that he had been a Conscientious Objector in the Great War (instead of an officer at Passchendaele) and had been paid by Winston Churchill to leave England in 1939 (instead of going into voluntary exile). Martin's wife, Eleanor, explained—during a magnificent lunch—that the furious expression in her portrait was provoked by Lewis' cynical criticism of patriotism, the royal family, important politicians and military leaders while he was painting her. The Dowager Marchioness of Cholmondeley, a friend of Henry James, received me in her Kensington Palace Gardens mansion, filled with portraits of herself by Lewis, Orpen and John. She had written love letters to Lewis in the early thirties and described their secret meetings in his dingy Ossington Street flat.

Hugh Porteus, Lewis' longtime friend and disciple, was my liveliest and most indiscreet informant. In three long meetings (and a dozen letters) he told me of Lewis' keen interest in his own sexual affairs and how jealous he was of the closely guarded Mrs. Lewis. Henry Moore, still handsome and energetic at eighty, dressed in a lilac shirt and affectionately stroking a piece of smooth-grained wood, expressed great admiration for Lewis as he showed me his studios and sculpture garden. As a young student, Moore was inspired by Lewis, whose books provided the stimulating gust of fresh air that liberated him from Bloomsbury's stranglehold on English art and confirmed his youthful hope that "everything was possible, that there were men in England full of vitality and life."

Moore's friend, Geoffrey Grigson, who impressively matches Lewis' fine presence and flashing intellect, also shares his reputation for stern standards and vitriolic severity. I approached

Grigson with some trepidation and, as he assured me of Lewis' kindness, was surprised by the warmth, patience and generosity that belied his own fierce image. After a dinner cooked by his wife (a famous chef), we walked out under the stars of Wiltshire, his lamp guiding our way. As he wiped the mist from my windscreen, bade me safe journey and asked me back to see him in the spring, I could not forbear confessing that I found him exactly as he had found Lewis.

Though most people were astonishingly generous with their time and help—and I was gratified that so many eminent people agreed to see me—a few uncooperative ones did not answer my letters: Basil Bunting (a friend of Pound), Morley Callaghan (who knew Lewis in Paris and in Toronto), Sir William Coldstream (who represented the Slade at Lewis' funeral), Malcolm Cowley (who met Lewis in New York), Henry Ford II (a patron in Detroit), Elsie Hirst (a friend of Mrs. Lewis, who had moved into a nursing home by the time I tracked down her address), Philip Johnson (a friend of Iris Barry), Alfred George Lewis (a New York relative), Rob Lyle (a friend of Roy Campbell), May Morris (an actress who lived next door in Notting Hill Gate), J. B. Priestley (who was drawn by Lewis), Lady Read (the widow of Herbert Read), William Roberts (a member of the Vorticist group and a total recluse), Martin Seymour-Smith, G. W. Stonier (a critic now living in South Africa), James Johnson Sweeney (who knew Lewis well in New York) and Pier van der Kruk (an elusive Dutch disciple). Perhaps some zealot can pin down and interview this remnant of witnesses.

The only people I was unable to find were Ida, the German model for Bertha in *Tarr*, who bore Lewis' first child and disappeared without a trace; and Alex and Ethel Lewis, Wyndham's half-brother and half-sister by his father's second marriage. Besides Mrs. Lewis, Burgon Bickersteth, Edmond Kapp, I. A. Richards, Allen Tate, Ruthven Todd and Anton Zwemmer died while I was writing the book.

## IV

The research, correspondence and interviews enabled me to clarify, for the first time, the major mysteries of Lewis' life: his family background; his mistresses and children; his secret mar-

riage; and the serious illnesses of 1914, the four operations of the
mid-thirties and the etiology of his final blindness.

The National Archives in Washington, D.C. supplied extensive
documents about the military career of Wyndham's father,
Charles Edward Lewis. The library of Nunda, New York, where
Lewis' father grew up, sent information about his family and a
copy of his article, "Escape from a Rebel Prison," published in the
*Nunda News* of February 18, 1865. I eventually found his parents'
marriage certificate in the London Registry Office, Charles' death
certificate in the Pennsylvania Department of Health, and his
Will in the Philadelphia City Hall. Family letters in Cornell
revealed that Lewis' parents separated when he was eleven years
old because of his father's love affairs.

Lewis had five illegitimate children with three different women
between 1909 and 1920, and abandoned all of them. Ida's child
was born in December 1909. I knew, from Lewis' unpublished
wartime letters to Pound, that two other children, a boy and a girl,
were born between 1909 and 1915, but had never been able to
trace them. After I had completed the biography and given it to
Routledge, I went to Manchester to see a major collection of
Lewis' drawings. The curator there, who was planning a major
Lewis exhibition in October 1980, had through a mutual friend
been put in touch with Lewis' daughter, who had told her about
her mother, her childhood meetings with Lewis and his mother,
and the later life of herself and her brother. Fortunately, I was
able to meet Lewis' daughter and add this new discovery to the
text before it was sent to the printer.

Iris Barry, an extraordinary woman, important film critic and
founder of the Film Library of the Museum of Modern Art, was
the mother of Lewis' last children, another boy and girl. Though
Iris' close friends, Lord Bernstein and Ivor Montagu, were
reluctant to discuss her, I found out about her life from material in
the Museum of Modern Art and from interviews with other
friends. Following up every vague lead, I telephoned a man whom
I thought might be her son—a very delicate situation
indeed—and he eventually agreed to meet me. He was a kind and
cultured professional man, who had a difficult childhood and
never knew Lewis. We became friends, I dined with him several
times while I was writing the book, and he told me about his
mother.

Lewis, who was a handsome man and had the gift of inspiring

feminine devotion, possessed an impressive number of attractive and intelligent mistresses, most notably: Ida, the "Rose Fawcett" of *Tarr*, Kate Lechmere, Beatrice Hastings, the wealthy novelist Mary Borden, Augustus John's model Alick Schepeler, Sybil Hart-Davis, probably Helen Saunders and Jessica Dismorr, Iris Barry, Nancy Cunard and Agnes Bedford. From letters and interviews I was able to reconstruct their lives and relations with Lewis.

I found unpublished photos of Mary Borden and Iris Barry as well as of Lewis' father, his literary mentor Sturge Moore, his patron Sir Nicholas Waterhouse (whose unpublished memoirs I discovered), Marshall McLuhan and his friend Felix Giovanelli, and Father Murphy. I traced the photos of Lewis by John Vickers, which the subject described as unspeakable icono-graphic insults. In the files of the London *Times* I dug up two superb unpublished photos of Lewis: an early one of the young artist standing before his lost painting *The Laughing Woman* (used on the dust jacket of my book) and a later one of the blind sage under his green eye shade. The Hulton Picture Library was also an excellent source of photos. In the *Times* and the Tate Archives I discovered six articles by Lewis that were not listed in the two recent bibliographies; a factual account of the Toronto fire described in *Self Condemned*, and two unrecorded interviews with the *Buffalo Courier* in 1939 and the *Daily Mail* in 1956.

The basic dates in Lewis' life, as listed in standard reference books like the *Dictionary of National Biography* and *Who's Who* (which erroneously states that Lewis was an adviser to the Library of Congress), are incorrect. He was born aboard his father's yacht in Amherst, Nova Scotia, in 1882 (not in Maine in 1884 or 1886, as he liked to say, to compensate for the years he lost in the War); and the date of his marriage was 1930, not 1929. When Mrs. Lewis could not remember the date of her wedding, I recalled her fury when W. K. Rose asked if she had really married Lewis and thought she might be trying to hide something from me. Though Lewis met his wife in 1918 and began to live with her in 1921, most of his close friends, who often visited his flat, did not know she existed. I could not locate a marriage certificate for 1929, but found that a Percy Lewis had wed a Gladys Hoskyns in Bristol in September 1939; and thought they had married just before leaving for Canada—until I realized they had already sailed when the coincidental Bristol marriage took place. A second search produced another marriage certificate of October 9, 1930, in which Lewis, who always camouflaged his private life, deliberately falsified nearly all the details. He spelled his wife's name Hoskins and described himself as aged 44 (instead of 48), an architect living at 22 Tavistock Road, Paddington (instead of 53 Ossington Street, Bayswater), the son of an English Captain in the Warwickshire Regiment (instead of a long-retired brevet Captain in the Union Army). If I had not known that Mrs. Lewis' father was a deceased florist named Joseph, it would have been impossible to verify their marriage. It is worth noting that couples do not have to provide proof for the statements they make on their marriage certificates.

The most complex aspect of Lewis' biography was his medical history. With the help of two close friends who are doctors and the Neuro-Pathology Department of Southampton University Medical School, to whom I lectured on Lewis' case history, I was able to determine that his disease of 1914–15 was gonorrhea (not syphilis), to understand and explain the sequence and purpose of his four operations for cystitis and urethral abscess between 1932 and 1937, and to establish the connection between the early venereal disease, the bladder disease and the nephritis that caused his death. I found three doctors—Millin, McPherson and Meadows—who had treated Lewis and showed that the pituitary tumor which caused his blindness by crushing the optic nerve had no effect on his so-called "paranoid" behavior. Though hospital records and x-rays are systematically destroyed seven years after the patient's death (and must therefore be rescued by biographers before then), I found, held and examined Lewis' brain—the final remnant of a mighty intellectual life. In the Pathology Museum of Westminster Hospital, where Lewis died in 1957, Dr. Antony Branfoot explained the slow growth of his massive tumor (which did not, as Hugh Kenner put it, "invade vital areas of his brain") and his autopsy report. It is entirely characteristic that Lewis' death certificate incorrectly states that he was 72 (instead of 74) years old and that his tumor was a cranio-pharyngioma (instead of a chromophobe adenoma).

All this research was extremely expensive; during 1978–79 I spent more than $6000 for travel, postage and phone calls, xeroxes and photos, books and magazines, paper and typing. I did not recover this money from the sale of the book; and received nothing for the time (an average of twelve hours a day) spent on research, writing and typing the long first draft. The "merit increase" I received from the University of Colorado for writing *Mansfield* was negligible. Biography is a costly, laborious, exasperating and profitless work, and can only be sustained by demonic devotion to the subject.

At the fag-end of literary criticism, when all major authors have been exhaustively analyzed, four kinds of books are being written: rare original critiques, variations of existing ideas, thinly disguised repetitions of what has already been said and sterile infatuations with structuralism and semiotics. In this decadent context a thoroughly researched biography, which is firmly based on extensive archival evidence and presents a massive quantity of new material as the basis for original interpretations, is perhaps the most valuable contribution to modern scholarship.


V


The Guggenheim grant enabled me to spend 1978–79 in London instead of in the intellectual isolation of Boulder. I took over a friend's old flat in Hampstead and was intensely stimulated by the close proximity of Lewis' friends and my own. I soaked myself in Lewisian locales, from the Tour Eiffel restaurant (now the White Tower) of the Vorticist days to the Golders Green crematorium, where he made the final journey accompanied by a Hammond organ. I built up enormous momentum to finish the book and wrote the 500 pages in six months. My editor at Routledge, who swore he would not change a comma without my permission, rushed the book to press as their lead title for the spring of 1980 and issued a paperback edition for Lewis' centenary.

Even if the publisher is reputable, I carefully oversee all the details of the publication of my book. I selected the photograph for the dust jacket, chose the binding, wrote the copy for the jacket and the publisher's catalogue, asked for proof of the jacket, photographs and captions as well as of the text, and made up the list of complimentary and review copies. To do otherwise is to invite disaster.

While writing the biography I also arranged with Athlone and McGill-Queen's University Press to edit a collection of eighteen

original essays on Lewis, which would stimulate critical appreciation of the depth and diversity of his fifty years of creative life and
appear at the same time as my biography. I sent out the first
invitations in December 1978 and had all the completed essays by
July 1979. Though I got most of the contributors I
wanted—including John Holloway, Marshall McLuhan and
Hugh Kenner, old friends of Lewis, leading Lewis scholars and
some younger enthusiasts—and they agreed to write on a
well-balanced range of topics, this book involved much more work
than I had anticipated. It was especially difficult to convince
distinguished scholars, who had helped me in my research on
Lewis, to make the revisions I suggested and raise all the essays to
the highest standard. In the end, however, both Athlone and the
reviewers were well satisfied.

My previous work on modern literature from 1880 to 1950 was
excellent preparation for the life of Lewis, whom Eliot called "the
most fascinating personality of our time." I discussed the Great
war in my books on T. E. Lawrence (a friend of Lewis); the
politics and history of the thirties and forties in my books on
Orwell (with whom Lewis quarrelled); the relation of art and
literature in *Painting and the Novel*; and learned the methods of
modern biography in *Katherine Mansfield*.

Like many geniuses—and Lewis deserves this title—he was a
multifarious man who assumed many roles, and the disparate
aspects of his character could not be focussed in a single
convincing image. But as the self-styled Enemy emerged from
obscurity, he could be clearly seen as an independent, intelligent
and courageous artist, and one of the most lively and stimulating
forces in modern English literature. If he had not composed
political tracts, had concentrated on perfecting his major works
and had devoted more time to painting, his reputation would have
been much greater. After his centenary year, it seems just and
proper to include him in the literary mainstream with Joyce,
Pound and Eliot—the "Men of 1914"—and as Auden said in his
elegy of Yeats, to pardon him for writing well.

CHAPTER EIGHT

# William Carlos Williams*

## PAUL MARIANI

### I

"I know of no critics in modern times," Leon Edel, the biographer of Henry James, has reminded us, "who have chosen to deal with biography as one deals with poetry or the novel. The critics fall into the easy trap of writing pieces about the life that was lived, when their business is to discuss how the life was told" by the biographer. From scanning the reviews which greeted (in one form or another) my own biography of William Carlos Williams, I know the truth of Edel's statement. This is a curious phenomenon in an age which prides itself on the attention it has given to the critical act. It is as though, in the case of biography, the reader somehow believed that the life the biographer has assembled for us existed in that form prior to the writing itself. For it is axiomatic that the biographer must always be true to the facts—the literary remains—which he keeps finding, trying to make sense of it all in something like a final ordering.

But it is the other half of the problem which I want to look at: the biographer as creator, the dustman reassembling the dust, like the God of Genesis breathing life into a few handfuls of earth. For the biographer is as much the inventor, the maker, as the poet or the novelist when it comes to creating a life out of the prima materia we call words. Is it not, after all, the *illusion* of a life which the biographer gives in the process of writing biography, something carried on perhaps over many years, a process of reassembling tapes and letters, discarded drafts and manuscripts, directives and memos, testaments and check stubs, the feel of names and places revisited, people known perhaps still among the living,

* First published in *New England Review*, 5 (Spring 1983), 276–296.

words transcribed, written, uttered, words, words and more words, which the biographer must shape and select and reorder, until a figure begins again to live in our imagination? It is extraordinary what the biographer feels when, finally, after writing and rewriting chapter after chapter of a person's life, after having lived for so long with the pale voices of the dead and perhaps with the still-insistent voices of the living who think that they were there, to suddenly feel something like light come streaming into the head, and to feel then the dust of all those words we call "facts" begin to take form, like the shape of the rose (to borrow an image from Ezra Pound) emerging out of the steel-dust particles when a magnet has been placed beneath their surface.

I remember how this moment occurred for me, and I keep learning that something like my own experience has been frequent with other biographers as well. Even after eight years of research, I was still finding Williams' letters in new archives or in private collections (a process, incidentally, which continues and which is bound to continue for some time). By then I had already collected thousands of such letters and was beginning to find a certain repetitiveness in the process. I decided at that point to play a game with the new packets of material which crossed my desk and, after looking at the date of a letter, try to guess what the general contents of that letter would be. I soon found that I could guess fairly accurately a good portion of the contents. It was like a tape going over in my mind: this was how Williams would have spoken to Pound at this point, this is how he would have addressed Louis Zukofsky or Allen Ginsberg or Denise Levertov or Robert Lowell. In a sense, then, the biographer had finally managed to become his subject. Other biographers have taken to wearing their subject's clothes or hat or shoes, others find their smoking habits and diets and tastes subtly or not so subtly changing to conform to their subjects', some have even gone so far as to interject themselves on the domestic scenes of their subjects, sometimes with an aggrandizement bordering on the violent, sometimes with filial piety. You cannot live another person's words day in and day out without running up against such occupational benefits or risks. Those risks will differ of course for each subject, and several good novelists from Henry James on have used the biographer as their protagonist. Most of these novels have been in the tradition of the comedy of manners, though from the biographer's own standpoint I suppose the genre most apt would be the romantic quest. And at the heart of the romantic quest, remember, is the moment of the Grail, the visionary moment, the moment of the breakthrough.

Let us call this moment of breakthrough the *illusion* of the saturation point. I stress the word *illusion* because any biographer worthy of the name wants to ingest everything available on his subject and the truth is that more dust—new letters, new manuscripts, new memoirs by others who remained silent while you were doing your own work or who were spurred into writing perhaps because of your work—has a way of collecting after your own work, you thought, was done. Such a state of things, this new stirring of the dust, is to be expected and even welcomed, for it shows a continuing or at least renewed interest in a subject that one already has found worth exploring. Call this renewal of interest a kind of second life springing from the first life of the biography.

The only thing which might really trouble the biographer would be, I think, to discover that not only had the dust been stirred again but that something like a new rose pattern radically reshaping the life the biographer had already shaped had been part of the stirring: to watch all the dust reassemble again in a new configuration, and one which seemed to suit the dust more fully. Harold Bloom speaks of the anxiety of the later poet coming into the presence of the father's text. But that is as nothing to Ptolemy's meeting up with a Galileo, the son who would rearrange the sense of the world according to his own discoveries and his own imagination. For is not the biographer's primal desire to father his subject, so that the "world" (i.e. one's interested readers) is satisfied with the illusion the biographer has given it and which can then pass for what one thinks of when one thinks of subject X? How many of us think of James Joyce without thinking of Richard Ellmann's Joyce, or think of Hart Crane without thinking of Horton or perhaps Unterecker, or of Henry James without thinking of Edel's composite of a life?

How then does the biographer go about accomplishing this rich illusion of a life, this essential fiction? First of all, of course, not all biographers are sufficiently concerned with the shape of their fictions. In this they are like certain novelists in the American realist tradition who want to tell the story without really giving much concern to formal considerations. There are those biographers who try to do the impossible by trying to get everything between the covers of two or five or nine volumes, in that attempt (frustrated from the start) emptying the dust bin over the grave of the dead as a memorial so that the dust sifts down and down in the shape of a pyramid, out of which monument the reader is then invited to make his own judgment, his own private portrait. This gesture of omnipresence and omnipotence on the part of the biographer is perhaps that writer's last infirmity, and many have, finally, wearily, succumbed to that temptation. This is not to make an oblique strike at the long biography, for there is often good reason to publish a book or even several books which may exceed even the thousand-page mark. Besides, having perpetrated a long biography myself, I suppose I would like to defend my own actions as well. But Williams died just short of eighty and up to almost the very end he was in the midst of one or another of those American vortices which, like their natural cousin, the hurricane, have a way of forming and splitting up with unseemly haste. But I still believe that eight hundred pages devoted to Keats or to the two Cranes, figures who died young, will appear excessive to all but the most devoted follower. On the other hand, Edel's five volumes on James, R. W. B. Lewis' biography of Edith Wharton, and Ellmann's life of Joyce, each certainly sustained meditations, seem to me appropriate in part because of the creative longevity of each of those figures.

Sometimes a case has to be made for presenting a particular life in detail even as one is in the act of recreating that life, and that strategy likewise takes time. No one would blink twice if another long life were to appear which dealt with Faulkner or Pound or Eliot or Frost (though it is interesting that Lawrance Thompson's three-volume life should already have contracted to a single volume). But what about Williams? Did he really deserve a long biography? To listen to one camp of critics: no. To listen to another: yes, and it was about time. For part of a biographer's art will have to deal with the question of scope, of size; to do a mural or a cameo or a portrait? You do not write a long biography by chance, and you will certainly not get it past a trade editor without making a very good case for the length of that life study. For myself, I was so frustrated by hearing the same myths about Williams—that he was incapable of serious, consecutive thought, that there was no real drama in the life of this New Jersey poet–doctor from a one-horse town, that *Paterson* and Williams' other poems were mostly pre-compositions, sketches for poems rather than poems, frenetically dashed off between delivering one baby and another—that I was determined to do what I could to set the record straight. With very few exceptions no one who had worked in any way with Williams' life and written of it had given the reader anything like a sufficient sense of just how complex and multi-levelled that life had been. Nor had anyone yet shown how intimately Williams had touched the imaginative lives of three generations of American writers in his time. Profoundly touched by my own encounter with Williams, I wanted to do what I could as life writer to see at least that Williams was not dismissed, now that something like a full picture of the man in his time could be presented. The story is there now, at least in place, and dismissal will have to come, if it comes, either out of gross literary incompetence, indifference or malice. When I was younger it was Richard Ellmann's biographical example in dealing with Joyce which had held me, and I see now that what I wanted to give American audiences in particular was a book about Williams peopled with his friends and enemies which would be a counter-part in every way except in tone to what Ellmann had offered in his homage to Joyce. I make no secrets about it. Call it hubris, but my book would be a way of paying homage to the father, of doing for Modern American Poetry what Ellmann had done for European Modernism. There would be shortcomings of course. There would be little on Frost or Sandburg or Robinson, and less than I would have liked on Stevens or H.D. or even Marianne Moore. But that would be because Williams had touched these lives only peripherally, if at all. In spite of this, he would be my candidate for one of the truly major American voices of our century, and here between the covers of this book would be my case.

## II

Looking back at what he had achieved in several biographies on late medieval princes and statesmen, Paul Murray Kendall wrote that the biographer has the nearly impossible task of grafting stone to rainbow. What he meant by this happy phrase was that the biographer must take the recalcitrant facts as they appear to exist—in memoirs, diaries, journals, the rest of it—to possess this material and to create out of it the rainbow, the living simulation in words of a life, from all that we can discover about that person. In the last poem he ever wrote, Hopkins spoke eloquently of this moment of inspiration, the moment of the rainbow, and of that moment's ability to keep *in*-forming its recipient, no matter how long it took the poem to come finally to term:

> The fine delight that fathers thought; the strong
> Spur, live and lancing like a blowpipe flame,
> Breathes once and, quenchèd faster than it came,
> Leaves yet the mind a mother of immortal song.
>
> Nine months she then, nay years, nine years she long
> Within her wears, bears, cares and combs the same:
> The widow of an insight lost she lives, with aim
> Now known and hand at work now never wrong.

The biographer is both like and unlike the poet, he also feels the same strong spur. But once the biographer has felt that fine delight, that moment of light streaming into the head, the moment of the rainbow, there is still that forbidding pyramid of dust to work with. The biographer may have caught something like the inner life of his subject, but how shall he go about taking all those index card entries and all of those interviews done on tape or in shorthand or by telephone and, in the case of the subject as writer, analyzing or at least accounting for all those marvellous poems and essays, those memoirs and letters and libretti, and transforming them all into a readable narrative which shall do justice to the subject? What tone shall he take toward the material, what distance assume in relation to the subject, what language employ? What strategies shall the biographer employ by which to reassemble the dust and reveal the pattern the biographer believes is somewhere in the midst of all of that?

Biographers seem to have worked, at least until quite recently, pretty much alone. First of all, they still come from widely divergent disciplines. There is, for example, the field sociologist, the journalist, the historian, the psychoanalyst, the feminist, the Marxist, the theologian, the professor of literature, even the professional biographer. Each comes to biography with different attitudes about the field, different presuppositions, different purposes. In spite of this we must still learn how to tell a good story if we are to tap the peculiar energies of the biography.

And how are we to do that? I think one answer to that question, if I have learned anything from working on Williams, will depend on the specific contours as well as the underlying myth which spurred a man or woman on and gave them their own deepest sense of self-definition. I mean anything of course but the public mask, the face most people see when they look at Hemingway or Hart Crane or Emily Dickinson or Thoreau or Emerson or Poe. I mean that it is the biographer's special agony and his glory to grasp *that* reality, that radiant gist, that energy and direction, which should inform, *in*-form, a thousand thousand otherwise disparate facts and make them dance together. For without that inner understanding we see as in a glass darkly, as in a winter snowstorm, the figures in the drama blurred, shadowy, halting, moving through a strangely cold and unrealized landscape. I think most successful biographers will tell you (or at least *could* tell you) that there was that moment of light when the inner life of their subject was suddenly revealed. At that point the earlier, partial images fell away and the inner consistency of their subject was impressed in upon the biographer. What were many images suddenly coalesced into a unified figure of many sides but nonetheless possessing a self, and then the dust particles—all those discrete facts—could be arranged into a major pattern. My experience has been that if this moment of light rings "true" to the biographer, then all subsequent finds will accommodate themselves to this pattern. If they do not, if the facts insist on squiggling still all over the surface, then the insight will have turned out to be partly light and partly an *ignis fatuus*, a shadow light beckoning into the swamps. Philip Horton, for example, published his biography of Hart Crane only three years after Crane's suicide, but he was not superseded by John Unterecker, whose life of Crane was published thirty-five years later and was nearly three times as long. For Horton managed to catch the truth of his subject and wrote passionately and to the point. In short, the pattern held.

Writing my own biography of Williams, I think the moment of realization came when I saw how central the myth of success through repeated failures had been for Williams. In teaching *In the American Grain*, for example, it became clear to me that Williams was dividing his protagonists into parts of a cubist mural composed in binary fashion of those who had "apparently" succeeded and those who had "apparently" failed. Among those who succeeded, Williams included Cortez and Jonathan Edwards and Ben Franklin, men whom Williams thought had failed to establish the intimacy necessary for genuine and lasting contact with their world. On the other hand there were such "failures" as Columbus and Montezuma, Père Sebastian Rasles and Daniel Boone, Aaron Burr and Poe. These figures were failures in the eyes of most Americans because they had not achieved the American Dream, ending their lives—all of them—in disgrace or loneliness, though what they all had in common was their contact with the ground, a grounding necessarily figured for Williams in the woman, as much the necessary counterpart for him in his art as in his life.

It became clearer to me as I worked with Williams that he had pursued this theme through twenty years while he wrote his Stecher trilogy and watched his family of immigrants (based as they were on his wife's family) become stranded on the desert shores of that same American Dream. I saw the theme again in Williams' dream of Washington, the father who had persisted in spite of repeated military failures on Long Island and Manhattan and the New Jersey coast until doggedly he had won through and made his dream of America a reality, at least for a short while. I could see the theme at work again more subtly as a way of *in*-forming his epic, *Paterson*, where the poet's desperate search for a language with which to marry himself irrevocably to a place became his all-important work. By then Williams' sense of place had become a cry, the cry Williams swore Poe had heard when that poetic predecessor had gone in search of a country. So Williams heard his country crying out against him with all the anger and frustration of a Marcia Nardi, the very real woman whose very real letters he placed into the fabric of his poem. They were a judgment which he was willing by then to bring against himself for his own hubris in attempting to speak for the whole tribe (America) in the first place.

Williams' photographic negative of the American success story, then, became the generative myth, the underlying poetics, if you will, which in turn *in*-formed my own narrative of Williams. Early on, Williams somehow became convinced that he was going to live a long and productive life. Somehow—perhaps because his grandmother had lived into her nineties and his mother lived to be a centenarian—Williams believed that the Fates would not cut his own life thread short, as they had cut short the life of Hart Crane. As a corollary to this act of faith, Williams also came to believe that he would have a very long and recurring creative springtime in which to get done what he knew he had it in him to do. In his early thirties he began to envision himself more and more as a revolutionary born into a time of revolutions: the revolution in American art signalled by John Reed and Big Bill Haywood and the Paterson strike of 1913, followed by Pancho Villa in Mexico and—most significantly—the Russian Revolution of 1917. Williams only began to come of age at that extraordinary period, and he knew he would need the next half century to work out the complex implications of his own revolution of the word. Incredibly, he nearly got the whole fifty years he had bargained for, though it cost him more dearly than as a young dreamer he would have thought possible. And it is just there—in the cross-currents Williams rode, the crest of the dream, the trough of rejection and misunderstanding—that my own biography found its own mythic impulse. Here was Williams' own version of the American success story lived out day by day in his own life drama.

Many critics and reviewers seem genuinely surprised that Williams could feel almost as if he had been physically assaulted by the rejections and dismissals of Eliot, Frost, and the New Critics, as though the critics who killed Keats (in Shelley's mythopoeic version of the tale) had resurfaced long enough to bring Bill Williams down. That of course is nonsense, as it was nonsense in Keats' own case, where tuberculosis had a prior claim. But literary infighting, the politics of art, did have its grinding effect on Williams, as it had its effect on Eliot and Pound and Hart Crane. And even Gerard Manley Hopkins, who published virtually nothing in his lifetime, could feel a critic's barb by inference and smile sardonically to his friend, Robert Bridges. If such oblique references and dismissal constituted fame, he wanted no part of it. For Williams, however, the case was far more interesting and severe, for it was easy once in American literary circles to laugh Williams off. The *Partisan Review* did it, the Princeton circle did it, including Blackmur and Jarrell and others, *Poetry* did it, and by extension the entire British literary tradition did it. Everybody did it, or so it seemed. And though Williams could forgive, as he forgave the editors of the *Hudson Review* and sent them, in his last years, some of his best work, he could not always forget.

So, when Robert Lowell tried to patch things up between Williams and Eliot in 1948, Williams was willing to go along with the reconciliation (he did after all admire much the Possum had wrought), but he was quick to warn Lowell (and the rest of us) that the younger generations would be hard put to comprehend what Williams' literary skirmishes had cost his battered spirit. Did Williams actually remember Frost's snub at Bread Loaf, offered in the summer of 1941; did he remember it ten years later when he returned again to Bread Loaf? Yes, Williams did remember, as he remembered Eliot's dismissive conduct in 1924, and DuChamps' barb in 1916 and Jarrell's final negative reassessment of Williams when *Paterson 4* was published in 1951. Williams remembered because literature mattered so much to him. It really did matter how a poet put his language on the line. In the long empyrean view, as we turn the pages of our Nortons or other anthologies of American poetry and see Stevens and Williams and Pound and Eliot and Hart Crane enthroned side by side like larger-than-life Byzantine presences, none of this much matters. But in recreating Williams' life, I learned early on that all of this of course does matter. It mattered because there was a political and social judgment implicit in telling the world that a poem could be made of anything. "I have said it many times," Williams reiterated towards the end of his life. "Anything is grist for the poem. Anything. Make it of this, of this, and this."

"Reading your biography," Williams' younger son, Paul, wrote me, "I can remember Dad's conversations over the dinner table. You brought them back to me. Apparently you were there too." For that is the job of the biographer: to recreate the inner drama of those literary skirmishes for those for whom literature meant life itself: the words of the poem, the words of attack, the words of praise. All these words matter in the recreation of a life. They matter as much as the victories and defeats of a Caesar, a Vercingetorix, a Nelson, a Pershing, a Patton, even though long after those battle sites have been emptied we may walk there in a tranquillity which we attribute to those earlier times . . . at our peril. What we want again in the literary biography is the hurl of voices shouting at or past each other, the words actually spoken in mid-passage and not the words remembered after the voyage is

over. Discovery by "seabord," Pound has it, not by Aquinas'
map.

## III

Literary lives, we should keep reminding ourselves, are after all
made up of words. And if a biography is composed of words, we
should look carefully at the ones we use. Is there, for example, a
particular kind of language better suited to the telling of subject
X's life rather than Y's, or at least a particular range of language
choices? I think there is, *if* the biographer is able to possess himself
of that language. The language used to portray a figure like Henry
James should be made to reflect the world of James, just as, in the
vast verbal kaleidoscope of things, another language could be
made to flesh the world of a Wallace Stevens and another the
worlds of a Hemingway or an Emily Dickinson. Some will, I
know, object to such an organic view of biographical language.
Some may, for example, claim that such a suggestion smacks of
what, in the days of neo-orthodoxy, was once called the mimetic
fallacy: the attempt to imitate reality with language, or (in this
case) the attempt to imitate the world of subject X by seeing that
world through the lens of subject X's own language. Imagine
doing Faulkner in the style of *As I Lay Dying* or Joyce in the style of
*Finnegans Wake* or Emily Dickinson in the style of her own poems
. . . or even of her letters? Other biographers will reject my
suggestion because they do not have the ability to reconstruct
either their subject's language or even the illusion of that
language.

Of course such a direct imitation is not exactly what I have in
mind either. What I mean is rather a simulation of the language of
the subject whose life we are retelling. This is not to say the
language which we hear in Williams' or Stevens' poems, or in the
novels of Faulkner or Hemingway, but rather a simulation of a
person's characteristic diction and syntax as we can discover
those in letters, tapes, and memories of their speech: in short the
language staple, the language as they themselves used it every
day. To tell the story, that is, from the eye and mouth of subject X,
rather than from the outside, or at least to do this as a strategy part
of the time.

Let me give an example of the kind of thing I mean. One critic took me to task for quoting some of the salty language and four-letter words which Williams finally managed to get into his written and spoken language. Williams was in his thirties before he apparently felt comfortable about doing this, having for so long been under his mother's injunction never to do or think a wrong thing. In allowing myself to reveal this darker side of Williams, this particular critic argued, I had revealed myself to be, like Williams, rather coarse-minded. By which he presumably meant using language unfit to be uttered in the presence of the truly great, like Henry James and Proust and Dostoyevsky, Mallarmé and Kafka. But it seems to me an easy enough trick for the critic to summon at least by name such an impressive pantheon, such a philosopher's circle, and yet never once raise himself above the humdrum quotidian of what passes for literary salon talk. There are very few of us indeed who have not at one point or another in our lives employed stereotypes in our language or found ourselves resorting to Chaucerian sub-standard English. Maybe it is because I am of a later generation, but if I had written the life of "Vinegar Joe" Stilwell I would not have agonized over Stilwell's characterization of polio-stricken FDR as "rubberlegs," as that fine biographer, Barbara Tuchman, worried about in writing *Stilwell and the American Experience in China* a dozen years ago.

It seems apparent to me that the biographer cannot afford *not* to reveal the darker shadows of his subject. For, like the novelist, the biographer must remain absolutely true to his subject. Biographers may well regret that their subjects used such language, just as they will probably regret the banal or vicious stereotyping of which their heroes were guilty (by which I mean comments about race, about religion, about sexual differences or preferences), but if it is part of the record, then certainly a representative portion of that material will have to be recorded or we falsify the story. The biographer *must* know not only what his subject said in the prepared speech before the podium in the glare of the public light, but also what the subject felt in the privacy of a letter or remembered in conversation with a friend, an enemy, an outsider. Such glimpses will be rare enough once the eulogizing and sculpting into marble begin. As a rule of thumb, therefore, the biographer would do well to learn from the linguist that all language—however highly charged—is acceptable if it helps to reveal the full dimensions of the subject, the chiaroscuro, the light and dark which renders the portrait plausible.

Let me add, so that I am not misunderstood on this point, that I have little patience with those biographers who seem to be out to reveal the little or big secrets of their subjects for the pleasure of the scandal itself, without taking the necessary responsibility of placing those shortcomings in their correct perspective. There are biographers, regrettably, who show no real understanding of their subjects, who do not have the ability to show us the underlying strengths of a figure, who set out to debunk in a way Lytton Strachey himself never did by holding up the shabby truths they have discovered like so much unwashed underwear. I find something disturbing, for example, about the treatment accorded Elvis Presley by his most recent biographer, Albert Goldman, not because he bares Presley's dark side, but because he seems to have gone to such disproportionate length to reveal what he learned from those figures, some of them mere hangers-on and some outrightly hostile to Presley, who surrounded the singer in his last depressed years. What this biographer fails to show us, however, is the very real hold Presley's music had for millions of Americans. We have the sordid facts of Presley's last years, the quantities of uppers and downers consumed, the casual sexual interludes, but where is the dream of the young singer before it soured, where is the truth of the legend which touched so many who make up the democratic ground of America? And why did that legend have the effect it did? It is not to be found, this other Presley, in Goldman's telling.

Norman Mailer, on the other hand, taking much less promising material in the life and death of convicted killer, Gary Gilmore, did manage to explore the reality of the American West and to place that world like the tragicomic inversion it is against the troubling and stark vision of the early Mormons coming by wagon train into Utah. Mailer's is not, perhaps, a "true" biography since he is enough of an iconoclast to break generic bindings when he can, but for biographical texture his book succeeds where Goldman fails. This is because Mailer had the imagination to find a vehicle for Gilmore's sense of reality in the relentless, quotidian, and ultimately stark quality of the language he himself used. This language employs the techniques of journalism in much the same spirit as Andy Warhol painted his meticulous reproductions of

Campbell's soups: a medium of flat, unadorned and even tacky sentences, precise as plastic rulers, the thin tissue of syntactical connectives simulating the thin tissue of unconnectedness which turns out to have been Gilmore's life. It is a life shared, except perhaps for its explicit violence, by millions of Americans. Goldman's language, on the other hand, strikes me as made up of a Madison Avenue confectionery of tinsel and plastic, half glitter and half functional, much of it having the texture of that imitation marble where Presley's body lies, and serving much the same purpose of preserving a corpse.

What then of the cool, detached stance of the narrator as the model for the biographer, the speaker keeping an objective distance? Again, it is a matter of literary strategy, and I can see where an aloof, objective tone would do well for a life, say, of the historian Gibbon, or for a life of Baudelaire or Flaubert. But for the most part this sort of scientific detachment belongs rather to the case history or to those situations where the biographer needs to employ an ironic detachment to best engage the reader. This mode comes close to the best reportorial prose, and might serve well in presenting a life of Nixon, say, or Kissinger. In most cases, however, where one is giving a life story, it should be the unfolding inner drama which asserts itself, whether that life reveals itself in the poems and novels of a writer, or rather in the realized places of the explorer, the soldier, the statesman, or in the operating room, over a Sunday dinner, on an assembly line, or on a lonely road lost somewhere at night. Let objectivity and distance be relegated to the preface of the biography or to the notes or the afterword or the index.

What we want, after all, in a biography is the subject alive and moving, and if this means evoking the Muse of the novelist as well as the more familiar Clio, that is all to the good. Let us see Hemingway driving his ambulance on the Italian front lines, or fishing for trout in Lake Michigan or beginning to go to pieces in his mountain home in Ketchum, Idaho. Let us see Faulkner stopping to chat with friends on the town green in Jefferson or drinking some of the local whiskey with the other hunters by a campfire at night, creating the Snopes clan half out of thin air, half out of the reality of the hill people. Let us see Dickinson stoop to stare quizzically at a bumblebee bumping about its work in the June sun there in the south garden of her home in Amherst, Whitman tracking through the dirty snow of a cobblestoned alley in the Brooklyn of the late 1840's, his head filled with an aria he had heard at the opera house across the river the night before. Let us see T. S. Eliot, tall and stoop-shouldered, in morning coat and frayed slacks, hair slicked and parted down the middle, a dog-eared copy of the Temple Classics translation of Dante's *Inferno* in his coat pocket, on a lunch break now from his wearying duties as clerk at Lloyd's, and staring down at the waters of the Thames, recalling that other great river with its brown gods, the Mississippi at St. Louis, along whose shores he had grown up. Let us see the mistakes and slights and economic worries, the estrangements and erotic engagements and the imaginative breakthroughs of these figures as and where they occurred, directly, and not through the clairvoyant eye of the omniscient and omnipresent narrator who, with deistic hindsight, looks out over it all and passes final judgement. We want the life, not the marble tribute.

And yet we do want to see what these figures managed to achieve in their lives as well, for we have not chosen this man or that woman to flesh out with ten or a dozen years of our own life without hoping to have something given in return. Writing a biography is, after all, rather like falling in love. At some point we must have seen something like a greatness in our subject, or if not that at least a uniqueness, demonic or otherwise, an achievement, or—if the life is minor—a uniqueness in the life, a hunger at least for something, an ideal, however flawed, which draws the biographer on day after day. It was Geoffrey Wolff in his biography of Harry Crosby, that minor luminary of the American 1920's, who said that it was his subject's determination to transform himself through his own suicide into the Great Poet which held him riveted. Harry Crosby determined, Wolff tells us, "to translate himself from a Boston banker into a Great Poet by the agency of Genius," a genius "he calculated to attain by the agency of Madness." What is more, the final weird apotheosis of that madness would take the bizarre shape of Crosby's self-immolation. By keeping his word, Wolff argues, Crosby authenticated his life. "It is awful," Wolff tells us, "to watch someone with good eyesight and all his senses on full alert walk with gravity and determination toward the edge of a precipice, and keep going." Wolff disclaims any design on his readers; he is clearly not after a type or a lesson in the figure of this American expatriate of the twenties. Nor, he argues, is it the biographer's task to shape a subject's life to fit to a standard of morality or conduct, since the life, if sufficiently grasped, is always greater and more complex than any code or system superimposed upon it. And yet, we read lives because they do teach us something about the human and moral condition, which none of us, I suspect, can ever escape or ever afford to dismiss. And they teach us even as they hold and fascinate us endlessly. A life unfolds, gathers to a greatness of momentum and complexity, and then inevitably begins to unwind, like those presences of Yeats' in the heavenly city of Byzantium, spinning in counterclockwise fashion, divesting themselves of the very lives they had spent the better part of their time on earth winding themselves into in the first place. This process of self-realization unfolds about us and within us every day, occurring to a billion people. And yet what infinite variety there is within that basic arithmetical pattern we call life, we call death, alpha and omega.

## IV

Which leads me then to a word about the esthetic strategy of endings and beginnings. Jay Martin began his life of Nathanael West with the moment of West's death. In a skillful narrative passage, Martin recreates the scene: a California highway, summer, 1941. West and his wife, Eileen, are slumped over in their new stationwagon, West's body resting on the horn, still sounding, the car demolished, the two of them dead. Having killed off his subject, Martin explained a few years ago at a session on biography at the English Institute at Harvard, he could get on with the business of recounting West's life that would lead up to this irrevocable terminus. Like a butterfly collector, Jay Martin had his specimen pinned in all its gorgeous colors on display.

Justin Kaplan, in his biography of Whitman, appears to have employed a variant of this killing off of the subject by beginning his life of the poet in old age, waiting for the very thing he had yearned after all his life: sweet death and surcease. Only in the fourth chapter, then, do we see Whitman's own beginnings. By adopting this narrative strategy, it seems to me, Kaplan allowed us to see Whitman at the end of his biography not in death, but as an old man at Camden, walking through the tall meadow grasses and summer flowers along the peaceful river, himself at peace at last, like that other bearded patriarch, Monet, in his gardens at Giverny. But such a death-in-life scene as a strategy for Williams seemed particularly inappropriate, since death was the very thing Williams had struggled all his life against. Even Williams' still lifes, Jarrell has reminded us, swarm with a life which most poets never get into their presentations even of men and women. How much more, then, is the life of the man himself.

I had more trouble with the opening passages than I had with anything else in the writing of my biography. I wrote and rewrote those pages, trying to discover the most effective way to begin that book and introduce the reader to my version of Williams. I did not want to begin at the beginning, at least not right away. Rather, I wanted to present an image, a scene, which would catch something of the man's gestures and vitality but which would also signal something of the underlying drama of that life. For a long time my original opening had young man Williams sitting in an open boxcar with a group of other teenaged boys as the freight train ground slowly over the Hackensack River. In that scene Williams, sitting on the wooden floor, watches as one of the boys, a local kid from Rutherford with the marvellous real-life name of Dago Schenck, dives from the boxcar and down into the muddy river below. Such a scene, I had imagined, would have suggested Williams' own early passivity, his own delayed springtime—sexual, emotional, creative—as he bided for his moment to make the great leap. It was a leap which came finally, in spite of his feelings of inadequacy and cowardice, only with the decision to begin *Paterson*, a decision which was made only as Williams approached his sixtieth year. This opening scene would have been the only partially fictive scene (at least to my knowledge) in the entire biography. By its placement as entrance song it would have meant that the biographer, if he is to make an artful biography, must use fictive devices to reveal the underlying truth of a person's life. It would have said, in effect, that in writing biography what the biographer must finally deliver, in spite of all the research one can do, is not the life itself but a reconstruction, a simulation, a dramatization, an illusion. In short, the biographer's reality is finally one more version of what Wallace Stevens meant by the Supreme Fiction.

Finally, however, I did not use that opening, because my own thinking had shifted as I moved towards the completion of the biography. The original opening had stood as a metaphor, which is what I thought I had wanted in the first place: a scene which might reveal in microcosm the essential direction of a life. But that scene had been partially manufactured, as if to say: look, in spite of the years I have lived with Williams' spirit, I cannot give you the whole truth about him. And then it struck me: what hubris to suppose I or anyone ever could have done that. For to do that would have been to deny the central mystery of the human condition which no one—not Darwin or Jung or Freud or the biographer—can ever fully reveal.

Once I understood this truth along my pulse, I could try another entrance into my biography. It would be a much humbler moment this time, and yet one filled with significance, if only its metaphorical significance could be made to resonate. Such oblique metonymical strategies, a method of appearing to address a subject directly while revealing something other by implication, had been one of the lessons Williams as poet and as man had taught me. Approaching seventy and with most of *Paterson* behind him by then, Williams was finally ready to do his public *Autobiography*. It is an effort filled with many good and true stories; indeed, it served as a primary source for my own biography, especially for Williams' earliest years. But it was a text filled too with significant omissions and distortions, and it was shaped according to its own *in*-forming myth, for Williams had meant to show the world how a small town boy and provincial doctor had stayed at home while the others—like Pound and Eliot and McAlmon and H.D.—had gone to Europe. Williams' reward for staying at home had been to catch the prize, for by age seventy he knew he had won through to being at least in some sense a representative American poet, a son in the venerable tradition of Emerson, Thoreau and Whitman.

In the final scene of the *Autobiography*, Williams leads the reader back to the river, to the Great Falls at Paterson, this time in company with a friend and Williams' own grandson, Paul. It is early winter and there are ice formations everywhere about the park above the Falls. Young Paul asks his grandfather to hurl one of those "ice cabbages," as he calls them, into the river below, and that act of hurling the object into the Passaic evokes in Williams' mind the image of Sam Patch, the local daredevil who had leapt from this very spot several times in the 1820's until the words, Williams tells us, failed him and he finally died. Young Paul is of course both terrified and fascinated by the sheer magnitude of the spectacle, and yet he wonders out loud how deep the river is at that point. So Williams ends his own life story here, at this place and at this moment, the present, with the son of his son calculating when and how he might ever duplicate Sam Patch's leap, the very leap Williams himself had finally willed himself into taking when he chose to begin writing *Paterson*.

It was with this scene, then, that I decided to begin my biography. In studying the original drafts for the *Autobiography* now at the Beinecke Library, I learned by chance that this visit to the Falls had taken place on New Year's Eve, 1950. The moment of Janus: the exact fulcrum on which the century itself rests, a looking forward and a looking back. By beginning just here, then, I would take Williams' own narrative closure and begin all over again for myself, telling Williams' story partially as Williams himself had seen it, but taking my own leap, as we all must, by restructuring Williams' rendering with my own. It would mean supplanting Williams' later version of the American success story as he had presented it in the *Autobiography* with the deeper version which had guided him all those years while he had had to fight like a bantam to achieve a voice and have that voice heard. And of course, on the darker side, I would have to fill in the omissions which Williams, his wife Flossie looking over his shoulder, had chosen to ignore when telling this official version of the story. And so I would begin by asking the same question which Williams had had his grandson—my own contemporary and (luckily my namesake)—ask: how deep did the river (of Williams' life) really flow? What, in other words, had it really cost this American of mixed ancestry (like myself) to pursue the dream of a language rising out of a particular ground, and to pursue that language and that dream daily for nearly eighty years?

The answers, such as they were, took over 800 pages of print, answers recapitulated for the reader once more in the biography's final pages. For the strategy of juxtapositions in that closure was meant to suggest that Williams' life, like the lives of his own heroes—Washington and Boone and Poe and even his own father-in-law—was both a vindication and a personal tragedy. The singleminded pursuit of Williams' dream had cost him dearly in terms of his own life and the lives of those dear to him, especially his wife, whom he had loved in spite of self-preoccupations and infidelities. I meant to suggest as much when I showed Floss discovering her husband's small and wasted body turned towards the wall after the man had suffered one cerebral hemorrhage too many, and then juxtaposed that death with Floss's own death one May morning thirteen years later. Floss remains in part a silent presence throughout the biography because, after all, it is her husband who is taking center stage here. But this death was hers. And when at the end we learn that Floss made the decision to be cremated and have her ashes scattered rather than rest beside her husband in death, it comes as something of a shock. I myself chose not to speculate on the reasons for that final decision, reminding the reader that, in *any* life, no matter how long, much must remain, finally, a mystery. That having been understated, I could then get on with the business of the literary and imaginative significance of Williams' life, the legacy that flawed giant had left us, his sons and daughters.

## V

Last, a word about the overall strategy of the biography. What I attempted there was something like a calculus of indeterminacy, a strategy of wresting success out of defeat. In my version of the metapoetics of the biography, I would inundate the reader with the river of facts surrounding Williams even as the reader should become aware that, if Williams' was a representative life, a life shared on many counts by many Americans in his roles of father, husband, lover, physician, citizen and artist, it had somehow managed to move along another, original axis as well. In spite of failure after failure in that life, therefore, a cross-current paradoxically makes itself felt in the biography which, especially with the decision to finally do *Paterson*, resulted in Williams' breaking through. He gives us a poetry commensurate with our particular sense of reality; with a people at cross-purposes with ourselves, yet jostling in our pluralistic society in a kind of antagonistic co-operation.

On this level, the biography was an attempt to reduplicate the central paradox of *Paterson*, which after all contains Williams' true autobiography; a poem which tells us finally that it is not any system of values which holds us together, whether we see those values as political, economic or societal. Instead, what we get in *Paterson*—and what I tried to duplicate—is the sense of a life caught in the flux of reality itself, a life which, while in danger of being pulled under by the overwhelming flood of events, dares to question at every turn, responding to the flood of experience as well as it can at every moment. If it is *Paterson* then that contains the most central Williams, it was my special task as biographer to respond as fully as I could to what that poem had to teach me as a life replica, my biographical form answering to Williams' more complex autobiographical one. "Weakness dogs him," Williams confesses towards the close of his epic,

> fulfillment only
> a dream or in a dream. No one mind
> can do it all, runs smooth
> in the effort, *toute dans l'effort*. . . .

It is the artist–father consoling the artist–son even in death. If I have told the life failingly, that too may be forgiven and may even be a virtue in the way we say that sweeping the dust together can be a virtue, apart from creating the elusive rainbow I earlier evoked. Williams for one knew that, being human, there could be no other way but to go haltingly when it is a man and not a god who is left to tell the story, to collect the dust and try to breathe life into it all again. *It is all in the effort.* Let that be the biographer's as well as the poet's final defense. That and the intercession of the text itself, and the man caught shimmering (perhaps) in all that dust.

CHAPTER NINE

# T. E. Lawrence

## PHILLIP KNIGHTLEY

Not many a biographer can say that he came upon his subject by accident rather than by design. Yet this is the way I came to T. E. Lawrence. I am still somewhat bemused by how it occurred, and if this account seems complex and sometimes bewildering it is because that is how it really was. It began in London in the summer of 1968. I had just finished writing with two colleagues on the London *Sunday Times* a book about Kim Philby, the Soviet spy who had penetrated the British Secret Intelligence Service, and, taking advantage of the seasonally small newspapers, was enjoying a comparatively leisurely existence. Unknown to me another colleague, Colin Simpson, an enterprising and resourceful journalist, was in the process of negotiating a deal which he hoped would prove a literary goldmine. All newspapers receive letters that are obviously written by eccentric or obsessive readers. No newspaper ignores them because, eccentric or obsessional people may, nevertheless, have a story to tell. The skill of the newspaper executive who deals with such letters is in deciding what resources he is prepared to devote to checking out a "crank" letter and in choosing which reporter is best capable of doing it. Leonard Russell, then literary editor of the *Sunday Times*, had both skills. The letter he received in May 1968, had come from Chester and was signed by Jock Bruce. It was succinct and well written. Only its contents had caused Russell to frown in disbelief.

It said that the writer had known Lawrence of Arabia from 1922 until Lawrence's death in 1935, that Lawrence had submitted to being beaten by him, that he had been trying to tell this story for years and that no one would believe him. Russell passed the letter to Simpson.

There was an easy course for Simpson to adopt. He could

154

telephone either Lawrence's brother, Professor A. W. Lawrence, or the solicitors who acted for the Lawrence literary trust, read out Bruce's letter, and see what the reaction was. Simpson chose a harder but possibly more rewarding approach. He went up to Chester to see Bruce. The meeting was a fascinating one. Bruce, a large but now unhealthy man, was cautious but convincing. He wanted to tell his story for money: he had a family, his working life was over, his future uncertain. He could authenticate all his claims but he did not want to give away too much until a financial arrangement could be agreed; he had been disappointed in earlier relationships with other newspapers. Simpson took Bruce through his life: date and place of birth, army service, times and occasions when he claimed to have met Lawrence. Back in London he checked the army records. There he discovered that Bruce had indeed been in the Tank Corps during Lawrence's period of service. Although Bruce had joined the Corps in Aberdeen and Lawrence in London, they had arrived at the Tank Corps depot at Bovington, Dorset, together. This lent considerable weight to Bruce's claim that he had joined at Lawrence's instigation and that Lawrence had "arranged everything."

Simpson went to see Bruce again. Encouraged by Simpson's belief in his story, Bruce was much more forthcoming. Simpson returned to London ready for a meeting with Professor Lawrence. To his surprise Professor Lawrence was frank and open. He had known about Bruce since 1935. Other newspapers approached by Bruce had come to him and been told that he had placed the matter in the hands of his solicitors. This had apparently discouraged their investigation. Simpson persisted. He said that his checks on Bruce's story had convinced him that Bruce was telling the truth. Was Professor Lawrence denying that Bruce had beaten Lawrence? No, said Professor Lawrence, but the circumstances were of the utmost relevance. The beatings were intended to achieve a subjection of the body by methods advocated by the saints whose lives he had read.

Simpson said that whatever Lawrence's motives, this was a matter of too great an historical importance to be left unwritten. Although the *Sunday Times* editor, Harold Evans, would have the final say, he was certain that this was a story the newspaper would want to publish. Professor Lawrence and Simpson then came to an arrangement. To help convince Simpson of Professor Lawrence's view of his brother's motivation, to enable him to get a full view of T. E. Lawrence, Professor Lawrence would break the embargo on the Lawrence papers in the Bodleian Library, Oxford. These papers had been collected from Lawrence's friends by Professor Lawrence and had been placed with the Keeper of Western Manuscripts to be kept secret until the year 2000. Professor Lawrence wrote a note which read "Dear Hunt: Will you kindly allow Mr Colin Simpson to read anything he may wish in the collection of T. E. Lawrence material you are holding incommunicado till 2000. Yours sincerely, A. W. Lawrence." In return for this unprecedented access, Simpson agreed that he would not sensationalise the story of Bruce's beatings but would treat the subject with sympathy and understanding. (What each of the parties thought this statement meant later became the subject of some dispute.)

Simpson proceeded to go through the Bodleian material as quickly as possible. Much of it was not surprising and merely added detail to what was already known. Some of it was new and startling. There was, for example, a letter from Lawrence to a Foreign Office official, J. B. Kidston, marked "please burn," which set out Lawrence's motives during the Arab Revolt. These motives were very different from those he had made public. Simpson did not feel competent to assess all this material.

But all of it was interesting and, with the added spice of "incommunicado until 2000," Simpson's journalistic instincts told him he had a marvellous scoop—an excuse to retell the romantic story of the Prince of Mecca, the British Imperial hero, and to add to it the human drama of a man so spiritually tormented that he had submitted to degrading beatings at the hands of a fellow recruit in the Tank Corps. Russell agreed with him and three "Review Fronts," the first page of the arts section of the newspaper, a prime position, were set aside for June. Simpson still had a great deal of research to do. There would have to be long and exhaustive interviews with Bruce and a thorough check of all his new information. Simpson would need help. Why not let him get on with the research and bring in Knightley as a writer? I protested slightly. I had not read *Seven Pillars of Wisdom* since my schooldays. I had not read any of the volumes of T. E. Lawrence's letters. I was not interested in T. E. Lawrence. If I thought about him at all, I saw a vision of Peter O'Toole burning his fingers with a match. "Perfect," Leonard Russell said, "You'll bring a fresh, unprejudiced mind to the subject." I went off on a fourteen-day

Mediterranean cruise to read *Seven Pillars* and to come back ready
to write 12,000 crisp words from Simpson's research.

The first article appeared on Sunday, June 9, 1968. It was
headed "The Secret Life of Lawrence of Arabia. Part One: The
Night of the Turks." It was largely devoted to retelling the story of
Deraa and Lawrence's account of his experience at the hands of
the Turkish Bey.

In keeping with Professor Lawrence's agreement with Simp-
son, I prepared the reader for Bruce's story—Parts Two and
Three. After saying that the Bey had homosexually raped
Lawrence (a view I was later to change) I wrote:

> It is understandable that Lawrence should feel that the Bey had
> subjected him to an indignity that no man should be asked to
> bear unscarred. But one would expect a normal individual to
> realise that it was beyond his power to have prevented what
> occurred and therefore to absolve himself of shame and blame.
> Lawrence was not a normal man. He had a horror of the flesh
> . . . and to find a way of atoning for Deraa became a quest that,
> as we shall see, was to occupy much of his later life.

But no amount of forewarning could overcome Professor
Lawrence's shock at the tone and presentation of the Bruce story.
It could only be told in Bruce's own words, and the detail and the
emphasis distressed him. Leonard Russell, as editor of the series,
took the blame, diverting the Professor's wrath from me, Simpson
and the newspaper by saying, incorrectly, that the decision had
been his and his alone. This left the editor, Harold Evans, room
for compromise with Professor Lawrence over the projected book.
For, within days of the first part of the *Sunday Times* serialisation,
offers from publishers had flooded the newspaper's telex room.
The highest bid was from McGraw-Hill of New York, which
offered $65,000 for US rights. With a British publisher (Nelson)
and contracts with publishers in eight languages, the gross
advances before a word of the book was written totalled over
$100,000.

Anxious not to endanger these contracts because of Professor
Lawrence's distress over the articles, the editor of the *Sunday Times*
wrote to him on July 26 saying that he was taking over the project
himself and would be happy to discuss the book's content and
presentation. To ensure that the tone was sober and scholarly, he

would allow Professor Lawrence to vet it. The letter was sent just in time. Professor Lawrence replied that he had been on the point of refusing collaboration of any kind (not an insurmountable barrier to our writing the book) and of denying use of any copyright material (a telling blow because of the need to quote Lawrence's actual words). He had reconsidered and was prepared to conclude "a gentleman's agreement." As so often happens, this gentleman's agreement eventually became a six-page legal contract with so many obligations involving so many other legal decisions that at one stage I felt that there was not a single lawyer in London who did not have a say in the biography that I was supposed to be writing.

At the time the main clauses did not appear too onerous. One was distinctly advantageous: Professor Lawrence had not only declined the editor's offer to vet the book but had incorporated in the contract an agreement that he would not be available for consultation and would not render any assistance.

The other main clauses were that Professor Lawrence would allow quotation of 4,000 words from Lawrence material on which he owned the copyright, 4,000 words from material controlled by the Seven Pillars of Wisdom Trust, 4,000 words from T. E. Lawrence material; that he would not revoke Simpson's access to the Bodleian material until the book was published. For its part, the *Sunday Times* contracted to publish an acknowledgement of this copyright material and a statement that neither Professor Lawrence nor the Trusts had given any help in writing the book. Somewhere in the book the authors would call attention to the passage written by Professor Lawrence in *T. E. Lawrence by His Friends* which reads:

> One of his friends . . . holds that he was a man perfectly clear in his way of life, who had achieved a balance between spirit, intellect and body to a degree few even imagine. . . . In my opinion he neglected the body's claims unfairly. He maintained this balance at a cost so terrible in waste and suffering, that its author would himself, I believe, have agreed that it was a failure.

The authors expressly agreed to state that none of the material relating to Bruce was obtained from papers in the Bodleian Library or from Professor Lawrence; that Clouds Hill (Lawrence's cottage in Dorset) should not be associated with beating; that no indication be given that a British soldier was involved in a sodomy episode described in a cancelled chapter of the *Seven Pillars of Wisdom*; that no indication be given of where in the unpublished text this cancelled chapter could be found; that the authors would submit to Professor Lawrence for his approval all references in the book to himself; and that they would supply to Dr. John Mack (a psychiatrist from Harvard University, who was working on a book on Lawrence) copies of all the material they obtained from Jock Bruce.

The financial terms were straightforward. In return for the use of copyright material, the *Sunday Times* would pay £2,000 on signature of agreement; £1,000 more when the book earned £30,000, and a royalty of $2\frac{1}{2}$ percent of the net earnings from the book. This money would be divided in the proportion of two-thirds to the Seven Pillars of Wisdom Trust and one third to the Letters and Symposium Trust.

The negotiations that led to this contract were going on in July and August 1968. Nelson, the principal publishers, had rashly promised their foreign counterparts delivery of the manuscript in February. I left Simpson to the negotiations while I tried to work out the shape of the book. It was obvious that the Bruce material, fascinating though it may have been to a newspaper reader, could be no more than a chapter or two in a book, say 6,000 words. What were the other 114,000 words to say? Leonard Russell's suggestion seemed soundest: if the Bruce–Lawrence relationship had been kept secret all those years, what other sides of Lawrence's life were waiting to be uncovered? He advised me to take nothing about Lawrence at face value and to re-examine every facet of his career.

This would clearly be a huge undertaking, but I had the considerable advance available to spend as I saw fit and the *Sunday Times*'s worldwide network of correspondents to call upon for research. I had the weight of the newspaper's name in making enquiries, its extensive clippings library, and all its support facilities—secretaries, typists, researchers, telephones and telex.

On August 4, 1968 I set up a "T. E. Lawrence centre" at the *Sunday Times* and assembled a team. At first it consisted of me, Simpson, Parin Janmohamed (a research assistant) and Anne Dark (a secretary). Simpson was to conclude negotiations with Professor Lawrence, continue his research at the Bodleian, re-interview Bruce, and then write down in as minute detail as possible everything he had in his head and notes about T. E. Lawrence. Parin was to classify the material we already had and get it into some chronological order, looking as she did so for areas that suggested further research. Anne was to help her and, eventually, type the manuscript that I would write. Within two weeks two others joined the team. The first was Suleiman Mousa, a Jordanian historian who, by coincidence, was working in the Public Record Office researching a book he planned on the Hashemites, the family of the leader of the Arab Revolt, the Sharif of Mecca. Mousa had read the articles in the *Sunday Times* and came to see me with a proposition. It would be a waste of effort to have two people going through the same papers at the PRO. He would extract for me anything he found during his research that was relevant to the Lawrence story. How I interpreted what he gave me would be my affair, but if I wanted an Arab view at any time he would be pleased to give it. I engaged him immediately. The other was Arabella Rivington, a middle-aged Englishwoman who had become fascinated by T. E. Lawrence, particularly his post-war life. She planned one day to write a book to be called "T. E. Lawrence, 1918–1935." In the meantime she was prepared to make her extensive files available and to do further research in the areas in which she had become an expert. She too was engaged.

I felt that I now had a reasonably well-balanced team. Mousa clearly thought that the Arabs had had a somewhat raw deal from the British, that the revolt had been a mistake, and that Lawrence's hands were not entirely clean. He might try to push his view. But I did not believe he would withhold anything he found in the PRO that did not support this view. He was an honest man and a scrupulous scholar, and I trusted him. I also had Arabella as a balance. She considered Lawrence to have been one of the greatest Englishmen who ever lived and could be relied upon to defend his reputation. If I could not resolve their conflicting views from the evidence they presented, I could always take an outside opinion. Simpson had no firm stance. As a journalist who had specialised in uncovering the strange practices of wine merchants and antique dealers, he had no illusions about his fellow men. The Lawrence–Bruce relationship had neither surprised nor shocked him. He was, at that time, in the process of buying a country newspaper and, after a discussion over lunch, he agreed to leave the editorial viewpoint of the book to me.

One last organisational matter remained: what was to be the relationship between the authors and the *Sunday Times*? Of course the newspaper could have simply said that the book was an extension of the articles, have directed us to write it as part of our editorial duties, and have paid us nothing more than our salaries. But the editor, Harold Evans, said that he wanted us to have some stake in the book's future. He proposed, and we accepted, an arrangement designed to recompense the newspaper, reward the writers, and enable the whole staff to share in whatever success the book might have. Basically, the contract provided for the paper to take fifty per cent of the profits of the book, for the two authors to receive 20 percent each and for 10 percent to be divided among staff members who had contributed to any way at all. With this incentive we settled down to work.

Research on Lawrence's early life produced little that was new. We were unable to resolve when and how Lawrence learned of his illegitimacy, whether or not he disturbed his parents having sexual intercourse, and many other points that in the end, we realised, mattered little.

We found we agreed with other biographers that the young Lawrence's relationship with the Oxford archaeologist, D. G. Hogarth, was important. But we drew different conclusions about the relationship. From what I had learned about espionage from my last book, it seemed to me that Hogarth was a typical pre-World War I British intelligence agent. He had some sort of loose arrangement with the Foreign Office to report anything he discovered of interest during his frequent spells abroad, especially in the Middle East. His relationship with Lawrence also struck me as a typical case-officer-and-recruit one; and although we turned up no positive proof of these theories, we advanced them in the book and they have since been accepted.

Our major source of new material turned out to be the Foreign Office archives in the Public Record Office. Until 1968 the embargo period for these papers was 50 years. Allowing time for classifying and indexing, much of the material relating to Lawrence would not have been available until about 1970. Then in 1968 the period of embargo was altered to 30 years and a variety of documents concerning Lawrence have been released at irregular intervals since then.

Suleiman Mousa was one of the first historians to go through them and the fruits of his research began to pour into the Lawrence centre where, from 10 am to 6 pm every day, I did little else but read them. From this reading emerged my view that Lawrence was the antithesis of his legend.

Far from having an emotional attachment to the Arabs, he did not care for them as a race; far from devoting himself to uniting their divided tribes so that an Arab nation would emerge, he believed that it was in Britain's interests to keep the Middle East divided; far from furthering the cause of Arab freedom and independence, he was intent on making the Arabs part of the British Empire. This double-dealing and the betrayal it involved gave Lawrence a lasting sense of guilt which explained much of his behaviour in later life. As this view clarified in my mind I began to write it. This meant leaping straight into the centre of the chronology before writing the first sections. This had dangers, but I wanted to get down what I believed would be the core of the book so as to have as much time as possible to revise it. As the pages came from the typewriter and Anne Dark distributed them, the first dissension threatened the team. Mousa felt that I was not being hard enough on Lawrence and that the new evidence justified a tougher approach—a view also held by Bruce Page who had been the principal author of the Philby book and who had also read my first Lawrence drafts. But Arabella Rivington, although admitting that this was not the period of Lawrence's career she knew best, insisted that everything she knew about his later life made the behaviour I was attributing to him completely out of character.

This dispute, postponed rather than solved, brought forward an idea I had been considering for some time. Arabella Rivington had often spoken of Lawrence's character, his personality, the sort of man he was. Lawrence had been many things to many people, but the book would clearly benefit from some impartial analysis of the man. Would it be possible, I wondered, to put all our research material before a psychiatrist, ask him to read it and then tell us what sort of a man he believed Lawrence to be—a sort of post-mortem psychoanalysis? I wrote to the secretary of the Royal Maudsley Hospital asking if one of his colleagues would be interested in such an idea. Eventually we heard that Dr. Denis Leigh, a distinguished psychiatrist and the secretary-general of the World Psychiatric Association, was fascinated by the project and would be delighted to help.

At the same time we initiated an investigation of the Deraa incident, which would obviously be crucial to the psychoanalysis. As we discussed how best to research the Deraa story one fact struck us. In every biography, every examination of Lawrence's account of Deraa had been an internal one. Every biographer had reached his conclusions about the truthfulness or otherwise of Lawrence's story by looking at the different versions Lawrence himself had recounted of his meeting with the Turkish Bey. No one had ever asked the Bey for *his* version. We immediately telexed our correspondent in Ankara asking him to find out who the Bey was, if he was still alive, and, if he was, to drop everything else and interview him as soon as possible.

The answer three days later caused mixed emotions. The Bey was Hacim Muhittin; but he had died in 1965, so we were three years too late. The good news was that his son had kept the Bey's wartime diaries, he had not only offered to make these available to us but had also volunteered introductions to his father's friends and enemies so that we could obtain a complete picture of him. The conclusions we reached from this research—that the Bey was an aggressive heterosexual and that although he knew of Lawrence's existence there was no mention of him in the diaries—was added to the stack of material prepared for Dr. Leigh.

With the end of the year approaching and the book only one-third finished, I had to abandon writing because of yet another legal complication. In the newspaper articles, part of Bruce's story concerned "the old man," a character invented by Lawrence to justify the beatings he wanted Bruce to inflict on him. Lawrence wove an elaborate fantasy in which, because of his debt to "the old man," he had to submit to a regime of punishment to improve his character. Instructions from "the old man" on the time and severity of the beatings would, in Lawrence's fantasy, arrive from time to time. Bruce would be recruited to help Lawrence by carrying out the beatings; Lawrence would go off to see "the old man" and return to tell Bruce whether "the old man" was satisfied or whether another beating was required. The "old man" did not, of course, exist. The fantasy was necessary to help persuade Bruce to carry out the beatings without questioning Lawrence's motives. But either because he believed Bruce might be sufficiently suspicious to check Lawrence's story or just to add verisimilitude to it, Lawrence gave the "old man" a name.

He chose that of Mr. Fetherstonhaugh Frampton, a distant relative, who lived in Dorset and who had sold Lawrence his cottage, Clouds Hill. We had told all this in the newspaper articles, and believed we had made it clear that there was no possibility that Lawrence's fantasy contained any element of truth and that Mr. Fetherstonhaugh Frampton had been made the unwitting victim of Lawrence's elaborate deception of Bruce.

But now Commander R. H. C. Fetherstonhaugh Frampton, D.L., R.N. Rtd. wrote saying that his attention had been drawn to the articles and "its allegations against my father" and requesting publication of a letter stating that his father had probably never even met Lawrence and was not the sort of person to have behaved like "the old man." On legal advice we published this letter with a note adding that we had found no evidence to suggest that the whole story of Mr. Fetherstonhaugh Frampton was anything other than a fantasy concocted by Lawrence for his own purpose. We also agreed to show the commander the text of the manuscript where it concerned him, thus adding his name to a growing list of people from whom we would need approval before we could publish the book.

The newspaper articles had brought a flood of letters from people who had known Lawrence and who wanted to add their bit to the story. Arabella Rivington, Simpson, and occasionally, a *Sunday Times* reporter, travelled the country to see them. This was laborious, expensive research which could have been done by letter, but we found that an interview—or, in some cases, several—always elicited better information than an exchange of letters or a telephone call. A leisurely chat seemed to help people recall incidents and conversations which they believed they had forgotten. As 1968 drew to a close, with most of these interviews done, the Bruce section of the book finished, the wartime chapters nearly written, and the file on Lawrence's period in the RAF filling out nicely, we felt we were making good progress. Then, in the week between Christmas and the New Year, we lost a whole chapter. The publisher had been worrying us as the deadline approached to deliver the manuscript as it was written. We had devoted one chapter to examining the charge that Lawrence was a homosexual, in retrospect an ill-advised effort, but since the book was being written under pressure and out of chronological order, it seemed a good idea at the time. An editor at Nelson wisely rejected it in its entirety with reasons we found impossible to dispute. He had once been a homosexual himself, he said, and it was clear to him that we had not the faintest idea of what it was all about.

By early February a draft manuscript of about 120,000 words was ready. I had been considering since the previous November a plan to submit it first to some neutral academic reader. The book was aimed at the widest reading public and the historical background had to be expressed with broad strokes. None of the team were historians by training, except Mousa, and I was eager for a second opinion.

In November I asked a friend in the Department of History at Edinburgh University if he could recommend someone. He suggested Professor Elie Kedourie, then at the Center for Middle Eastern Studies at Harvard. I wrote to Kedourie and he replied saying he would be interested, but before I could reach an arrangement with him Leonard Russell said he thought that Elizabeth Monroe, of St. Antony's College, Oxford, should read the draft.

It was sent to her the first week in March. She replied almost immediately to say that having read it she was sorry but she would have to decline the task. She had found the assessment of Lawrence's character "detached, to the point, and interesting." She differed on what we had labelled new, and it was clear that this difference would have arisen no matter which academic had read the manuscript. We had used "new" in the sense that the material had not been available to the *general reader* before. Mrs. Monroe—and later other academics—took exception to this because the information was known, or available, in *academic* circles. Thus, Mrs. Monroe wrote that a government report we had called new was not so, "partly because it has been available in the Austen Chamberlain papers at Birmingham for some years, partly because important sections of it appeared in a White Paper in 1939 and enabled several historians, including myself, accurately to guess the rest, and partly because an article by Dr. Véreté, of Jerusalem, will appear before your book."

We decided that we could live with this criticism. Two other points by Mrs. Monroe were more serious. First, she said that our emphasis was wrong because "you have sent researchers into the jungle of the PRO without enough background knowledge of

known history." We put this to the person who had done most of
the PRO research, Suleiman Mousa, by then back in Jordan. He
replied: "Historians seldom agree on interpretation or emphasis.
You are writing about an individual, not the history of the period.
The book is intended to be a popular and controversial one, not a
doctoral thesis. Have the courage of your opinions." We were
suitably chastened. Mrs. Monroe's second point was to disagree
with our statement that Hogarth was some sort of private
intelligence officer before the war. Mrs. Monroe said that this was
not true. But then she went on to write:

> He did, until the war, exactly what many of us have done. If,
> after travel in a little known area, an archaeologist, or even a
> journalist like myself, sits next to a Foreign Office or a military
> intelligence man at dinner and tells where one has been and he
> asks for a written account, one writes what one knows. Lots of
> travellers in the Ottoman Asian provinces did so without being
> engaged in political intelligence work, except casually, and
> without thinking of it as such.

We decided that Mrs. Monroe had actually confirmed what we
had written about Hogarth and stuck to our allegation.

For the rest, Mrs. Monroe was most helpful. Although she had
declined the formal assignment, her scholarly instinct would not
allow her to overlook our errors and she had meticulously
corrected these as she had read the manuscript. She wrote that she
offered this as a gift but would be grateful if we would refrain from
using her name in any way, either with Nelson or with the
American publisher.

By late March, already six weeks behind on our delivery date,
we began to realise the extent of our legal commitments. Dr.
Leigh, having read the manuscript, said that it would be of great
value to his analysis of Lawrence if he were able to see Lawrence's
army medical records. We asked the Ministry of Defence if it
would make the records available to Dr. Leigh. It replied that it
would, providing that Lawrence's next-of-kin, that is Professor
Lawrence, agreed. But we were under a legal obligation in our
contract with Professor Lawrence not to contact him during the
writing of the book. We took a chance and wrote to him. His
solicitors, Kennedy, Ponsonby and Prideaux, replied setting out
the conditions under which Professor Lawrence would agree: Dr.

Leigh should keep the information confidential but should pass it
to Professor Lawrence; anything he wrote from the records should
be subject to approval by Professor Lawrence and the Ministry of
Defence.

Next, on April 1, Kennedy, Ponsonby and Prideaux wrote
pointing out that we were in breach of the agreement to show to
Professor Lawrence all references to himself by March 31.
Professor Lawrence would soon be going abroad; unless these
references were supplied within the next few days he would be
unable to see them until the end of August. This, of course, would
have meant postponing publication, announced for September
29, until the following year, so we worked around the clock to
deliver the relevant sections on April 8. Kennedy, Ponsonby and
Prideaux replied ten days later.

Professor Lawrence had made a number of minor changes and
we accepted these. He also insisted on revisions and deletions. We
had written: "T. E. told one of his brothers that while he was at
home recovering from the injury to his foot he had accidentally
come upon his parents having sexual intercourse and that this had
been a great shock to him." Kennedy, Ponsonby and Prideaux
said that this should be omitted; nothing of the sort was ever told
to Professor Lawrence by T.E. or anyone else and it was unlikely
that it had been reported by any of T.E.'s other brothers. We had
written: "From one of the Lawrence trusts set up to handle money
derived from royalties, a small payment was made to help the
education of Bruce's son." This was changed by Professor
Lawrence to: "an annual payment of £4 was made as the result of
a request by Mrs. Bruce for the benefit of Bruce's son." We had
written: "Professor Lawrence believes that the salient features of
Bruce's account are probably a true version of what Lawrence
told him." Professor Lawrence changed this to: "Bruce has given
a true account of what Lawrence told him about the anonymous
uncle and the mode of life his non-existent relative required of
him." None of this really seemed worth quarrelling about and we
accepted all of Professor Lawrence's points.

In the meantime Commander Fetherstonhaugh Frampton had
been sent the references to his father, as we had formally agreed to
do. He replied asking that we remove all references to his father's
name because two new points had convinced him that it was
impossible for his father to have been this person. The facts were:
Bruce had written to him to say that he had never revealed the

name of the Old Man to the *Sunday Times* or anyone else (this was true; we had identified Fetherstonhaugh Frampton from clues in Lawrence's story); Professor Lawrence had written to say that he had letters of Bruce proving that Lawrence had told Bruce that the mythical persecutor was an uncle, "a relationship Lawrence chose because he had no living uncle, thereby widening the field for speculation." Since we had decided that the story Lawrence told Bruce was fantasy, there seemed no point in insisting that we be allowed to name Featherstonhaugh Frampton as the model Lawrence used for his fantasy, and we agreed to drop the name.

At the same time as we were dealing with the references to Professor Lawrence, we were trying desperately to fulfil the most onerous clause of our agreement with him. We had to obtain from the recipients of Lawrence's letters (copies of which we had found in the Bodleian) permission to publish them in our book. Most of these people were dead, so we had to try to trace their next of kin, or their literary executors. Some had moved abroad. Some proved untraceable. Yet we were legally obliged to have their written permission, otherwise Professor Lawrence, in whom the copyright of the letters was vested, would refuse copyright clearance.

Just what this could mean is best illustrated by the Kidston letter. Vizards, the London solicitors, acting for Kidston's executors, refused to grant permission. This was obviously a bluff. The copyright to the letter was vested in T. E. Lawrence and had never passed to Kidston or his executors. We had already published the letter in the newspaper articles so it had been read by four million people in Britain and had appeared in syndicated serialisations throughout the world. Yet—and to this day we do not know whether Vizards realised it or not—although they had no legal grounds for preventing us from publishing the Kidston letter, their refusal to agree to a request that was basically a courtesy one, would have effectively stopped us because the agreement with Professor Lawrence made his copyright clearance contingent on Vizards' "courtesy" permission. We took our own legal advice and tried our own bluff. We assumed that Vizards did not know of Professor Lawrence's strictures, so we wrote to them saying that the letter was an important historical document and that we considered it would in no way infringe on their clients' rights if we were to publish it without their approval. However—and now came the lure—we said that time was short and that since we did not want to become involved in a long disagreement we would suggest a compromise: if the executors of the late J. B. Kidston would agree to our request to publish the letter we would delete Kidston's name and refer merely to "a Foreign Office official." To our relief, Vizards replied agreeing to our suggestion.

There were other set-backs about which we could do nothing. Kennedy, Ponsonby and Prideaux wrote saying that our request to use an extract from a letter written by Lawrence to his mother was subject to the same stipulation as the Bodleian letters—the consent of the recipient or the recipient's heirs was necessary. In this case, the heir was Mrs. Lawrence's eldest son, Dr. M. R. Lawrence, and he was not prepared to give his consent. The hunt for the heirs of other characters in the Lawrence story was arduous, despite some assistance from Kennedy, Ponsonby and Prideaux. Colonel Stirling's wife was living in Tangier; Mrs. Reider, a language teacher at the American mission near Beirut, was dead, but Professor Lawrence thought she might have had some distant relatives living near New York (consent was eventually waived in this case); Major-General Dawnay died in 1938 and the only address for his youngest son was ten years out of date. In other cases the recipient of Lawrence's letter was often a literary person as well; literary persons tend to have literary executors and it became necessary to obtain consent from *all* the executors, no one executor being prepared to take the responsibility himself. Or the executors simply referred us to their solicitors, who wanted to enter into a long correspondence about the matter.

At this stage our publisher struck. They wrote saying that they had concluded deals with a number of foreign publishers on the clear understanding that the present manuscript represented the final version of the book, so "we cannot at this stage accept any further changes to the text." This had been prompted by the publisher's discovery of our agreement with Professor Lawrence. Fortunately the last of our permissions came through and Professor Lawrence's final changes to references to himself were minor, and we were able to persuade the publisher to accept them and pass them to the overseas publishers.

We thought the period while waiting for final proofs would give us a chance to wind down, but Kennedy, Ponsonby and Prideaux had other ideas. On July 18, two months before publication, they wrote to say that they had discovered that bound xerox copies of the typescript of the book were circulating in the uncorrected form and that at least one of these copies had come onto the market. Professor Lawrence would take a very grave view "of what must amount to a breach of the Agreement." The copies should be withdrawn immediately. We replied saying that a draft typescript had been circulated to overseas publishers to enable them to obtain translation and printing estimates. This was normal practice. The actual publishing would be from the master, corrected manuscript. We did not know how a London bookseller had obtained a copy, but we could say that he had decided to withdraw it from sale and return it to the vendor. Kennedy, Ponsonby and Prideaux were not entirely satisfied because, as they pointed out, there was nothing to stop the unidentified vendor from putting the purloined typescript on the market again. But, as they recognised, there was little we or anyone else could do about it.

*The Secret Lives of Lawrence of Arabia* (the publisher's choice of title) was published in Britain on September 29, 1969. The first printing of 25,000 had sold out before publication—helped, no doubt, by extracts published in the *Sunday Times* throughout the month of August. It was the Literary Guild choice in Britain and the Literary Guild Alternate choice in the United States. There were to be German, French, Italian, Spanish, Swedish, Norwegian, Dutch and Japanese editions. We felt justified in holding a modest launching party and invited everyone we had spoken to who had known Lawrence, including Jock Bruce, Edward Robinson (in the desert), Tom Beaumont (his gunner) and L. B. Anwyl (in the RAF). Bruce had an argument with one of Lawrence's admirers and left early. Harold Evans and I made brief speeches and we sat back to await the reviews.

The first was in our own newspaper, the *Sunday Times*. It was harsh. The reviewer was Professor Elie Kedourie, the academic with whom we had corresponded about reading our manuscript before we settled instead on Elizabeth Monroe. After saying that we had interpreted our documentation wrongly—especially that relating to British–Arab relations and dealings between the Zionists and Sharifians—Professor Kedourie concluded: "In this respect therefore the book does not add to knowledge but only promotes and deepens those feelings of guilt in which so many of the intellectual classes of this country like to luxuriate." We entered into an abortive public correspondence with Professor Kedourie over what our documentation did or did not prove. In retrospect, it would have been better to have remained silent.

After this the reviews picked up. The *Evening Standard* said the book was "biographical dynamite"; the *Sunday Telegraph* that it was "required reading; fascinating." The *Times*, the *Daily Mail*, and most of the provincial press praised the book. In the United States it was called "indispensable": "the mere fact of its appearance constitutes a restructuring of the Lawrence myth." There were news stories, and Simpson and I were interviewed on television and radio. We awaited the more scholarly reviews with interest.

The first was the *Times Literary Supplement*. On October 2 it carried a three-column review combined with the Aldington biography, presumably re-published to take advantage of the Lawrence boom. The anonymous reviewer (it was *TLS* practice then not to publish the reviewer's name) said that much of the material we claimed as new was not so; that we lacked a sense of historical sequence; that we were wrong in our assessment of Lawrence's role as an intelligence officer; that the book, though so full of faults, was immensely readable. We puzzled over who this reviewer could be. Then the answer leapt from the page. Writers tend to repeat their own felicitous phrases. The reviewer had written "their researchers galloped through the jungle of the Public Record Office." This was the very phrase used by an Oxford academic to criticise our manuscript. The reviewer was none other than Mrs. Elizabeth Monroe.

Other reviews raised a question that concerns all biographers. Literary editors tend to give biographies to a reviewer who knows about the subject and is competent to see the flaws in the author's conclusions. But the reviewer has often gained this competence because he has already written a biography of the subject or—worse still, from the author's point of view—he is currently working on one. In the first instance the reviewer will naturally tend to feel that the new work does not measure up to his own. In the latter case, he will resent the fact that he has been beaten to publication. Two reviews of *The Secret Lives* illustrate my point.

Anthony Nutting, former minister of state for foreign affairs under Anthony Eden, reviewed our book for *Mid East*. It was a generally unfavourable review. But Nutting is the author of *Lawrence of Arabia* and he began his review with these frank and illuminating words: "It is never an easy task to review a book by another author on a subject about which one has written *a definitive work of one's own*" (my italics). In the autumn issue of 1970 the *Middle East Journal* carried a very unfavourable review by Dr. John Mack, the Harvard psychiatrist whom we had been obliged to help under our agreement with Professor Lawrence. Nowhere in the review does Dr. Mack mention that he himself is engaged in writing a biography of Lawrence, *A Prince of Our Disorder* (which was eventually published in 1976 and won a Pulitzer prize). I see no easy solution to this problem except, perhaps, a frank and prominent statement of the reviewer's position.

The Lawrence project was financially rewarding. The total cost including money paid to Bruce and Professor Lawrence was about £14,000 (then $33,600). Total net revenue was about £34,000 (then $81,600) from which each author received (over and above his salary during the writing of the book) about £6,000 ($14,000). There were other intangible returns. I learned a lot about Middle Eastern history and politics and remain interested in the area. I still keep in touch with many of the people who helped with the project. And I met, as a result of the book, many authors with similar interests (including the editor of this volume).

Literary biography is extremely difficult because at its heart is one unresolvable conflict. You have chosen your subject because he is interesting. He is interesting because he was controversial. If you side with his friends then beware of his enemies, and vice-versa. If you stand in the middle you are hit by the bricks from both sides. And if he was a figure of some public stature you will have the legend to contend with as well. Not to mention the lawyers.

# CHAPTER TEN

# T. S. Eliot

## LYNDALL GORDON

Eliot told Mary Trevelyan, his closest friend in the 1940's and early 1950's, that he hid behind impenetrability.[1] As he shed his American youth, he cultivated the anonymous front of the proper English gentleman. He surrounded himself with the props of respectability: the polite, modest manner, the voice so measured as to sound almost deadpan. His gestures of weariness and his appointment book kept people at bay. Although he used to see Mary about three times a week, he preserved a fiction that minimized the relationship. She must agree, he insisted, that over all those years they had met only once a fortnight. His letters to her show that, even to a constant companion, he was guarded and changeable, and liked playfully to adopt an alias. In time, she learnt to read simpler signals—his fingers drumming on the table spelt bad weather—but he remained, after twenty years, still incomprehensible. The interest of Eliot's life, as well as his work, lies in a game of masks and unmaskings. His elusiveness is the essential problem for a biographer but this is, to some extent, pre-empted by practical problems.

Eliot's decree that there should be no biography has been faithfully upheld by his much-younger widow. There is, in addition, a ban on quotation of Eliot's unpublished writings which must be published by Faber. Vast amounts of Eliot's criticism still lie buried in journals. Often his most telling pieces, say an informal interview or a more relaxed talk to boys at his own school in New England, are tucked away in obscure and almost unobtainable magazines like the *Milton Graduates Bulletin* and the *Grantite Review*.[2]

Another practical problem is Eliot's letters which are scattered far and wide. Eliot was too guarded to be a great writer of letters, but there are some more confidential batches: to Virginia Woolf,[3] to Conrad Aiken in 1914,[4] and to Bertrand Russell after Eliot's disastrous first marriage.[5] The letters to Eliot's college friend, Aiken, tell us what Eliot was writing during the obscurest period of his life, the years immediately before his first publication in 1915, and there are tantalizing plans for a sequel to "Prufrock" in which the speaker will attend not a teaparty but a masquerade.[6] He will go as St. John the Divine, wearing only underwear.

For the last ten years the publication of Eliot's letters has been talked of as imminent but, so far, only one really important letter has been published, to Stephen Spender in 1931, suggesting what may be Eliot's first impulse to write his masterpiece, *Four Quartets*:

> I have the A minor Quartet [of Beethoven] on the gramophone, and I find it quite inexhaustible to study. There is a sort of heavenly or at least more than human gaiety about some of his later things which one imagines might come to oneself as the fruit of reconciliation and relief after immense suffering. I should like to get something of that into verse before I die.[7]

Yet, even when the letters are published, they must be incomplete without the 1000-odd letters to his first, long-lasting love, Emily Hale, sequestered at Princeton until 2020 by which time, presumably, any questions will be futile.

Although Eliot died in 1965 there has been, for these reasons, no authorized biography. It was quite indirectly, through an initial interest in the development of Eliot's religious ideas, that I came to write a biographic study of Eliot's early years. I began to see that it would blur the picture to keep Eliot's life as rigidly separate from his work as critical dogma dictated. And then, the more that I found out about Eliot's life, the more it appeared that life and work were, in this poet, inseparable. For the patterning of the poetry on the familiar model of spiritual biography was reflected in a life that was, to a curious degree, patterned itself, almost as though Eliot's life were an invention complementary to his work.

At this point an intellectual problem loomed: it became necessary to disregard the dogmas that had gathered around Eliot's career and, more difficult, to test his own claims to poetic impersonality and European tradition. These claims had become dogmas because Eliot himself invented, enacted and reinforced them in a series of memorable pronouncements: "The progress of an artist is a continual self-sacrifice, a continual extinction of personality."[8] "The more perfect the artist, the more completely separate in him will be the man who suffers and the mind which creates."[9] How do we reconcile the moments of intimacy ("I am moved by fancies that are curled / Around these images"[10]) with the classical allusions that stud the surface of Eliot's poems? The quatrain poems (1917–1919) strike at pathetic targets—pimpled youths, ludicrous women—with loathing and hilarity. We are drawn into some underlying and unspeakable emotion and, at the same time, distracted by Eliot's deft allusions. The allusion to Greek tragedy at the end of "Sweeney Among the Nightingales" implies that the menace surrounding Agamemnon, about to be murdered by his wife, offers a key to the fate of Sweeney, a comic figure of brute lust but somehow in the toils of Rachel *née* Rabinovitch who tears at grapes "with murderous paws."[11] Such allusions, if followed too slavishly, can take us away from the poem. But the emotions in Eliot's letters to Pound, with their undisguised anti-Semitism and misogyny, would help us to understand that the quatrains were rooted in the peculiar circumstances of Eliot's life: the misogyny connected with his hellish marriage, the anti-Semitism with anxieties over money.[12]

This kind of link could easily become reductive, for the point of Eliot's career is how he managed to transmute almost maddening states of mind into a universal spiritual drama. Here, the best commentaries are Eliot's essays. In "Cyril Tourneur" he claims that loathing and horror of life may legitimately, even "consummately," exceed objective truth with characters "projected from the poet's inner world of nightmare, some horror beyond words."[13] This nightmare—and it is here that Eliot reveals his dazzling leap to a spiritualized vision of his career—"is a triumph; for hatred of life is an important phase—even if you like, a mystical experience—in life itself."

A biographer might safely assume that for most writers there will be public and private selves but, in Eliot's case, façades invade, almost take over the poems as they entirely take over the life. Every reminiscence of Eliot has reinforced the mocking self-effacement of the man in "a four-piece suit" (as Clive Bell described him[14]), the Eliot of the famous photograph, impeccable in his bowler hat, leaning lightly on a carefully rolled umbrella, and smiling shyly en route to his irreproachable editor's job at Faber & Gwyer. Eliot enjoyed the act (as he later enjoyed being

an Old Buffer[15]) and played up his tease in "Lines for Cuscus-
caraway and Mirza Murad Ali Beg":

> How unpleasant to meet Mr. Eliot!
> With his features of clerical cut,
> And his brow so grim
> And his mouth so prim
> And his conversation so nicely
> Restricted to What Precisely . . .
>                                    (*CP*, p. 137)

Two ways of getting past this façade were to examine Eliot
manuscripts and to frame the right questions. These two efforts
were simultaneous: the questions were determined by the manuscripts and the manuscripts combed with questions already in
mind. These were, first, who were Eliot's models? What was his
native tradition? Auden once remarked that no genuine European
could have made Eliot's celebrated statement that tradition is not
inherited but acquired by great labour.[16] I assumed that Eliot's
acquired tradition was to be found in his "objective correlatives,"
his elaborate term for the historical or literary parallels by which
he attempts to universalize private states of mind. But was there, I
wondered, an inherited tradition nevertheless, obscured by an
international frame of reference, but latent in attitudes to nature,
to women, even to religion? Did his Puritan forebears leave any
residue, that line of New England divines or hanging Judge Blood
who made himself conspicuous in the punishment of witches?
Hawthorne was prepared to recognize that "strong traits of their
[the Puritan] nature have intertwined themselves with mine."[17]
The Dimmesdale element in Eliot might be worth pursuing, the
excruciation of a sinner of high spiritual gifts, gazing absorbed
into the mirror of election with its associated dangers of pride and
despair:

> To the high mountain peaks of faith and sanctity he would have
> climbed, had not the tendency been thwarted by the burden,
> whatever it might be of crime or anguish, beneath which it was
> his doom to totter. It kept him down, on a level with the lowest;
> him, the man of ethereal attributes.   (*The Scarlet Letter*, ch. 11)

Yet it was this very secret burden that gave the minister the

Tongue of Flame, capable of expressing the highest truths through the medium of familiar words and images.

Towards the end of his life, Eliot himself confirmed a native tradition in his poetry: "in its sources, in its emotional springs, it comes from America."[18] This aspect is still neglected, but the dominant forms of American writing, soul history and sermon, give a curious backing to Eliot's impenetrability. He shares with Emerson, Thoreau, Whitman and Dickinson a guarded mode of confession. Unlike St. Augustine or Rousseau who draw us into intimacy, these Americans throw the onus of introspection back into the lap of the reader. Their confessions, like *The Waste Land*, are fragmentary and, left so deliberately incomplete, demand a reciprocal effort. The point lies not in their content but in the act of self-discovery and judgement. Its ultimate purpose is not to expose the speaker but to create the reader. In short, it is a form of sermon.

Another question was what does Eliot's work tell of his life? Eliot's early notebook with poems dating from 1909 and his folder of miscellaneous poems in the Berg Collection were, more than letters, the main clue to the invisible Eliot. The unpublished poems and drafts are less guarded and more obviously autobiographical than the published work. And they show, too, how Eliot achieved impersonality either by the simple exchange of pronouns, "one" and "we" for "I," or very subtly by an effective extinction of his own meditative, prophetic voice against a cacophony of hollow, determined voices from different quarters of a doomed civilization. The failure to sustain the prophetic voice—it appears briefly in part I of *The Waste Land*—together with ephemeral glimpses of sublimity, is the essential problem in the poem and a necessary preamble to part V, according to the manuscript the earliest in origin and to Eliot "the only part that justifies the whole, at all,"[19] where the elevated voice, resonating with the thunder, comes, at least briefly, into its own.

The longer I looked at the manuscripts side by side with the published poems, the stranger Eliot appeared. He became less and less the familiar figure of the schoolroom and critical text. In the earliest fragments of *The Waste Land* manuscript, written before Eliot left Boston, in other poems of that time, "The Burnt Dancer" and "The Love Song of St. Sebastian," the polar opposite of decorum struggles for an acceptable form of expression. A would-be martyr lashes himself wildly to stimulate higher faculties in recoil from the flesh, but masochistic passion turns easily to murderous violence. Eliot's St. Sebastian is a repository for fantasies of anarchic abandon, emotional and physical, which are only in the most primitive sense, religious. Moral judgement is conspicuous by its absence: the young poet inspects an obsession with chastisement carried to intoxication. There was no sign of the controlled discipline which an earlier generation of Eliot's readers, the generation under the spell of his visible presence, took for granted.

It was the conviction that I was on the track of the elusive Eliot that made practical problems, at least at first, fade into comparative insignificance. For the Berg manuscripts suggested that, contrary to the critical dogma of the last half-century, there was no break in Eliot's career, no sudden switch from atheist to Christian but that Eliot's was a singleminded, even obsessed career. Atheist and Christian stances are familiar enough but Eliot's religious development, for all its eventual orthodoxy, might, it began to seem, defy understanding. As a schoolgirl, reading Eliot with my mother, I was struck by her impression that Eliot had, from the start, some sort of half-mocking religious temperament, which was borne out perhaps by Prufrock's "hundred visions" and the fourth Prelude's "notion of some infinitely gentle/Infinitely suffering thing."

When, as a graduate student, I looked at the hoard of early manuscripts, I felt the exhilaration of a scientist who, trying out a mere hunch, gets astonishing results. When I found "Silence" (dated June 1910), the 1st and 2nd "Debate between Body & Soul" (dated 1910 and 1911), and the martyr poems (undated, but about 1913–14), it was clear that even very early details in Eliot's career fitted the set pattern of the rare life that strains for perfection: his American Puritan inheritance, his mother's poetry which maps the states between loss and recovery of grace, his own obsessive reading in the more bizarre psychology of religious experience and his 1914 comment to Aiken that, if he could slough off petty worries, he might look forward to the luxury of divine discontent.

Other holographs, the almost demented vigil poems, written in Paris in 1911 and culminating in "Prufrock's Pervigilium" (a passage eventually cut from "Prufrock"), filled in the story of a psychic nightmare which Eliot was to define, later, as a visionary triumph and which, it seemed by Eliot's dates, followed the intimations of election in "Silence" and the "2nd Debate between the Body & Soul"[20] where Eliot speaks of the wind beyond the world and the appalling fall from sublimity when Time begins again its remorseless work of attrition. Still, the timeless moment does promise a brilliant transformation: it would be possible to shed the chrysalis of the flesh and burst out ingenuous and pure. Another unpublished poem, "The Little Passion," foretells the route of the lifespan as an *imitatio Christi:* the line of street lights leads inexorably to a cross on which souls are pinned and bleed. A letter to Aiken from Marburg in 1914 speaks of a magnum opus to be called "The Descent from the Cross." It was to include a Fool-house section in the manner of "Prufrock," an insane section, a mystical section, and "The Love Song of St. Sebastian."

These initial discoveries gave an irresistible momentum and direction to routine biographic research. I simply went ahead with a conviction that the truth would speak for itself. The excitement of detection drove me from one library to another, from Hamilton, Ontario to Charlottesville, Virginia. These journeys (paid for by night classes at Hunter College) were never tedious because this research had never been done so that there was always the hope of a find. And, incredibly it seemed, at every library there *was* a find for even the smallest facts added to my growing sense of the weird inevitability of Eliot's career.

Once I had questioned the division of the career, the impersonality of the poetry and the absence of American tradition, it became easier to question another assumption: the monstrousness of Vivienne Haigh-Wood, Eliot's first wife. Vivienne suffered at least as much as her husband and, to be fair, something had to be said for her early understanding of his gifts and for her own flair for writing. Since sides were taken after the couple's separation in 1933 and since almost all their friends, including Vivienne's brother, sided with Eliot, some imagination was necessary to fill in Vivienne's case with the help of her diaries which are unfailingly loyal to the man who abandoned her. Still, her dramatic efforts to lay claim to Eliot became increasingly awkward and she was certified insane. It is curious to note Eliot's comment to Virginia Woolf that Vivienne was *not* mad, simply talked herself into states. During the Battle of Britain, Mary Trevelyan, concerned for Vivienne, suggested to Eliot that she might be moved to safety. Eliot replied that he had no authority to contravene court orders.

In the 1920's Eliot was hailed as the spokesman for his generation. His friends were therefore taken aback by the epigraph to "Sweeney Agonistes." "The soul," he quoted from St. John of the Cross, "cannot be possessed of the divine union, until it has divested itself of the love of created beings." Eliot was only superficially a man of his time. I have suggested that his natural ties were with American Puritans of the seventeenth century, but he was also drawn to the Catholic mystics of the Middle Ages. His is not the cultural despair, the dead-end alienation of Modernity but the purposeful withdrawal of monastic tradition.

As these conclusions emerged, my main problem was intellectual isolation. I used to take the subway from 116th street down to the Berg Collection and come back home every day having spoken to no one but accompanied all the time by self-doubt: how dared I, an obscure graduate student, contradict many critics? Yet there was also a detective excitement, particularly in the dating of *The Waste Land* fragments, that made up for loneliness. Eliot himself was the best support at that time for he taught me to laugh at postures, at the sycophantic backwash of the campus uprising of 1968 and at the plaintive tones of a vastly successful professor who muttered "I am dying, Egypt, dying" over a dingy cup of coffee.

There was another diversion. This was the voice of a fellow-student who occupied an adjoining cubicle at the top of Butler Library.

"Are you there?" he would call.

The story of his unhappy marriage poured through our open windows. (It was stifling in summer.) His wife was depressed.

"Try," I ventured, "to hear what she says."

"She liked that," he said next day.

It was much too intimate for us ever to want to meet. But out on the campus I used to wonder if this man or that was the Voice.

At this point I still had not faced the practical problems. The research had flourished solely on the basis of Chaucer's advice to

> Flee fro the prees, and dwelle with sothfastnesse
> Suffice unto thy good, though it be smal.[21]

Impatiently, I had put aside thoughts of permission, publishers and contracts and, though this may seem unworldly, it worked. Eventually, when the research was written up, top Eliot scholars welcomed the findings with exemplary openmindedness. A.

Walton Litz suggested that the unpublishable quotations could be replaced by very close paraphrase, as Carlos Baker had done in his biography of Hemingway. And though I never sought Mrs. Eliot's backing, when the findings were first published in an article on *The Waste Land* manuscript, quite unexpectedly she asked me to lunch at the Eliot flat. I saw at once that questions would be impertinent, so decided to enjoy myself and we talked mainly of novelists. Mrs. Eliot was persuasive about Dickens as an influence on Eliot and, later, made a few brief corrections of the typescript. Their marriage, I had written, lasted for the last seven years of Eliot's life. "I was married for eight years less six days," Mrs. Eliot wrote, "and would not lose a minute." Some reviewers thought that *Eliot's Early Years* could have been done only with her co-operation but the truth is that there was no contact until it was virtually finished.

In retrospect, I should like to propose that the impossibility of official biography may be, far from a handicap, an actual advantage, not because of the licence this offers but because of the chance to invent a new form. The full-scale biography, though it is easily done, is simply unsuited to an imaginative understanding of Eliot's life. And this is, perhaps, one reason why he forbade it. Eliot made it clear whatever is worth recording in a poet's life will not be found in wills and obituaries, nor in legal papers presided over by the lean solicitor, nor even in well-intentioned recollections, the webs woven over the career by a "beneficent spider." The whole force of the career is contained in

> The awful daring of a moment's surrender
> . . . . . . . .
> By this, and this only, we have existed.
> (*The Waste Land*: V)

For Eliot, what he called "unattended" or "essential" moments are when, rarely, he lost himself in a religious vision. They are transforming moments, invitations to a new life. To find these moments, the biographer must pare away the trivia of the external life for, said Eliot, in "The Dry Salvages":

> Our own past is covered by the currents of action.

Eliot used the word "waste" for the empty stretches of the lifespan that are not worth recording in the light of a sublime moment:

> Ridiculous the waste sad time
> Stretching before and after.
>     ("Burnt Norton": V)

In the first draft of "Little Gidding": II he uncovers the essential moments of his own history: the agonized all-night vigils in Paris in 1911 and the emotional quickening that came to him as a young man as he sailed off the coast of Cape Ann:

> Remember rather the essential moments
>   That were the times of birth and death and change
>   The agony and the solitary vigil.
> . . . . . . . . . . . . . . . . . . .
> The fresh new season's rope, the smell of varnish
>   On the clean oar, the drying of the sails,
> Such things as seem of least and most importance.
> So, as you circumscribe this dreary round,
>   Shall your life pass from you.[22]

These moments are so inward that only the poet can reveal them. In this sense Eliot will always remain the master of his biography, concealing and revealing with the utmost calculation. The most the biographer can do is to check the life, as far as it can possibly be known, against this revealed life. And to check is to realize that Eliot was scrupulously honest, about his guilt, say, for his treatment of Vivienne (transmuted into the drama of Harry, Lord Monchensey, who believes that he has murdered his wife and is haunted by Furies). He was honest, too, about religious experience, careful never to assume too much. The clearest intimations came extraordinarily early, at the age of 21, when the poet sees the noisy city streets of Boston shrink. At that moment his everyday preoccupations, his past, all the intimidations of common experience are wiped out by this peace which he calls "Silence."[23] He concludes that there is nothing else beside it.

Apart from Eliot's poems, I learnt more from the comments of people who knew him in his early years than from posthumous comments. Eliot's living contacts knew him only in his years of great fame when, I imagine, he was harder to know. They must have had to accept Eliot as he presented himself: this, I would guess, was his pre-condition for any sort of relation. One of Eliot's confessors spoke of his respect for reserve, another of his humility. This suggests that only in his poetry did Eliot give a full account of the religious drama that dominated his life, a drama in which the only real character was Eliot himself as he prepared to meet a remote God whose attributes were unknowable except in so far as they transcended nature: "the unimaginable / Zero summer."[24]

Eliot was so singleminded that his life and work redefine, repeatedly, the same drama, the private search for salvation. To him, "the life of a man of genius, viewed in relation to his writing, comes to take a pattern of inevitability, and even his disabilities will seem to have stood him in good stead."[25] If we applied Eliot's theory to his own life, its inner coherence is obvious. If we followed, say, his relations with women, it is curious to see how they were absorbed into what seems an almost predetermined pattern. Emily Hale prompted the sublime moments; Vivienne the sense of sin and guilt, and provided, throughout the first marriage, the living martyrdom. Later, sensible, efficient Mary Trevelyan served her long stint as support during the years of penitence. For her their friendship was a commitment, for Eliot quite peripheral. His passion for immortality was so commanding that it allowed him to reject each of these women with a ruthless firmness that shattered their lives.

The shape of Eliot's life is one of paring down, concentration. So much had to be discarded to make his life conform to the pattern of soul history and there is a constant tension between an idiosyncratic nature and an ideal biography. *Eliot's Early Years* was about his acceptance of this pattern. The later years turn on the question of its fulfilment. Its drama lies in efforts to close the gap between nature and perfection—at whatever personal cost, revelling to some degree in that cost and inspecting his suffering as the distinguishing brand of his election. Yet, to become one of the chosen, he had to purify the very spiritual ambition that set him going. And so the moral drama of the later years, beginning with *Murder in the Cathedral*, centers not so much on the earlier festering of primitive violence, epitomized by lust, as on the subtler taints of public dignitaries, epitomized by pride. Eliot always calls for judgement but, we can never forget, for divine not human judgement.

At best, a biography of T. S. Eliot would be, then, but a
complement to work which speaks for itself. The writer in Virginia
Woolf's *The Waves* is intently aware of some future biographer
dogging his footsteps. To forestall the predictable roadmap from
pedigree to grave, this writer speaks directly to a future reader:
"Take it. This is my life."[26] What he offers is an alternative to the
standard biography which he calls "a convenience, a lie."[27] All
our stories of birth, school, marriage and death, he argues, are not
true because lives turn on "moments of humiliation and triumph"
that happen now and then but rarely at times of official crisis or
celebration.[28]

In Sweden in 1948 to receive the Nobel Prize, Eliot was shaving
when a procession of six girls, dressed (it seemed to him) in
nightgowns and carrying crowns of lighted candles, marched into
his room.[29] By stretching an arm round the bathroom door he
reached his overcoat and appeared before them. They sang
solemnly while he stood there feeling foolish. The Nobel Prize was
peripheral to the moments on which his life turned, like the
moment in 1926 when he fell on his knees before the *Pietà* in Rome.
His actual marriage was peripheral to "the awful daring of a
moment's surrender." And his Harvard education was peripheral
to the Silence in the streets of Boston, the hour in June 1910 for
which, already, he had waited when life, he said, was justified. In
the case of a writer like Eliot, where the center of interest lies in
private events that are the sources of creativity, it would be
perverse for critical biography to imitate the schema of historical
or political biography where the center of interest lies in public
action.

To recount Eliot's life in the usual compendious form would be
to miss the point of the poetry. The core of existence, he says
repeatedly, was the hidden life where words, as in poetry, reach
into silence:

> It seems to me that beyond the nameable, classifiable emotions
> and motives of our conscious life when directed towards action
> . . . there is a fringe of indefinite extent of feeling which we can
> only detect, so to speak, out of the corner of the eye and can
> never completely focus; of feeling of which we are only aware in
> a kind of temporary detachment from action. ("Poetry and
> Drama," 1951)

Virginia Woolf detected the same unknowability in Henry James, "something incommunicable, something reserved."[30] This, she said, is the "aloofness and loneliness of the artist's life."[31] Here is the almost insuperable challenge for Eliot's biographer: not the technical obstacles of the present, but the sources of creativity in the silent spaces of the writer's life.

# CHAPTER ELEVEN

# Bertolt Brecht

## RONALD HAYMAN

I met Brecht only once—on June 29, 1956, six weeks before he died—and, judging from my diary, my first reaction was one of disappointment. A charwoman took me up some stairs and pointed to an open door. I nearly went in without knocking, thinking I was to wait there till Brecht was ready, but the sound of voices halted me. A man and a woman. Was it Brecht? The clothes were right. Thin material, proletarian cut, high lapels, no tie and a glimpe of pinkish shirt. But could Brecht be such a small man? I had expected a Hemingway and found a monk. The grey jacket hung low and loose, and the thin hair was brushed forward to give the impression of a tonsure. But he came forward, held out his hand and said: "Brecht." Even his voice was monkish. I had expected it to be deep, incisive, commanding, but it was gentle and quite high-pitched.

The word "monkish" recurs in the description that follows of our conversation. He had "the tired, patient, teaching voice of an abbot." Only once or twice in the interview did he become animated. When he talked about the absurdity of trying to produce Shakespeare in the same style as the Elizabethans, he said: "It would be like an old film. The audience would laugh. You know what it is like to see a film of fifty years ago. Think how the banquet scene in *Macbeth* would be with the people all eating with their hands." And he made gestures of chewing and throwing bones over his shoulders.

But his charm was more in evidence when he talked about Khrushchev's speech at the 20th Party Congress. This was his sensational denunciation of Stalin and the cult of personality. "That changes things a great deal, and it's impossible to predict things like that. Who could have said that was going to happen?" He was saying he had not read *Les mains sales* since Khrushchev's speech, so he could not judge it. Generally it was impossible for Sartre to be objective. His plays were "gut aber nicht ganz gut. They help to alter society now, but in fifty years time society will be changed and no one will read them."

Already, in 1956, one of my closest friends was urging me to write a book about Brecht's plays, but the idea did not excite me. And five years later, when I translated *Im Dickicht der Städte* (*Jungle of the Cities*) and directed it at Stratford East, I did inexplicably little research.

In 1980, when I was nearing the end of my Kafka biography, my publisher proposed that Brecht should be my next subject. My only hesitation was prompted by Klaus Völker's biography, which I had not read. It has been translated into English, and if it performed its function, what need would there be for another biography? So I read it.

When I am approaching the end of writing a biography, I usually feel that I know the subject better than I know any of my friends, and I was not relishing the prospect of parting company with Kafka. In the final weeks of his illness, I felt like an accomplice of the tuberculosis that was killing him. I was working to make the end approach faster. How could I do that to him?

Brecht seemed more lovable to women than he possibly could to a biographer but, there were strong incentives for saying yes to the commission. Völker had made no serious attempt to explain (or even to understand) the personal motivation behind the political actions Brecht took. Völker had obviously been nervous of offending those who wanted to keep the Brecht legend intact. He fails to mention the changes Brecht made to *Lucullus* under pressure from the East German government, while the events of 17 June, 1953, which included skirmishes between German building workers and Russian tanks, are described in his book as "emotional scenes." Brecht is characterised as "a staunch lover and friend" and the question of his cowardice is raised but not treated truthfully. At the end of reading the book I felt that Brecht's biography had not yet been written.

An Englishman is at an obvious disadvantage in attempting the biography of a man who spoke another language. Quite apart from the difficulty of reading what he wrote, always with the danger of misunderstanding something vital, there is a barrier to intimacy. Working at a biography, I always feel a bit like an actor who needs to steep himself so deeply in his character's habits of thinking that he can say the words as if they were being spoken for the first time. With de Sade, with Nietzsche, with Kafka and with Brecht, I needed to give myself the actorish feeling of being able to assume the character, to stretch out in the foreign consciousness as if it were a warm bath. Even if they had all been English, the consciousness would still have been foreign, and I would have needed to go on reading, thinking, rehearsing, working till the moment came when it did not *feel* foreign. When I was an actor, I did sometimes convince myself, if only with 98 percent of my mind, that I was inside the character's skin. Probably it is even more arrogant to think oneself capable of being Kafka or Brecht than it is to think oneself capable of being Hamlet. (Not that I ever played Hamlet.) But I need the same degree of identification, and though a foreign language, however familiar it is, makes the identification harder to achieve, the identification, once it is there, gives me the feeling of having solved the language problem. This is no guarantee, of course, against minor mistakes based on misunderstanding. And I am not saying these do not matter. But what matters most is to take the reader inside the man's mind, to show how it works from moment to moment, to give a full answer to the question "Who was Kafka?" "Who was Brecht?"

What I always do when starting on a biography is to read in chronological order all the subject's published work. This invariably teaches me a great deal, even when re-reading books or plays I know. I begin to form an impression of growth and to escape from the insidious image (determined by pictures) of the writer at a fixed age. (At first I found it quite hard to visualise Nietzsche before he grew his formidable moustache.) Without making any conscious effort to study the life as distinct from the work, I begin, when reading the work chronologically, to see it in its context. Experiences described in letters or diaries cast their shadow on stories or plays; anxieties and preoccupations are creatively mastered: instead of merely being their victim, the writer asserts his dominance by making use of them.

The biographer probably does the most important part of his work when he is more passive than active. It goes without saying that research will involve a good deal of activity, persistence, resourcefulness, fact, persuasiveness and so on, but a good researcher may be a bad biographer, though a good biographer will never be an unconscientious researcher. He will be a good story-teller and—like a writer of fiction—gets many of his best ideas without conscious effort. It is a matter, mainly, of noticing connections, and noticing them early enough for them to determine or at least influence one's principle of selection. After all it is easy, in a diary, to devote as much space to a year as one will have for a man's whole life: if you have, say, 150,000 words to deal with 70 years, you will average only a little over 2000 a year.

With Brecht, I knew from the beginning, one of the main problems would be to discover how much continuity there was between the two apparently discontinuous halves of his life. Before he committed himself to Marxism in 1928, he was not interested in politics. *Drums in the Night* (1919) is set in Berlin during the Spartacist rebellion, which, said Brecht, "was of no more interest to me than Vesuvius is to a man who wants to cook a saucepan of soup on it." In the early thirties, when millions of Germans, suffering from the consequences of the Depression, were adapting to circumstances and joining the Nazi party, Brecht did not adopt a disapproving stance. On the contrary, the view he put forward in the first version of *Man Is Man* (1925) is that since life is so very short, one must live it to the full, ignoring the suffering that may be caused and wasting no time on resistance to change in the political environment. The central character in the play, Galy Gay, represents a "new sort of type," mendacious, optimistic, adaptable. He wants to survive, even at the cost of becoming someone else, and instead of being punished by the play's action, he ends up in a stronger position. His attitude is like the one Brecht expresses in the "Ballad of Poor B.B.":

> In the earthquakes that are coming I hope bitterness
> Won't make me let my cigar go out.

So how much continuity would I find between the cynical egoist and the Marxist who wrote didactic plays and equated bad conscience with deviation from Party orthodoxy? It was a question I could hope to answer gradually as I began to unearth the facts.

Reading Brecht's poems, plays, newspaper articles, interviews, letters, stories, novels, theatrical writings and so on in roughly chronological order, I studied the political background and read reports by other witnesses. I tried, while dipping into assorted books, to let a story tell itself to me—the story of what was happening inside and outside Brecht—and I began to write the story down. This is the way I always work, making very few notes and scarcely attempting to do any original research until I have finished my first draft. I then have a framework, a complete set of pigeonholes. I will know where to put any new information I get. The danger is that I will finish the book too quickly without having digested all the information and established all the necessary interrelationships between one element and another, but I prefer this risk to the risk of chewing the cud for too long. I could never take ten years on a biography. I try to preserve in the narrative a residue from my own excitement at getting to know my subject better. If the narrative had to be written up from notes that had been stored in ring-books for seven years, the momentum of the story I told would have nothing to do with the learning process as I experienced it. The insights would have gone stale, and I set a higher value on insights than on facts. My aim in this book was to explain what made Brecht tick in such different ways at different phases of his life. What mattered to him? How did his consciousness function?

One of the difficulties, I soon discovered, was that Brecht could not be trusted in the way that Kafka could. Kafka devoted a great deal of effort to the hopeless task of arriving at an understanding of himself, and the evidence he set down is scrupulously truthful. He believed in writing as a means of gaining access to the inaccessible Law, and it would have been sacrilege to write untruthfully. He used fiction as a means of telling truths that could not be told factually.

Brecht, even before his conversion to Marxism, detested the idea of individuality, and while he had a boundless appetite for physical gratifications of different kinds, he was interested in self-knowledge only in so far as it would help him to make decisions. Most young writers practise their art as a technique for discovering and relaying the truth about themselves; Brecht, even at the beginning, was less interested in truth than in power. The main point about literature was that it could be useful. His youthful journalism helped to gain a reputation for him, and the reputation induced those in authority—teachers, and later army officers—to give him preferential treatment. His poems could be performed to guitar accompaniments, and his performances not only impressed his school friends but made girls easier to seduce. He also discovered early on that his verse would be still

more serviceable as an instrument for enhancing his glamour, if
he used it to make his own activities into something like a legend:

> No-one's awake but moon and cats
> The girls in bed already,
> Bert Brecht is crossing the Rathausplatz
> His lantern held high and steady.

Many of the early ballads are autobiographical, but the autobiography in "Ballad of Poor B.B." is not to be trusted. He got into
the habit of rewriting personal history long before he became a
Marxist, and the habit, of course, continued. Many writers—Sartre is the Kafka in this respect—have a stong autobiographical impulse: they want their past to go accurately into aspic,
and where they mislead future biographers, it is mainly through
lapses of memory. But a biographer of Brecht finds that his most
important witness is unreliable. There is accurate evidence about
the present in both the early diaries and the *Arbeitsjournal*, but the
references to the past are often as fictional as the account Brecht
gave in the Kremlin, when he was presented with the Lenin Peace
Prize in 1955, of his youthful feelings towards Soviet Communism. He pretended that he was still a medical orderly when the
rebellion broke out in 1918. The biographer needs to become like
a father who knows his son so well that it is obvious when he is
lying. This is easy; what is difficult is to get at the truth behind the
evasions and distortions.

Like Shen Te in *The Good Woman of Setzuan*, Brecht found it
difficult to reconcile the commandment "Be good to yourself"
with the divine commandment "Be good to other people", but he
had no doubt about which commandment was to be given
priority. The habit of deviousness was formed in his dealings with
schoolteachers and girlfriends. Obedience and loyalty were not
virtues to be cultivated but flags to be flown when it was
expedient. The double-dealing that characterised his behaviour
with translators and collaborators would later extend into his
relationships with the East German government. This was one
strand of continuity I discovered. In 1921 he was telling both
Marianne Zoff, who was pregnant, and Paula Banholzer, the
mother of his two-year-old son, Frank, that he wanted to marry
them. In April 1949, angling for Austrian citizenship, he wrote: "I

repudiate the idea of repatriating myself in Germany." Six
months later, when Wilhelm Pieck was installed as first President
of the German Democratic Republic, Brecht saluted him with a
poem titled "To My Compatriots."

Working through Brecht's writings I became familiar with all
this double-dealing and distortion; what was dismaying, when I
started my original research, was to find that many of the other
witnesses were equally unreliable. The daughter of his marriage
to Helene Weigel, Barbara (born 1930), tried to give me the
impression that he was an excellent father, deeply concerned
about her and her brother Stefan (born 1924), even if he could
spare little time to spend with them when they were children.
And, intent on proving that he went on loving her mother, Helene
Weigel, Barbara describes an occasion when she had to wait in a
car while they went into the woods together. "When they came
back, it was quite obvious what they'd been doing."

Not that Barbara is alone in trying to sustain a legend. When I
went to Berlin in May 1982, many of the people I interviewed
were surprisingly loyal to this disloyal man. The actor Heinz
Schubert says: "He liked actors very much and never screamed at
them. He screamed at technicians. Like Hitler." But he with-
draws the comparison immediately. "Not like Hitler. He apolog-
ised afterwards." Later Ekkehard Schall, Barbara's husband, will
tell me that he did scream at actors. "But he could do it without
losing his temper. He might yell something and then whisper:
'Let's see what effect that has.' Then yell again." On details of
what went on in rehearsal, actors' memories are unreliable. Some
say he directed mainly from the auditorium, seldom going up on
stage; some say he spent a good deal of time on stage.

Naturally I seize any opportunity I get in interviews to find out
more about the most under-documented areas, such as the
relationship with Weigel. According to the 71-year-old Heinz
Kuckhahn, who first met them in 1931 and worked as Brecht's
production assistant in Berlin after the war, "She had no sense of
humour at all. Brecht was always complaining about that. . . . Of
course they weren't living together even between 1931 and 1933.
Sometimes, when I went into the room when she was in bed, she
used to roll over. I didn't realise then that it was an invitation."
But is this man to be believed? I talk about him to Manfred
Wekworth, who is now running the Berliner Ensemble. He is
dismissive about Kuckhahn, and maintains that Weigel did have

a sense of humour, though it was very different from Brecht's. She was a typical Viennese Jewess, he says, more intellectual and sophisticated than Brecht. From another former production assistant, Hans Bunge, I learn that Weigel, though she was nominally the artistic director of the Berliner Ensemble, was not allowed to join in the discussions Brecht had with his assistants. He admired her as an actress, and he gladly let her take care of all the administration, but she must not try to interfere on questions of production. Sometimes, when she persisted in having her say, he was extremely rude to her.

As proponents of the Brecht legend, the former girlfriends are hardly less fanatical than the daughter. Commitment to Communism rubs shoulders here with loyalty to the dead man. His last girlfriend was the attractive Isot Kilian, who was married at the time to Wolfgang Harich. ("Divorce her," Brecht advised. "You can marry her again in a few years' time.") Kilian talks about his relations with the government and the part he played in the shaping of a new state. He had frequent meetings with the architect reponsible for the new buildings in what was then called the Stalinallee. (This surprises me. Visually, to judge from his productions, he had excellent taste.) Käthe Rülicke is no less loyal to the man or to the Party, but she talks more critically about the demands he made on his production assistants, keeping them so busy that in summer they never had time for a swim. He was jealous of their wives, and he was equally possessive, according to Wekworth, about his girlfriends. He made a point of telephoning them all twice every evening, once early, once late, to make sure they were at home.

In Berlin I discover how published material is being weighted to keep the legend alive. Barbara is doing all she can to minimise the importance of Brecht's relationship with Ruth Berlau. In the collection of his letters which has been published, there are only 27 letters to her, but in the archive there are nearly 500. The librarians and archivists have to carry out Barbara's orders, and when I ask to see the Berlau letters, I am told they are not available. Fortunately the catalogue quotes key passages from most of the letters, and they cannot refuse me access to the catalogue. In 1953 Brecht's reassurances that he loved Berlau are scarcely less ardent than the declarations he made in 1940. He still needs her badly, he says. He will explain why if she wants him to, but it is not really necessary, because so far as he is concerned, nothing has changed. With most of his girlfriends he made no promises of fidelity, but with her, at one stage, he did promise. He may even have kept the promise until he was absolved by her infidelity to him.

Hans Bunge has prepared a book containing interviews he conducted with Berlau, but the publisher who had accepted it withdrew, having been intimidated by Barbara, who wields enormous power, through control of the Brecht estate in East Germany. According to Bunge, Berlau made a great many suggestions when Brecht was working on *The Caucasian Chalk Circle* and Brecht incorporated nearly all of them, though he used none of Weigel's. According to Barbara, he accepted all the suggestions her mother made for the play, and rejected all Berlau's. Here it is not hard to make up my mind whom to believe. Berlau was pregnant when he was working on the play, and besides doing his utmost, in the script, to present maternity in a favourable light, he was asking her advice. When their son was born, he was to be called Michael, like the child in the play, but he lived only a few days. Berlau was one of the most important women in Brecht's life; later, when I am collecting illustrations for the book, I receive a message from Barbara, who would prefer it if I do not include a photograph of Berlau. This desire to make Berlau disappear into an oubliette is of course typical of Communist historiography, but if Brecht had written an autobiography, Berlau would have been prominent in it.

The work I did in the archive was illuminating in a number of ways. I was surprised to discover that Brecht had taken an early interest in the work of Wilhelm Reich, and that his preoccupation with the Salvation Army derives partly from Lenin. The work of the Berliner Ensemble is probably better documented than that of any previous company in theatrical history, and I learned a good deal from the transcripts of notes taken and recordings made at rehearsals. This was one way in which Brecht used his production assistants—they had to record what happened. The records show that he had his distinctive way of stimulating actors and making them relax. Sometimes he gave actors notes on their performances in writing. He did this with Ernst Busch, who played Galileo. According to Wekworth, Brecht was scared of Busch; according to Käthe Rülicke, he was scared of no one.

I also saw in the archive a photocopy of the diary kept by Elisabeth Hauptmann, his assistant and girlfriend, in 1926. I saw his notes for an adaptation of *Macbeth* (1927) and his reworking of *Waiting for Godot*—presumably he was considering it for production at the Ensemble if Beckett agreed to the changes. Brecht typically cuts the first line, "Nothing to be done"—there was always something to be done—and he makes the first Pozzo-Lucky sequence into a dream, leaving Vladimir asleep throughout, and making Estragon take over many of his lines.

The unpublished letters included several to various departments of the East German government, making complaints—about the unnecessary rudeness of frontier policemen, for instance—and making constructive suggestions. I saw a great many loose notes, some of them fragmentary, and it was enlightening to study the underlinings and marginal annotations in some of his books and magazines—especially the ones he did not take into exile, for with these, the markings can be dated as having been made between the date of publication and 1933. Some of his early reactions to Hegel, Marx, Engels and Lenin are particularly revealing. One reason dialectical thinking attracted him was that it provided a rationale for what he had done instinctively, enjoying both halves of a contrast or opposition instead of choosing one half and rejecting the other. One way of looking at his method of directing plays is to see it as an application of the dialectical method. He liked to provoke disagreement, encourage criticism, discover anomalies. Wekworth, on arriving to meet Brecht for the first time, was ushered into a rehearsal and told to write down everything he disagreed with. Brecht would then weave into a production or a performance elements that at first seemed to contradict other elements, but eventually came to enrich the texture of the whole.

I would have preferred, naturally, to do everything I needed to do in Berlin during a single visit, but on my ante-penultimate day there, Bunge offers to let me read his interviews, if I read it in his flat. And on my last day Barbara offers me access to a large collection of unpublished poems. So I make a second visit in June, and pick up even more useful information from the interviews than from the poems.

When I get to the end of the research—a point determined more by the passage of time than by the feeling of having done enough—I start on the third phase of work, which is probably the most important in giving the narrative its flavour. I try not to do too much explaining or interpreting or judging. What I have

learnt about the man should be present in the book, but in
suspension, not as something separate from the events, physical
and mental, I am describing. I do not want to force my
conclusions on the reader, but I want to illuminate the facts as
fully as I can. I want the reader to arrive at his own understanding
of what it felt like to be Brecht, how his mind worked, what his
priorities were, how his energies were divided, how he was
changed by age and the strange incidence of success at the
beginning and the end of his life—it was uncomfortably missing
from the period of exile, which lasted from 1933 to 1948.

Nothing about the man is more congenial than his insistence on
having fun and his ability to involve other people in it. Fun could
be a matter of arguing or trying to answer a deceptively simple
question like "What is acting?" He was good at rejecting
preconceived notions, at forcing himself and others to start
debating or rehearsing with a *tabula rasa*. I came to understand
something I had not understood when I met him but could not
have understood so fully if I had not met him—that for him
thinking and action were inseparable. He liked to get up in the
middle of a conversation and act out what he was saying. "A face
is different according to the angle you see it from," he told me and,
unnecessarily, he got up to peer at my face from different angles.
Unnecessarily? It was necessary to him, just as it was necessary to
pace about while he was working. He could not sit still for very
long at a writing table. In every sense he was a man who had to
keep on the move. One of the reasons he could keep actors
interested throughout rehearsal periods that sometimes stretched
over nine months was that he could always make it seem possible
to improve on what had been done before. No phrase was more
foreign to him than "Nothing to be done."

So what can I finally say about the momentum that carried me
through this questionable enterprise? We take biography for
granted, but is not it rather odd that one man should give up a
substantial part of his life to reconstructing another's? Does
retrospective envy play a role? Do I secretly wish I had been
Brecht? Did Sartre secretly wish he had been Flaubert? Is the
biographer no more than a masochistic parasite, a professional
dabbler in vicarious living? When I was working on Nietzsche's
life, I sometimes had the feeling I was trespassing in his bathroom.
What would I say if he suddenly appeared and magisterially
expressed surprise in the interest I was taking in the dirty

underwear and unwashed socks in the linen basket? But then isn't Sartre's biographical writing integral to the development of a man who was arguably the century's greatest thinker? Certainly he could not have written *La nausée* if he had not, from his twenties, been irresistibly attracted to biographical writing. He would go on to devote more of his working life to biography than to fiction. The duel with Flaubert was fought to the death.

I do not feel I was duelling with Brecht, though certainly I disapprove of his ruthlessness towards the girls he made pregnant—"Let the little Brechts be born"—of his double-dealing, his opportunism and his support for the East German regime. I was explicitly asked by an East German diplomat not to be "unfriendly" toward his country. I have spent quite a lot of time in East Berlin, and I did not answer. I have done my best to be objective. No doubt Marxist readers of my book will disagree with many of my judgments and interpretations. The Marxist must believe that it is easier for a Marxist to be objective; I believe that I was at an advantage in not having any answer to the many people who asked me what my "angle" was going to be. I did not know. I was not trying to prove a thesis or to defend Brecht or to attack him. I simply wanted to find out as much as I could and then tell the story as well as I could.

In spite of everything I dislike about the man, I admire his genius, his self-discipline—he prided himself on working every day, even in exile—and his vitality. Not that this wholly explains his attractiveness to women, which is one of the many mysteries I enjoyed trying to solve. One of the best explanations of his attractiveness comes in Marianne Zoff's rather good contribution to Paula Banholzer's rather bad book, *So viel wie eine Liebe: Der unbekannte Brecht* (Munich, 1981). She liked his persistence, his brightness, his "amazing musicality" and his lack of inhibition. When he sang, his "grating metallic voice" sent shivers down her spine.

Ferdinand Reyher once said of Brecht and Weigel: "These are tough babies who would not hesitate to trouble a republic for a safety-pin." One of the reasons I liked working on him was that private needs constantly brought him into public and political confrontations. The choices he had to make involve issues and polarities that are crucial to twentieth-century history. He was a key figure in the development of modern theatre, but his influence would not have been nearly as great if he had not—after years of hesitation—settled in East Germany, giving his support to a viciously undemocratic regime. But in so far as his devious and original mind was still capable of sincerity, he sincerely believed that the Stalinist government of Ulbricht and Grotewohl offered the one alternative to the resurgence of Nazism.

# CHAPTER TWELVE

# Samuel Beckett

## DEIRDRE BAIR

A few fortunate biographers, when telling how they came to write a given life, present an organized and reasoned tale beginning with their identification of a subject, determining its feasibility, following with their methods of conducting research and ending with the happy fact of the printed book. Everything proceeds in such a logical manner that their stories might almost serve as a model for theoretical inquiry in one of the social sciences rather than what they actually are—the unfolding of a life, with all its random haphazardness.

I always wonder, when I read these carefully delineated accounts of research that always reach proper conclusions, of lives that seem to have been lived according to a clearly defined plan and easily discerned thesis, of books that virtually allowed themselves to be written from easy start to smooth finish, is there no other biographer whose work originated in such an accidental, serendipitous manner as mine did?

I have heard any number of stories since the biography of Samuel Beckett was published in 1978, all told by responsible people who believe them to be true, of how I came to write that biography. Perhaps this is the time to try to recall the circumstances of thirteen years ago that led to the seven-year process of writing it.

It is a curiously reversed position I find myself in now, no longer the biographer in search of the facts and events of the life of Samuel Beckett, but rather, the biographer in search of her own history, or "the book about the writing of the book."

The facts, then, are simple and few. I was a graduate student at Columbia University trying to persuade myself that I was happy working on a dissertation topic that I had selected more for its manageability than for my genuine interest in it. It meant at most

199

eighteen months of sitting in the library, translating a manuscript from Latin and Old English, and then making critical comments about its relevance for several modern writers. One day, in a moment of idle boredom, in the effort to stave off the irrational panic and the increasing urgency of time passing without progress, I took the names of the five or six contemporary authors I was hoping to write about once I had finished the translations, put each one on a small file card, alphabetized them, found that Samuel Beckett came before Joseph Conrad, James Joyce, and the rest of the list.

I had an easy familiarity with Samuel Beckett's writings—Joyce's literary heir I was then calling him—because I had written a master's thesis on the question of literary influence and the creative process and I had used Joyce and Beckett for that work. At that time (1969), I had read all of Beckett's then-published writings. The attraction I felt was immediate and lasting, and I had every intention of continuing this scholarly interest after the dissertation, when I envisioned having both the time and the occasion to treat the entire canon in depth.

However, at the end of 1970, I found that I was becoming increasingly more reluctant to work on my original project because I wanted to write about Beckett. I began to read all the existing criticism. Of the initial group of scholars who wrote about Beckett, I had slightly mixed feelings. For the majority I had great respect, as their theories and interpretations represented my own thinking. But a few of these studies left me dissatisfied, feeling that something crucial was missing. Still, I had no idea then what the crucial missing element could be. Of the succeeding "generations" (as Beckett scholars tend to label themselves when they describe the appearance of their writings within the chronological hierarchy of those who write about him), I had even more strongly mixed reactions. By the summer of 1971, I had come to the conclusion that many of them were simply inventing different vocabularies to say the same thing, metaphorical dogs catching their own tails and running in circles not of their own making.

I had not yet begun to consider the possibility that what was missing might be a biographical element even though each time I returned to one of Beckett's writings, I was almost overwhelmed by the sensation of the authorial presence within it. The life-giving and, at times, life-denying dynamic projected first by Beckettian characters, then Beckettian voices, made me uncomfortably aware of a presence in these texts that other critics seemed comfortably able to evade or avoid. What it all came down to for me was a sense of Beckett's presence within his writing, a feeling or recognition of—and here, at this point, I always seemed to come to a critical dead end.

To step briefly outside my own story and into history, the New Criticism was in its death throes and the full force of the invasion of French critical theory was well underway. Good graduate student that I was, I could not even bring myself to hint that the element I found to be missing in my work on Beckett might be biographical because biography was something I read to be able to fit authors into appropriate time and place, but I had been trained to believe that critical exegesis could only proceed through the total absence of biographical consideration.

Then, a serendipitous accident occurred: why not take a summer weekend away from the typewriter to see Jack McGowran perform the dramatic pastiche, "Beginning to End," my dissertation advisor suggested. He was sure that pleasure in the performance would lead to some sort of scholarship. McGowran was a personal friend of his as well as Beckett's, and perhaps McGowran's comments about what it was like to have worked with Beckett on this successful adaptation of fiction into dramatic performance might be of value to my own study.

I still remember that performance with a vividness and clarity that only a handful of the more than several hundred interviews I conducted over the years has had for me. The weather in Lenox, Massachusetts was cold and rainy that July night, and everyone in the tent shivered as the wind blew in. Metal parts used to support the tent clanged at inappropriate moments, and I was not at all sure if McGowran was modulating his voice because of the role's exigencies or the need to shout over the noise of the downpour and the flapping of the tent's sides.

Perhaps it was because McGowran felt so sorry for his audience's discomfort that he gave such an inspired performance, and perhaps it was the euphoria of the performance that made him so eager to recapitulate it afterwards (here, as biographer, I will not assign definite meaning but will only surmise his intentions). Whatever the reason, we spent several hours in the small room of the old house where he had his dressing room, each of us facing the other on a hard straight-backed kitchen chair, often reaching out to touch in astonishment or agreement at some shared opinion of Beckett's writing.

McGowran was Irish like Beckett, and his background, religion and education were all vaguely similar. He told a delightful tale of the time he and Beckett, drinking in Paris, discovered that their families had lived four or five miles apart in Ireland. He was full of marvelous theatrical imitations of many people in Dublin who were only names to me then; indeed several imitations were so successful that I could never talk to those people without thinking of McGowran.

This biographical dimension of Samuel Beckett's writing struck me so forcefully in my initial conversation with Jack McGowran that instead of finding a suitable topic as my advisor had hoped, I found myself unable to do any writing at all. Biography seemed to be in the air around me then, as one of my classmates and friends at Columbia had just published a landmark feminist biography; another was embroiled in a troubling, time-consuming debate with a literary executor who had suddenly withdrawn permission to use essential materials; and even my advisor had just published a biography which had been nominated for the National Book Award. I began to read biographical essays and criticism, to speculate about the validity of biographical criticism in regard to Beckett, to inquire whether I might submit a biography for the dissertation.

All my biographer friends were amused by my speculation and indecision, but all agreed that I should do nothing until I spoke first to Samuel Beckett. In July 1971, I wrote him a letter that I blush now to think about. It took me two days to write it, and even then, I think I sent it off more because I was exhausted by composing it and disgusted with my inability to sound sufficiently scholarly in it. I spent the main part of the letter telling him why I thought a biography was necessary, then I described my conversation with McGowran in some dramatic detail, and because I felt that if I were he, I would want to know something about the writer of this letter, I ended with a brief account of my personal history, which I hoped would induce him to allow me to write his biography.

The mail to and from Paris has never been as fast as then: eight days after I sent the letter, I received his reply. His life was "dull and without interest," he said, and was "best left unchampioned" because "the professors know more about it than I do." All this was written in a very careful handwriting, easily readable and proceeding from left to right in a steady horizontal line. But after that there was a curious paragraph far more representative of Beckett's writing (as I learned when I spent the next seven years agonizing over the squiggles he spewed haphazardly across the pages). In it, in a larger and less careful hand, on lines that started bottom left and ploughed steadily uphill to the right, he wrote that any biographical information he possessed was at my disposal and that if I came to Paris, he would see me. My astonishment was so great that I almost wore the paper through, rubbing at these words, convinced I was not seeing them properly, but that if I only rubbed hard enough, they would be revealed in their true clarity. I suppose I knew this was impossible—untrue as well as useless—but unconscious emotions are often stronger than intellectual thought. When I was convinced these words were really written, I planned a trip to Paris.

We were supposed to meet in October 1971, but Beckett was ill with a cold that lingered so stubbornly he was afraid it would become something more serious, and so he went unexpectedly to Malta for several weeks. Never one to waste time, I went off to Dublin, where I familiarized myself with places mentioned in his writings and met people who had known Beckett when he lived in Ireland. Then I went to London, where I interviewed a number of his professional associates in publishing and the theater.

On November 17, 1971, Beckett sat across from me for the first time in the dreary lobby of a small Left-Bank hotel. He tapped his thin elegant fingers steadily against the unsightly glass ashtray that sat between us on the table. He leaned forward to stare at me with such intensity from those pale blue eyes, the "gull's eyes" he gave to a number of his fictional creations, that I found myself shaking and stumbling through a series of replies that probably had no meaning or coherent connection to his questions. We talked about the weather in Dublin and London as well as Paris, we talked about chess, the American theater, mutual friends. In fact we talked about everything, including the fact but not the interpretation of his writing.

It was not until some months later that I learned he had only recently had his second cataract operation, and the only way that he could really see someone or something was to stare straight at it from a very close distance because he had neither depth perception nor peripheral vision at that time.

Nevertheless, his stare was almost as disconcerting as our conversation. Did I think I was the first to suggest that a biography was necessary? Well, no, I didn't really, but why then had he agreed to see me and not any of the others? He evaded my question, lit another in a steady succession of his short and slim brown cigars and asked who had I seen and talked to in Dublin and London. There followed an interlude which was probably the one which most closely approached hilarity in all our meetings. It was a sort of "do you know . . ." or "did you meet . . ." and depending on my response, he volunteered bits of their biography or telling (and in some cases, sarcastic) comments, or else told me something about himself in relation to these people.

Suddenly, his attitude changed. As swiftly as he had been joking, he became serious, even abrasive. He did not want me "prying about, bothering people, inquiring into my life." I must have blushed—I remember stammering—I was embarrassed by this remark, and I remember leaning my elbow on the table and lowering my head into my hand, saying "oh dear, I really don't think I'm cut out for this biography business." Again, there was a sudden change of mood on his part. My embarrassment caused him to become embarrassed, and I had one of my first glimpses of the old world courtliness of his manners and demeanor. He apologized for his seeming harshness, and at that point made the remark that I innocently quoted in the preface to the biography, and which has been interpreted in so many different ways since then.

"You are free to do as you choose," he told me, for he would "neither help nor hinder" my work. "I will introduce you to my friends," he said, "My enemies will find you soon enough." And so I pressed him for some further definition of this "neither help nor hinder" phrase. I had arranged to meet professional associates in Dublin and London, but had avoided his family or persons I believed to be close personal friends until I had secured Beckett's permission to write this book. Now, it seemed that he was telling me he would do nothing to stop my book, but I wanted to know what, if anything, he would do to help it.

Would he introduce me to his family and friends? I should contact them on my own, he replied, but if they asked him if they should grant interviews, he would tell them that he would "neither help nor hinder them," they were "free to do as you wish in this matter of Deirdre Bair's book." (I saw this sentence in any number of letters he wrote to persons who asked, I heard it from countless others who spoke to him.) What about letters or other written materials, I wanted to know—would he make them available to me? He was not about to stop living his life in order to resurrect a version of his past, he assured me. He was writing any number of things just then and could not stop in order to contemplate "this thing" called his life. However, I was free to use whatever my research led to and he would not censor anything. What about unpublished writings or variants of published ones—how would I receive access to them? The reply was curious but in keeping with the conversation: if I were to discern the existence of such materials, then of course I should be granted access to them. I decided to let that one rest for further interpretation at a later date. Well, then, what about people? I already had a list of persons I thought I should interview, but how would I know if it were complete, or even if the persons on it were or had been important in his life. He seemed to be waiting for this question because he brought his palm smartly down on the table and smiled a very broad smile. That, he said in a manner I can only describe as coy, would be for me to discern, wouldn't it, for remember, he would "neither help nor hinder" the course of my research!

And so we continued for almost two hours, a round first of methodological inquiries on my part followed by some clear response tempered with banter and evasion on his part, followed either by my embarrassment at my question or my inability to ascertain how to proceed, followed by his courtly concern for my feelings, and so on. I remember how the German round song, "A dog came in the kitchen. . . . And dug the dog a tomb," that Beckett used in *Waiting for Godot* buzzed on the edges of my consciousness then, and how, without either of us pressing for a definite statement of agreement, I probably became Beckett's biographer at that moment. As I write this now, I remember the seven years of writing that biography and how many times I sang that song in solace to myself because of the seemingly endless concentric and overlapping circles my work had generated.

Because I have a personality that seeks clarification and definition, I found myself insisting that he gave me something more to go on than "neither help nor hinder." What about himself—would he permit me to interview him? And if so, would he answer my questions fully? Would he volunteer information? Would he volunteer to correct any misinformation, misinterpretation, misrepresentation? There was another smile, again seemingly coy, but this time he leaned back in his chair and did not seem to care about eye contact. What did seem to matter was his deep inhalation of that little cigar. He replied at a particularly ungraceful moment, with smoke pouring from his nose and mouth, and although I think now that I must have compared him to some sort of devil then, I am too afraid that it might be hindsight to insist upon it now. He would reply, he said, to greater or lesser degree, as he saw fit. He would answer or not, as he saw fit. He would not volunteer information, for it was my book that I was writing and it was not up to him to influence the content, direction or interpretation.

At that time, and for a long time after, this last remark bothered me greatly, but as I reached the end of that book, and as I began to write a second biography of a living subject, Simone de Beauvoir this time, I came to value the independence and objectivity that such a statement gave me. For what if he had been an intrusive subject who insisted upon volunteering reams of information that may or may not have been germane to the understanding of the life, or what if he had been the kind of subject who would make strenuous objections and throw legal obstacles in the way of any interpretation of the life but his own? And, once having had what I came to realize is the ideal situation in which to write the biography of a living subject, I also came to realize that I could not write a life in any other way.

But I am abandoning chronology here, and must return to Samuel Beckett on November 17, 1971. At just about this point in our conversation, I reached down into my capacious purse and pulled out a stenographer's notebook and a pencil because I thought the time had come to make lists of whatever kinds of information I thought I would need. He nearly jumped out of the chair. What was I doing, he sputtered, were we not having a friendly conversation, just two people talking? Didn't I know that he did not give interviews, that he never allowed pencil and paper, and certainly the question of tape recorder was one I should never bring up.

I was so flustered by this outburst that I really do not remember what I said at that moment, but I do remember that it was another of the "oh dear, perhaps I'm not cut out to be a biographer" instances. He sat there silently for a moment, then continued as if neither his outburst or my embarrassment had ever happened. Then I asked a few questions of my own: if I could not take notes, nor could I tape record, how was I to amass information that I could use? That, he told me clearly, was a situation I would have to resolve without any assistance from him.

Resolve it, I did. Throughout our six years of "conversations," I learned to rehearse questions in my mind until I had them memorized, and then to re-arrange them according to his response. If a question elicited a negative, strained or hostile response, and it was only one of a series I had planned to ask, I learned to shunt the series to one side of my mind and go on to a less objectionable question, to return to the series only when the climate of the interview seemed hospitable. If one of a projected series of questions resulted in an answer that raised an altogether new area of questioning, I learned how to shunt that series to a siding and to pursue the new line of inquiry to its logical conclusion. The mental strain of this technique was enormous.

Usually I prepared for an interview with Beckett over a series of weeks, writing each question on a single small file card, laying out the cards and arranging and re-arranging them until I thought I had the perfect order and had committed them all to memory. The night before an interview I seldom slept, and then only fitfully, as I went through my questions in a dream-sleep, nightmare rehearsal of the interview. The day of the interview, I always had a nervous stomach: I was unable to eat, could not stand any sort of human contact and usually (because we generally met around 2 p.m.) spent the entire time before the interview pacing the floor of my hotel room and playing and replaying the questions in my mind. But when the interview actually took place, I not only had to perform the mental gymnastics of holding questions in my mind and reshaping the direction of the interview with each response, I also had to train another part of my mind to hold the reply as close to verbatim as possible, for he would not permit pencil and paper to be even within his eyesight, let alone at my command. I told him at the first of these sessions that I would probably return to my hotel room at the end of the interview and "talk" the entire session into a tape recorder in an effort to capture the exact wording of his

every response, and that I would also, in my own voice, try to
capture his exact inflection on every single word so that every
interpretation I gave would be as accurate as possible. That was
entirely up to me, he said; all he cared about was that we would
have "conversations," because he never gave "interviews." I was
amused throughout the times we met and talked to notice that
whenever he had something he particularly wanted me to quote
accurately, he always found a way to repeat it more than once,
and I always found myself in those instances nodding my head
strenuously so that he would be sure to understand that I had
made note of it.

I have been abandoning chronology to discuss methodology,
for we are still at my initial meeting with Samuel Beckett. I
wanted answers about what his role would be as I wrote the
biography, and I was annoyed by the "neither help nor hinder"
catchphrase, which he seemed to take great pride in having
coined, but which was quickly losing any real meaning for me.
Finally, I decided to be blunt and direct. I told Beckett that my
personal circumstances precluded my spending inordinate
amounts of time on something that might never come to fruition. I
had to write a dissertation, and by its very nature, it had to be
founded on fact, documentation, verification. There could be
nothing in it that was not fully reasoned, carefully thought out,
scrupulously exact. It had to be scholarship free of speculation.
Also, I would have to elicit financial support for this book,
probably from research foundations and other grant-giving
agencies, and therefore I needed to be able to state exactly the
degree of his cooperation. My own personal and economic status
was such that I could not afford to spend several years conducting
research only to be told that he had changed his mind, withdrawn
permission, forbidden publication.

"My word is my bond," he replied simply. "The rest is up to
you to decide." "Then I can't do it," I replied, equally simply and
just as directly, for I did not know this man yet, and I had no idea
of the solemn and binding weight such a declaration carried for
him.

"What will you write instead?" he asked. Later, when I knew
him better, I realized how important this seemingly innocent
question was: it was his way of telling me that he wanted me to
write about his life. In fact, for all the indirection of this question,

it was one of the most direct statements he made. It was one which seemed to be allowing me to make up my own mind (i.e. "What will *you* write?"), but which insured that my writing would be about him (i.e. *instead*). I replied that I would try to find a suitable topic about his writing within critical inquiry. Our first meeting ended with still another round of the by-then meaningless catchphrase, and my strong feeling that Samuel Beckett did not want me to give up the idea of writing a biography but could not bring himself to tell me directly and openly that I had his permission to do it.

I returned to the United States and began to write a partially biographical dissertation. I decided first to compose a preliminary chapter that would contain all the then-known details of the life that might have correlation to the work. That chapter was finished fairly quickly because there was not all that much that would be included in it. Then I thought to try my hand at a chapter which would combine several different kinds of research. I had had several interviews with the late George Reavey, who had given me a collection of letters Beckett had written to him when Reavey was acting as Beckett's literary agent and trying to find a publisher for *Murphy*. This chapter required a combination of paleography (Beckett's handwriting is execrable), translation (some were in French or German), collation (they were shoved into shoeboxes and pages and envelopes were misplaced or missing), dating (through internal evidence in many cases), interpretation (was he serious or jesting, for example), and exegesis. It also involved literary detective work, as the manuscript of *Murphy* had long since disappeared and the letters provided strong clues about the composition and content of the novel. The final chapter was one which combined oral history (i.e. interviewing persons involved in theatrical productions), dramatic criticism (of the plays themselves) and the kind of social and cultural history (because the subject of this chapter was the publication and production of Samuel Beckett's plays in the United States). All this was followed by a chapter of concluding summation.

By early April 1972, I had completed a first draft, and I wrote to Beckett and asked if I could come to Paris to talk to him about it. He agreed, and so I found myself on his birthday, April 13, sitting beside him this time, on a banquette in a café near my hotel, flipping through the dissertation page by page, telling him what I had written because he insisted, "Oh, I never read anything anyone writes about me."

Line by line we read through the dissertation. "I'd quite forgotten all about that," he would say about something; "You are absolutely right about that," about another; "I don't think that is correct" to something else; or "You'd better talk to Person X about that incident/writing/place/event" (whatever was the subject at hand). At the end of this very long afternoon, he seemed pleased by my work, and so I decided to take the plunge: "Look here, Mr. Beckett," I began, and then went on to tell him that I wanted to expand the dissertation into a book as soon as I received the doctorate.

I will not quote his many repetitions of the catchphrase except to say that interspersed before, after and around it, we came to the agreement that I should conduct interviews, be allowed to read documents, correspondence and unpublished manuscripts, and whenever I came to Paris, he would meet me for "conversations," and "perhaps" answer my questions. In other words, the direction of my research, the formation of my opinions, and the shaping of the final manuscript would be entirely up to me. I think it says a great deal about Samuel Beckett's character, that he was able to relinquish whatever control he might have retained had he chosen to direct the course of my inquiry, to let me write a fully independent book.

Very little was known about Samuel Beckett's life when I started my research, and most of that was incorrect. I knew that I would have to conduct many interviews in the three countries where he had lived throughout his life: Ireland, England and France. I realized how fortunate I was to be doing this in the early 1970's, because so many people who had known him at various stages of his life were still alive.

Originally, I thought I would follow the procedures for interviewing used by oral historians; that is, to ask the same questions in the same order with the same inflection or lack of inflection to every subject. I soon discovered that this would not work if I were to create a relaxed and conversational atmosphere with the interviewees, and so I adopted a basic question-and-answer interviewing technique instead.

Then the problem of interpretation became crucial. I decided that I would not use any fact, no matter how "Beckettian" it seemed, unless I had a minimum of three sources who agreed in their interpretation or remembrance of it. In a number of cases, where I thought the information required the utmost in scrupulous interpretation and documentation, I insisted on five sources of verification. How I mourned the several anecdotes that never saw the final manuscript because I only had one or two sources, and they were not entirely reliable.

This question of the source's reliability was one I think I solved—fortunately—very early in my research. For example: I had spoken to one person who claimed to have been seated at the right hand of every significant literary event in modern literature, to have correspondence, documents, and other materials from every important European writer in the early twentieth century. The Samuel Beckett he told me about was a complex and troubling person, and as this was one of my first interviews, I was reluctant to believe this source's version of my subject. I interviewed another person at the same time, the very model of impeccable honesty, rectitude and decorum. He told me of a Samuel Beckett homogenized, pasteurized and sanitized beyond human existence, and this was exactly what I wanted to believe and to write about.

I say "fortunately," when I speak of interviewing these two persons, because it turned out that the first speaker was entirely honest, able to produce verification for everything he said, and the second was a terrible liar and entirely untrustworthy. I had to keep these two persons at the forefront of my consciousness throughout my six years of interviewing because I discovered that my natural predisposition to like or dislike persons had very little to do with their reliability as a biographical resource.

I learned also how to interpret documents as well as to understand personalities. For example, I was fortunate to be given several large collections of Beckett's correspondence to three separate persons that ranged over long periods of time. These letters came to me at differing times during my writing, so that one instance serves as a perfect example of this problem of interpretation. One collection of letters to a friend then living in London told of a Beckett happy to be living in Ireland in the 1930's, making his peace with family, profession and country, and this is what I wrote in my first draft. Then the question arose: if he had been so happy, why did he leave so abruptly for Paris, never to return to Ireland? Several months later, another collection of letters came, this time to a friend in the United States. In these, Beckett was miserable because he could not decide what he wanted to do with his life and he was angry with several cliques of Irish writers who would not admit him to their friendship. But other than that, these letters read, he was happy living at home and in Ireland. The question of why he left for permanent residence in France still loomed large, but in the second draft of the manuscript I thought I equivocated fairly successfully around it.

Then I gained access to the third collection of letters and found throughout an entirely different Samuel Beckett. This one hated Ireland and could not wait to leave. This one spent all his time drinking himself into oblivion because he could not find work, could not write, and hated his widowed mother with venomous passion. In each of the three collections of letters, there were many written to the three recipients on the same day, and the dissimilarity in their content and tone was astonishing. I knew that the third recipient, Thomas McGreevy, was the only person Beckett had entirely trusted and confided in throughout the course of the correspondences because every single person I interviewed insisted this was true and Samuel Beckett verified it in conversation.

Therefore, I knew that only the McGreevy letters contained the truth about Beckett's feelings and that only they should be trusted. They came to me fairly late in the writing of the biography, and I remember how many times I was grateful that I had instinctively distrusted the earlier collections and had continued to look for "just one more source" to verify my hunches.

Since finishing the biography, I have often thought about what I call "the tyranny of the printed document" because of the natural human tendency to want to believe that what is printed or written is the most accurate record of history. I think of my own inclination to write different things to different people in letters, and I wonder how much literary history might be changed if only one more letter or document would come to light in the lives of many of our other writers.

One other decision I made was not to insist upon a unifying thesis for this biography. Samuel Beckett had lived his life in such privacy that I felt it incumbent upon me to allow it to unfold in print as it had happened. If I did any shaping at all, it was to be as chronologically full and inclusive as possible until 1950, the period that coincided with the great fame brought on by *Waiting for Godot*. Many of the persons involved in his life had either died by 1977, when I had finished the actual writing, or they felt such distance from the various situations that they no longer considered themselves subject to embarrassment. In some instances their literary executors granted me permission to write fully of their role in Beckett's life. After 1950, the situation was quite changed, and a careful reader can discern how from that period of time until the present, I generally gave catalogues of activity that traced Beckett's role in the publication and production of his work more than I wrote about the personal incidents of his life.

I was well aware that "warts and all" is the motto of many contemporary biographers, and I also knew well that I had discovered many in the life of Samuel Beckett. "Warts" for their own sake would not do, but there were very few of those, and they were mainly the anecdotes I referred to earlier in this essay which I did not use because I did not trust the teller's veracity or intention. But there was, for example, a major "wart" in the question of Beckett's psychoanalysis in London with Dr. W. R. Bion. This was a delicate subject and one which I originally thought I would either omit in the book or pass over without trying to interpret. However, when I discovered that Dr. Bion had taken Beckett to hear Jung's lectures at the Tavistock Institute, I realized that this was something of deep and lasting influence which Beckett had used repeatedly throughout his writings and which had helped very strongly to shape the direction of his so-called "mature" writings. This information helped me to formulate my theory of what should be included within the biography; namely, that any "wart" which had any degree of connection to the writing should appear, for this was after all the life of a writer, and there were very few writers of any period of literary history who had so entwined life with work as Beckett.

One of these "warts" in the life has haunted me since the biography was published in 1978. Beckett's cousins and some old family friends all told me the same incident of how, when he was a child, he would throw himself down from the higher branches of a pine tree with his arms outstretched, willing himself to fly and trusting to the low-hanging branches to break his fall if he did not. His mother beat him repeatedly to try to break him of this behavior, and each time she used a switch taken from the already-offended tree. There was not anything in his writing by

1978 that reflected this incident, but it was only one of many throughout the first thirty or so years of Beckett's life in which his will and his mother's collided, and so I used it in the biography.

Imagine my surprise when *Company* was published in 1980, and this incident, almost as I wrote it in the biography, appeared in his fiction. I have not yet decided the relationship between life and art here, between the creative originator and the imitator. But I do feel that Beckett's literary use of this instance of his life only grants further support to my contention of how intertwined they are for him and how correct I was to interview so many disparate people, to include so many seemingly unrelated facts and facets of the life in order to create what became a detailed chronology.

And so I proceeded throughout the writing of that book, collecting information, sifting fact from supposition, collating all versions of the same moments of the life, gradually forming and writing my own opinion. I learned that contemporary biography cannot follow older models because lives are no longer of interest when they present, let us say, a great person larger than life. The concept of "Re-visionism," which is most closely associated with the feminist re-writing of our history in order to determine women's role within it, is also applicable for contemporary biography. We need to see the human figure in much more detail now, and the fine line between personal privacy and public accountability is one which requires ethical sensibility as well as consideration of legalities.

The contemporary biographer must be aware that lives are not lived outside of and apart from society, but rather in the midst of all the complexities of modern life. The contemporary biographer must be critic, historian, cultural observer, intellectual arbiter, psychiatrist, physician and minister. In my own case, for example, I spent months, sometimes years, becoming expert in such matters as the French Resistance in World War Two or the small artists' colony that flourished in the 1930's outside Dresden, so that I could write of Beckett's involvement in both. In the first, most of a chapter resulted, in the second, only a few sentences, but both were crucial to the unfolding of his life. A situation particular to the biographer of a living subject resulted: friends of Beckett's in several countries came to depend upon me and my family in ways which none of us enjoyed. We nonetheless tried to help them with as much grace and generosity as we could muster.

Lately, there is much debate over the role of contemporary

biography in literary scholarship. Some scholars argue that it will
be the necessary middle ground between what they describe as the
dead end of historiography and the arid excesses of deconstruc-
tion. Others feel that it will signal the return of humanistic
discourse to scholarship. Others call it a necessary social tool that
helps us to understand the complex interplay between the
individual and society. I am not yet sure where my work falls
within this broad spectrum of theoretical speculation, for as I
write a second biography of a living subject and find that most of
the methodology I conceived to write about the life of Samuel
Beckett is unsuited to the writing of the life of Simone de Beauvoir,
I only know that biographical scholarship, for me, becomes the
ideal combination of literary, intellectual and social inquiry.

CHAPTER THIRTEEN

# Albert Camus

## PATRICK McCARTHY

Leon Edel says that in a literary biography "the initial impulse, more often than not, has been a response to the writer's work."[1] This was certainly the case with my book on Camus which, although it is a critical biography, grew out of my longstanding admiration for his novels. The aim of a critical biography, as I perceive it, is to reconstruct the life of a writer, to examine the relationship, however complex, between his life and his work and to set both of them in the context of their period. As my book advanced the biographical and the historical segments grew more important and I grew ever more interested in the concept of period: in the way that a writer is shaped by and also shapes the intellectual and political forces of his age. Yet my book began as a re-reading of Camus who was an important part of my adolescence and whose works have continued to intrigue me.

Since few biographers are altogether free of narcissism, my book is indirectly about me and the period in which I grew up. Clearly this cannot be of much interest to the reader either of my book or of this essay but it is probably significant, for example, that I was an adolescent in the Europe of the late 1950's when the Cold War was still raging. Much of Camus' post-war journalism and philosophical writing deals with the dilemmas of the Cold War which also caused him considerable personal suffering, and my interest in and judgment on the positions he took draw on my adolescent impressions of the Cold War re-examined twenty years later.

In the 1950's Camus was not to me a political figure and I had not read *L'Homme révolté*. Nor did I know anything about his life except that he loved the theatre and that he was a French Algerian and hence deeply disturbed by the Algerian War. I began spending my summers in France during the Algerian War and, without knowing much about it, I supported the Front de Libération Nationale partly because as a fledgling member of the British Labour Party I knew a little about the independence struggle in Kenya and Ghana and partly because it was apparent from conversations with ordinary French people that they were sick of the war and wanted it to end.

But this too had little to do with my interest in Camus which began when I read *L'Etranger* at the age of sixteen. Since it was only the second book I had read in French (the first was Françoise Sagan's *Bonjour Tristesse!*) I do not claim to have understood it but, like countless other readers, I was struck by Meursault's sensuous yet chilling view of the world. I went on to read *La Peste* where I was initially less impressed by the ethic of courage and fraternity than by the masterly way that Camus tells his tale, while at the same time undercutting it and casting doubt on his narrator's statements. I also felt that Camus, although frequently described in the press as an atheist, had a thoroughly religious temperament as he demonstrates in his depiction of Paneloux's death. Then—as now—the contemporary English writer I most admired was Graham Greene; and while I was writing my book I came across the passages in Camus' diaries where he quotes from Greene's *Heart of the Matter* and which seem to me to demonstrate an affinity between the two men. As an adolescent I also read *La Chute* and I was intrigued by this false confession which still seems to me Camus' best book.

I was eighteen when Camus was killed in the Villeblevin car accident and the English newspapers were full of photographs of him wearing a trenchcoat and smoking the inevitable cigarette. Along with millions of other people I felt that an unusual and sympathetic voice had fallen silent. I came to understand the nature of Camus' appeal a little better that summer when I worked in one of the Abbé Pierre's communities just outside Paris. Among the social workers and administrators who ran the community there were many who were well versed in con-temporary French writing and were indeed excellent examples of that endangered species called "the general reader." They read for pleasure, for the sheer love of language and also for the moral, psychological and political insights that their favorite authors offered them. Of these writers Camus was both the most admired and most liked. Most of my new acquaintances had been through the Second World War and several of them had lost parents or brothers in it. They felt that Camus had understood better than any other writer the experiences through which they had lived.

When I questioned them about it they grew reserved (as Camus himself did) and fell back on phrases like "he knows what he is talking about." But from their remarks about his individual works it was easy to piece together what they thought. *L'Etranger* had caught the bleakness of the 1940's and the second half of the book depicted graphically how social institutions could lose their legitimacy as they had done under the Vichy government. *La Peste*, which most readers at that time considered Camus' best book, marked the triumph over the seeming nihilism of *L'Etranger* and I remember long discussions in the community about the values of courage and fraternity. Rieux was to my friends the model to follow: taciturn, courageous, a rebel doctor with an unusual concern for his patients and a man to whom friendship was important. Not surprisingly *La Chute* puzzled my acquaintances because it contradicted the evolution from pessimism to revolt of which Camus himself had spoken. One of them went as far as to say that Camus had given what he had to give in *La Peste* and had nothing more to tell us.

The affection with which these men spoke of Camus marked his special place in his generation. Although they also admired Sartre they did not think of him, as they did of Camus, as a wiser elder brother. That same summer of 1960 Sarte had just published *La Critique de la raison dialectique*, which is today seen as a major influence on what would become the New Left but which could not attract the audience that had flocked to Sartre's plays in the late 1940's. To my friends Sartre's voice was less sympathetic and lacked the breadth of experience that was filtered through Camus' terse sentences.

Moreover Camus was not associated with any particular dogma. In the Abbé Pierre's community there were Catholics and ex-Catholics, some of whom had ties to the worker-priest movement, socialists, ex-Communists although no card-carrying Communists, anarchists and sceptics. Most would have described themselves as left-wingers and of course there were no women in the group. It seems to me that the prototype of Camus' readers would be male, left-wing and shaped by the Second World War. I remember thinking that, while Camus had attracted readers of extraordinarily quality, it could not have been easy for him to live up to their expectations. He was a prisoner not so much of his

success as of the sympathy he had aroused. My book would be
very much a re-examination of the 1950's view of Camus: the
chapters of literary criticism reassess this earlier estimation of his
writing and the biographical chapters are an attempt to discover
the man behind the legend.

In the course of the next decade I read Camus' other books.
Aside from the short story *Le Renégat*, which reveals a confused
violence that is suppressed in Camus' novels, they did not alter
my picture of him. Meanwhile the criticism that appeared on
him—much of it excellent—reinforced the impression I had
already gained. A new stimulus to my thinking came with the
publication of Conor Cruise O'Brien's little book in 1970.[2]
O'Brien offered a different interpretation of the Cold War debates
and a more favorable view of Sartre in the Camus–Sartre
dispute. Presumably reflecting on his own experience in Katanga
and Ghana, he was severe on Camus' role in the Algerian War.
Yet it is absurd to read O'Brien's book as an attack on Camus, if
only because the different picture he paints allowed him to
perceive the full significance of the enigmatic *La Chute*.

In general, O'Brien offered insights into literary problems like
the evolution of Camus' narrative technique and into his political
battles. O'Brien also raised the question that immediately
fascinated me, namely, Camus' links with French Algeria. What
was it like to grow up as a young, very poor boy in that Algeria?
What sort of a city was Algiers then? That French Algeria had by
now vanished; that it could not be reconstructed merely by
traveling to post-independence Algeria made the problem all the
more enticing. Biographers are usually concerned with
time—with the tricky task of reconstructing someone else's time in
one's own; but I was conscious from the outset of place, of Algiers,
Oran, Tipasa and all the places that Camus described so lovingly
and which seemed an essential part of him. Clearly politics could
not be excluded from this discussion for French Algeria, as its very
name affirmed, offered the contradictions of a colonial society.
But that was not for me the dominant consideration; my prime
aim was to reconstruct Camus' Algeria.

In the meantime I was working on a writer who must be the
exact antithesis of Camus, Louis-Ferdinand Céline. Where
Camus was a model to his contemporaries, the anti-Semitic Céline
was a pariah. Where Camus' life appeared as a struggle, Céline's
was a series of flights and hallucinations. It was as if he were

determined to mislead his hapless biographers who were left the task of sifting the tedious truth from the more colorful tales that Céline told about himself. In their use of language Céline and Camus were equally far apart. Despite such differences, however, both men belonged to the period of the Second World War. As someone who had not lived through the war but was surrounded as a child by adults who had, I was interested above all in such writers. So when I felt that I had recovered from the painful years spent in intellectual cohabitation with Céline I set about writing about Camus.

When I began work on the biographical section of my book, I discovered that there were certain obstacles which came from Camus' strong sense of privacy. Dismaying as it may seem to a biographer, an author's desire to cast a veil over his life is eminently reasonable. But it is also intriguing and in itself offers clues to his character. Although Camus did confide in friends and especially in women and was capable in his letters of expressing deep and intense emotion, he hid his life from most of his acquaintances. Sometimes this was simple reserve: he rarely spoke of his early poverty or of his special, difficult relationship with his mother. More often and especially as he grew famous he made a conscious effort to preserve a private realm into which outsiders could not penetrate. This is also a feature of his writing where his narrators tell us less than they appear to and where questions are left hanging at the end of the book.

Unlike Céline then, Camus relied on silence to deter his future biographers and his heirs have generally followed his wishes. Although some of his letters have been published, most have not, and there are several voluminous correspondences which may well offer fresh insights into his life. New pieces of his diary may surface and his medical records may still exist. As he was dogged by tuberculosis they would be particularly important but neither I nor any other researcher has been able to unearth them. His own statements and impressions gained by friends with no particular medical expertise cannot be a substitute for more precise information, especially since the role of tuberculosis in the lives of artists is such a complex topic. The old notion that tuberculosis causes violent oscillation between depression and ecstasy would seem to explain the moods of Camus' essays and even of *La Peste*. However recent medical research indicates that tuberculosis does not in itself have such an effect. So its role in shaping the cycles of despair and renewed vigor in Camus' life remain enigmatic.[3] Similarly it would be interesting to know precisely which drugs he was given because their side-effects are better understood now than in the 1950's.

Most biographers would agree that there is no such animal as a definitive biography but certainly there can be none unless the full range of sources—diaries, both sides of correspondence, manuscripts and the like—is available. I did not pretend to write such a biography and sought only to put down what seemed to me the most important aspects of Camus' life, subject to later addition and correction. For this I used two main sources: firstly Camus' journalism, the reviews of his theatrical experiments and information on his political activity which I was able to cull from French-Algerian newspapers, magazines and memoirs of the pre-1939 period; secondly the much greater store of information that is available from post-war French documents and that deals with the last fifteen years of his life. To complement this I conducted an extensive series of interviews with people who had known him.

In 1979, when I was half-way through this research, Herbert Lottman's biography of Camus was published.[4] Lottman used some of the same sources as I and interviewed many of the same people. But he did a more complete job of bringing together the detailed facts of Camus' life. Indeed in his opening pages he uncovered one fact that Camus himself never knew, namely, that Camus' paternal ancestors did not come from Alsace-Lorraine in the aftermath of the Franco-Prussian war but from other regions of France such as Bordeaux and the Ardèche. It was a part of what one might call Camus' personal mythology that his family had chosen to remain French when Alsace-Lorraine was annexed by the Prussians in 1870; he saw in this a patriotism which had both moral and cultural overtones and which he himself was renewing by his repeated assertion of France's cultural heritage during and after the Occupation. That his forefathers did not come from Alsace-Lorraine proves perhaps nothing more than that a personal mythology need not be grounded in fact. Still it is paradoxical that a biographer would know more about his subject's background than the subject himself did.

This is only one of many cases where Lottman's scrupulous and resolute efforts unearthed new information about Camus' life. Until his book appeared there had been only the notes in the

Pléiade edition of Camus' work along with similarly brief and frequently inaccurate notes that appeared in studies of his writing. Now there was a long biography which I along with all other Camus researchers was able to use and which also allowed me to concentrate on the "life and work" and "life and times" aspect of my book.

I did much of my work in the Bibliothèque Nationale on the rue de Richelieu in Paris. The BN is familiar—perhaps all too familiar—to students of French culture, many of whom remember it in the old, unreconstructed days when its catalogue was bewilderingly complex and its service irritatingly slow. One felt that it had been deliberately designed to prove that sociologist Michel Crozier's work on the shortcomings of French organizations was correct. Now the BN has been partially reorganized, and if the information one is seeking happens to be in a reorganized section, it can be obtained easily and swiftly. Documents from pre-1939 Algeria were, alas, in a yet-to-be-reorganized section which meant that some had to be sent from Versailles. This seemed to take longer than if they were being sent from Nice and proved that the old French habit of treating the Paris suburbs as if they were remote provinces is very much alive.[5]

Fortunately, however, the Algerian newspapers had not been microfilmed. This was fortunate because few of the microfilm readers worked properly and some of the copies had been so badly made that they were virtually illegible. Camus' post-war newspaper, *Combat*, was an unreadable microfilm, while the original had altogether disappeared. To read *Combat* I went to the Bibliothèque de l'Arsenal which had an original set and where I was able to take my lunchtime strolls in the newly renovated Marais district or on the île Saint-Louis.

Perusal of the Algerian files in the BN sometimes brought me valuable finds. After many battles with the catalogue I succeeded in finding a set, although incomplete, of the *Revue algérienne*, a little magazine edited by a family with whom the young Camus was friendly. Not only were its pages open to Camus and his circle but the *Revue* published pieces on the plays he staged and the exhibitions he helped organize. Indeed it reads like a history of the young Camus' development while providing information on everything else that was going on in Algeria. Temptations also lie in wait for the researcher and in perusing *Alger-Républicain*, the newspaper of which Camus was assistant editor, I found myself irresistibly drawn to the sports pages. I must have "wasted" hours reading the articles on Algerian soccer and on the early career of Marcel Cerdan, the future middle-weight boxing champion and lover of Edith Piaf who was then becoming the idol of the Algiers sports fans. Of these there were enormous numbers and one of the most fervent was Camus. I later met Paul Balazard who covered soccer for *Alger-Républicain* and who told me that he, Camus and a gang of part-time reporters used to sit around in the paper's office on Sunday evenings while the sports results came in from all over Algeria. It was a scene of shirt-sleeves, cigarette smoke and outbursts of cheering or hissing as each man's favorite team won or lost. Such occasions were important to Camus who played soccer avidly before he contracted tuberculosis and whose schoolmates remember him for his sense of balance and his skill at dribbling the ball.

Paul Balazard was only one of Camus' friends and acquaintances whom I interviewed. In general they were helpful, although many shared Camus' sense of reserve. Those whom Camus had met after he became famous at the Liberation were frequently journalists and writers who were accustomed to being interviewed and knew precisely what they did and did not want to say. The men and women he had known during his Algerian youth seemed to me some of the most sincere and most interesting people I had ever met. Except for the novelist, Emmanuel Roblès, their names would mean little to an Anglo-Saxon audience. They were architects, sculptors, painters, writers, lawyers and political activists, some of whom had belonged to the cell which Camus had organized during his Communist period and others of whom were socialists or anarchists. All had lived through the Vichy years and, although some had come to France after the Liberation, many had also lived through the Algerian war and had usually been caught in the middle. Most had relatives or friends who were killed in that war, some had come to France in the flight of the *pieds-noirs* in 1962 and others had remained in Algeria after independence.

It was clear from my conversations with them that Camus was a man capable of inspiring great affection and loyalty. Indeed the unusually close bond he had established with these early friends seems to prefigure the relationship he had with his millions of post-war readers. It was equally clear that the quality of the friendship they offered him had confirmed his belief that fraternity was a touchstone of all values. In this group which Camus began to form while still in school and which he steadily enlarged until he left Algeria in 1940 lie, so it seems to me, many clues to his character and behavior. The edge of aloofness which he preserved, the eagerness to be kind which led him to perform countless small and large favors, his confidences which were all the more dramatic and sincere because they were rare and his dislike of pretension and arrogance are all traits which his friends remember. Indeed almost the only episode of his early life which they were not able to elucidate was his relationship with his mother whom they scarcely knew. This all-important bond can be and has been analysed by Freudian critics but the biographical details of Camus' childhood will probably never be known.

In talking about him they were also reconstructing their own youth and I soon discovered that I could learn more about Camus from such a reconstruction than from asking specific and detailed questions. So I altered my style of interviewing, asking each person to tell me what he thought was significant about his friendship with Camus. After much initial reluctance people began talking about themselves and in this way, for example, the debates and tensions within Camus' theatre group became clearer. Moreover there was for the interviewer the added and undeserved pleasure of seeing the discussion grow more interesting because it entailed a reliving of the past rather than a collection of data.

It would be wrong, however, to deny that many of Camus' friends have objected—often bitterly—to my interpretation of his life. Most, although not all, of their objections were directed not at the first half of the book but at the second half, which deals with the Camus of the post-war period. As I collected the information and set about writing, it seemed more and more to me that there was a huge gulf between the heroic public personage of the Nobel Prize and the troubled human being who was toiling at *La Peste* and *Le Renégat*. Although I tried to be as objective as possible, it is likely that I was influenced by the way I had come to be interested in Camus. This led me to challenge the view instilled into me during my adolescence that his work was a message of hope and revolt, even as my own re-examination of the Cold War led me to see much validity in Sartre's criticism of *L'Homme révolté*, namely that it did not offer fresh possibilities of emancipation. It would then be impossible for me to deny that I was pre-disposed to see gloom in Camus' life.

It seemed to me that Camus' post-war years were a series of public victories and secret defeats. His newspaper, *Combat*, brought him fame as a moral arbiter, but it was unable to define a coherent political line and in 1947 it collapsed in a welter of financial difficulties and personal squabbles. The success of *La Peste* and the reputation it brought Camus as the man who had found the answers that a generation was seeking aroused unrealistically high expectations that no writer could have satisfied and that helped plunge him into a period of sterility. And so it continued: defeat, in the eyes of French if not of Anglo-Saxon intellectuals, in the quarrel over *L'Homme révolté* which not merely ended his difficult friendship with Sartre but also left him isolated in Paris, and the trauma of the Algerian war which helped poison the Nobel triumph. Not that Camus ever gave in to these or to the more strictly private problems that beset him; when he was killed in 1960, he was trying his best to recover after a particularly painful few years. There was nothing fatalistic about Camus, who had always considered life as a struggle.

Yet it seemed to me that this was a bleak life rendered all the bleaker by the public perception that it was a hero's or a saint's life. Like Sisyphus, Camus had his rock to push uphill but in his case it was the huge statue erected to the author of *La Peste*. Recently, when reading Graham Greene's autobiography, I was intrigued to discover how irksome Greene found it to be hailed as a great Catholic novelist and to have readers ask him how they could save their souls. Camus would surely have appreciated Greene's irritation. It also appeared to me that Camus' life was all the sadder because it was an exile from Algeria, from his youth and from the images that inspired his early writing.

To point this out seemed to some readers and reviewers an act of at least disrespect and at worst treason. It also appeared to a certain number that I had deliberately blackened Camus. This brings up the whole question of what the biographer's attitude towards his subject should be. Although I believe my view to be quite traditional, I feel obliged to restate it. Like all other human beings, Camus had faults; he was, for example, capable of extraordinary self-righteousness, as his 1952 letter to Sartre shows. This is more complicated and more interesting than it seems because he was also incapable of taking himself seriously and could see the comedy in almost every situation. The latter trait is to most people a virtue and the former a weakness but to omit one or the other would surely be a betrayal by the biographer. It would also in Camus' case have a special defect, for to stress the humor without the self-righteousness would simply reinforce the general view of Camus the saint without correcting or enriching it. In which case why bother to write yet another book about him?

To put the question then is to turn it against Alfred Kazin, who in an otherwise generous review of my book wrote that I was too harsh on Camus and wondered "what induced McCarthy to write about Camus at all."[6] The answer is that the man and his work seemed more interesting to me than the way they are usually presented, that the mixture of irony and self-righteousness was more intriguing than irony alone and that the bleakness of this life seemed to have been largely ignored. In saying all this I am merely saying that the biographer—like the critic or the historian—must blend empathy with distance and try to demonstrate that he has both the imaginative sympathy to enter his subject's world and the detachment to consider it objectively. Whether I succeeded in doing this or not is not for me to decide but such was my intention.[7]

My next task was to examine the relationship between Camus' life and work and between his life and the time in which he lived and wrote. For me these were overlapping matters and I hoped to integrate them. However, many people consider them quite separate, so I would like to explain how I perceive the links.

As early as 1957, when he published *Literary Biography*, Leon Edel was protesting against the separation of biography from criticism and the tendency by many critics to excommunicate biography. Modern critics, he writes, "are trying to narrow down the critical act far more than is necessary."[8] Since then this trend has continued until today the squabbling schools of literary theoreticians agree about little except the exclusion of biography. Edel attempts to bridge the gulf by arguing that the text is an integral part of the author's life. Using the methods of Freudian analysis he works from the text to the life and then back to a new consideration of the text. Of these two stages the first—from text to life—appears to him more important for the biographer.

The methods of psychoanalysis might be most useful in considering Camus and there are two excellent Freudian studies written on him, although both deal with the writer rather than with the man.[9] But I would also suggest that there may be many different kinds of relationship between the text and the life. One kind, not the most important but in Camus' case significant and paradoxical, is the way, already indicated, that the text rebounds on its author once it has been recreated by the reader. Writers are changed by the books they write and still more by the way they are read, and it is tempting to suggest that an artist's mature life is determined by these complementary yet conflicting phenomena.

The relationships between life and text are multiple, they vary from author to author and they may be examined in many different ways. Diaries and letters offer the best examples of the overlap between a man and his work. The recently published letters of Evelyn Waugh are fascinating as pure language and one does not need to be interested in Waugh's life to enjoy their concision and humor which are distinctive features of his novels. Yet these letters are also projections of Waugh's self and a means of contact with other people, and they offer excellent insights into his life.

So a biographer collects all the texts he can: diaries and letters give Camus' written version of his life as he felt he was living it while interviews with friends are oral texts which explain how they perceived his life. After reading this material—for biography like literary criticism is a re-reading—the biographer undertakes his own reconstruction. One part of it is to analyse his author's major texts—his works of imagination. The "I" of a novel may usefully be compared with the "I" of a diary or an event that finds its way into fiction may also be described in a letter.

This does not mean that life and work may be indiscriminately merged into an indeterminate jumble. The point of view from which a letter is written must be compared and contrasted with the point of view from which a novel is written and the contrasts may be the most interesting feature. In his life Camus was fascinated by street-talk—the use of Algiers slang or snatches of conversation heard on the Paris buses. But, although he notes examples in his diaries, his use of street-talk in *L'Etranger* is quite different. Shortened and juxtaposed with Meursault's observations, these fragments of conversations appear as the expression of a consciousness that is different from Meursault's but not in itself coherent.

Such comparisons and contrasts seem to me important, and in

the literary criticism chapters of my book I tried to do no more—since there is so much excellent criticism written on Camus—than to examine them. I juxtaposed, for example, the gloom of Camus' life in the mid-1950's with the more distant narration of *La Chute*, his rare utterances about his mother with the way she is depicted in his early essays, and his attitude towards Arabs with the way he depicts the murder of the Arab in *L'Etranger*. One might organize this analysis in many different ways. In general I divided the literary criticism from the biography and put it into separate chapters but this was merely for convenience sake.

In moving to the topic of "life and times" I can do no better than start with a quotation from Robert Gittings: "We no longer see any man and woman in isolation, divorced from his or her class and economic situation."[10] As I have already stated, I felt that Camus could not be understood without a knowledge of French Algeria as well as of post-Liberation France. In the first half of my book I inserted a chapter of the politics and culture of pre-1939 Algeria which places Camus' youth in its context and also looks forward to the analysis of *L'Etranger* in a later chapter of literary criticism. In the second half I was bolder or sloppier for I tried to integrate the political background and the biography by grouping characters around such themes as the *Combat* newspaper or a particular historical moment like the early Cold War. Clearly this involved sacrificing what one might call the biographical flow both because the events of Camus' private life did not coincide with political developments and because it was necessary to interrupt the chronological order with political analysis. The biographer's delicate task is to avoid leaving the life in isolation while preserving the individuality of his subject.

The best example I know of the integration of biography and period and the major influence on my own thinking is August Anglès' *André Gide et le premier groupe de la "Nouvelle Revue Française"* (Gallimard, 1978). It is unfortunate that this book, although greatly admired by students of the *Nouvelle Revue Française*, has been neglected as an example of a historical reconstruction. Perhaps significantly it is not in the ordinary sense a biography for it deals with a group of writers and the magazine they founded. This enables Anglès to set the lives of his writers—and especially Gide's life—in the context of many other cultural, social and political phenomena. Similarly Gide's writing, read as it was first published in the magazine, becomes an expression of the group and a voice of the period.

The problem of how one relates an individual's life or a text to their broader context is resolved by Anglès in a sophisticated manner. Moving at once from the concept of class to that of "milieu," he establishes the diverse strands in his writers' backgrounds; then he defines certain "zones" of readers who are linked by age, sensibility and political opinions. In this way the *NRF* becomes a "circuit" of interwoven themes and styles and behind each page lies a historical structure that can be recreated. To take only one example, the *NRF*'s initial refusal of Proust's novel is in part the rejection of Proust's fashionable and thoroughly Parisian background by a Gide who came from a very different segment of the bourgeoisie, one that was Protestant and provincial.

Such an example gives only a hint of the complexity of Anglès' work. He was unfortunate in writing about Gide who himself had a flair for burrowing into his period and who was a great letter-writer. Letters are the raw material of Anglès' book because they reveal the series of debates that constitute the circuit. Clearly it was also valuable for him to choose to analyse a magazine where each work is illuminated by the work published before or after it. Although much in Anglès' work is either intuitive or else the result of his decision to saturate himself in the period, the conceptual tools he created may be separated from his own achievement and used by biographers. The result of his work is to fuse the life, the writing and the times of Gide so that each page of Gide's writing is a fragment of the historical mosaic.

Although I could not hope in my book to equal Anglès' achievement, I borrowed some of his techniques. In studying the Camus–Sartre dispute I went back over the last few years of *Les Temps modernes* in order to set the quarrel in the context of the magazine's evolution. I also tried to see the young Camus as part of a group, which seems to me to throw light on *L'Etranger*. Young writers in French Algeria were engrossed in writing "the great Algerian novel" and Camus was the one who succeeded.

In analysing political topics the biographer's task is to maintain that blend of sympathy and distance which is his trademark. This is not as easy as it seems because the way one views political history, especially such a troubled and recent period, is shaped by how one lived it or, if one did not live it, by how it is related to the present. In particular the politics and culture of the Cold War are now being re-examined as East–West detente has given way to a time of greater conflict between the US and the Soviet Union.

I freely admit that in my own study of the period and while trying to be as objective as possible, I was struck both by the repetitive nature of the debates which had all been rehearsed in the late 1930's and by the way that anti-Communism became in Western Europe an autonomous force directed not merely at Communism but at supporting the reconstruction of Europe along Keynesian but still capitalist lines. It seemed to me that Camus fell into the trap of anti-Communism in *L'Homme révolté*, which is a long diatribe against messianic Marxism but offers few other political possibilities. The peculiar merit of Sartre was that he understood better than Camus or almost anyone else the way in which anti-Communism was being used and that he sought to combat it. Not that he entirely succeeded because in *Les Communistes et la paix*, which is his real answer to Camus, he falls into the trap that awaits "anti-anti-Communists," namely, he espouses uncritically the positions of the French Communist Party.

This led me to the view that the Camus–Sartre battle was a victory for Sartre in that he convinced a greater number of French intellectuals, but was a draw in a more real and lasting sense. Such timid hesitation has not spared me political attacks. The most comprehensive has come from Norman Podhoretz who has accused me of having an "anti-anti-Communist passion."[11] Part of Podhoretz's argument is about *L'Homme révolté*, which he considers excellent political writing. With this I simply disagree although not for political reasons. Whatever my own political opinions I can appreciate *Darkness at Noon*, where Koestler's hatred of Communism acts as a jealous passion that enables him to burrow through the many layers of Communist deceit. By contrast Camus' anti-Communism leads him to vague and repetitive rhetoric that does not offer many insights into Communism. However I do not wish to skirt Podhoretz's attack and I will say that while I do not feel passionately about anti-anti-Communism—if only because it is difficult to feel passionately about a double "anti"—it is quite true that I see dangers in the kind of anti-Communism which flourished in the 1950's and which has been revived in France by the now not so new philosophers and in the US by Podhoretz and his friends. I feel, therefore, that he has correctly defined the difference between his political perspectives and those of my book. Such are the tribulations of the biographer who strays into political debate.

I would like, however, to conclude on a different note by reaffirming my belief in the genre of the critical biography. Leon Edel is unkind about this genre which he defines in a rather narrow way. It seems to me that whatever its impurities the critical biography can offer better insights into a writer than mere biography can. I do not, of course, claim to have invented or perfected the art. Indeed I stumbled onto critical biography when I was working on Céline because it seemed to me that, if people were ever going to read Céline's novels, it was necessary to drive a wedge between Céline the novelist and Céline the virulently anti-Semitic pamphleteer. From this came my attempt to compare and contrast the "I" of Céline's life with the "I" of his novels and the "I" of his pamphlets.

Provided that these relationships are examined rather than blurred or destroyed it seems to me that critical biography is a useful genre. The separation of biography and criticism has now taken institutionalized form: university presses publish criticism, while commercial publishing houses favour biography. Both the language used by the writers and the circle of readers they hope to reach are quite different. This division between the university public and the educated but non-specialized public is unhealthy and not the least merit of critical biography is that it may help to overcome it.

# Notes

## Introduction: *Jeffrey Meyers*

1. Imaginative portrayals of the biographer's work appear in James' "The Aspern Papers" (1888), Mann's *Doctor Faustus* (1947), Henry Reed's "A Very Great Man Indeed" (1971) and Malamud's *Dubin's Lives* (1979).

2. An interesting sub-genre, which flourished in the 1920's and 1930's, is veiled autobiography—books substantially written by the subject but published under another's name: Robert Graves' *Lawrence and the Arabs* (1927), Florence Hardy's *The Life of Thomas Hardy* (1928–30), Gertrude Stein's *The Autobiography of Alice B. Toklas* (1933) and Herbert Gorman's *James Joyce* (1939).

3. W. H. Auden, *A Certain World* (New York, 1970), p. vii.

4. Carlos Baker, *Ernest Hemingway: A Life Story* (New York, 1969), p. vii.

5. Bernard Crick, *George Orwell: A Life* (Boston, Mass., 1980), p. xxiii.

6. Henry James, *William Wetmore Story and His Friends* (New York, 1903), p. 125.

7. Somerset Maugham, *A Writer's Notebook* (New York, 1949), pp. 68–69.

8. George Painter, *Marcel Proust: The Later Years* (Boston, Mass., 1965), p. 126.

9. See Jeffrey Meyers' reviews of: Elizabeth Longford's *A Pilgrimage of Passion*, *8 Days* (London), 1 (August 11, 1979), 34; Mark Holloway's *Norman Douglas*, *Sewanee Review*, 86 (Winter 1978), xxiv–xxvi; Nigel Hamilton's *The Brothers Mann*, *Virginia Quarterly Review*, 55 (Autumn 1979), 748–756; Phillip Knightley's *The Secret Lives of Lawrence of Arabia*, *Commonweal*, 93 (October 23, 1970), 100–104; Ronald Hayman's *Nietzsche*, *Financial Times*, April 19, 1980, p. 12.

**1  Samuel Johnson: *Donald Greene***

1. James L. Clifford and Donald J. Greene, *Samuel Johnson: A Survey and Bibliography of Critical Studies* (Minneapolis, 1970).
2. See E. L. McAdam, Jr., *Times Literary Supplement*, July 21, 1961, p. 449, and Donald Greene, *TLS*, October 13, 1961, p. 683.
3. See Donald and Mary Hyde, *Dr. Johnson's Second Wife* (privately printed, 1953) and James L. Clifford, *Dictionary Johnson* (New York, 1977), p. 118. Boswell also suppressed a conversation in which Mrs. Johnson's companion Elizabeth Desmoulins recounted that, before his wife's death, Johnson engaged in passionate fondling of Mrs. Desmoulins on his bed (Boswell, *The Applause of the Jury, 1782–1785*, ed. Irma S. Lustig and Frederick A. Pottle [New York, 1981], pp. 110–113).
4. The title of an article—one of many such collections of "good ones" out of Boswell—by W. H. Chamberlin, *Saturday Review*, September 4, 1965, pp. 14–15.
5. H. F. Hallett, "Dr. Johnson's Refutation of Bishop Berkeley," *Mind*, LVI (April 1947), 132–147.
6. A blurb on the dust-jacket of W. Jackson Bate's *Samuel Johnson* (New York, 1977) by the late Robert Lowell pays tribute to "the presence of Dr. Johnson" in the book. Yet Lowell listed none of his own many honorary doctoral degrees in his entry in *Who's Who in America*.
7. James Boswell, *The Life of Samuel Johnson, LL.D.*, ed. G. B. Hill, rev. by L. F. Powell (Oxford, vols. I–IV, 1934; V–VI, 1950; 2nd edn. of V–VI, 1964), II, 352, n.1 (hereafter referred to as *Life*). No one, so far as I know, has attempted to explain why Boswell in his title chose to designate Johnson as "LL.D." (Legum Doctor) instead of "D.C.L." (Doctor of Civil Law), the actual Oxford degree.
8. The honorees are listed, *sub anno* 1773, in *A Catalogue of All Graduates in Divinity, Law, and Medicine . . . between October 10, 1659, and October 10, 1800* (Oxford, 1801). Mary Hyde, *The Thrales of Streatham Park* (Cambridge, Mass., 1977), p. 72, was, I believe, the first Johnsonian scholar to call attention to this academic extravaganza. The celebrations, in which the degrees were conferred on their recipients *in propria persona*, lasted the better part of a week. Johnson had to be content with the conferral of his "by diploma"—i.e. *in absentia*.

9. October 18, 1982, p. 45.

10. Hester Thrale Piozzi, *Anecdotes of the Late Samuel Johnson* [1786], ed. Arthur Sherbo (London, 1974), p. 130.

11. Boswell relates the incident in *Life*, II, 53. It has been observed that Boswell was often incapable of appreciating Johnson's abundant dry humor.

12. Helen Louise McGuffie, *Samuel Johnson in the British Press, 1749–1784* (New York, 1976) lists between 3,000 and 4,000 published comments on Johnson during his lifetime. A great many, perhaps the majority, were hostile.

13. *The Prose Works of William Wordsworth*, ed. W. J. B. Owen and J. W. Smyser (Oxford, 1974), III, 75 ("Essay Supplementary to the Preface"). Wordsworth is quoting Pope's *Epistle to Arbuthnot*, which satirizes Addison for surrounding himself with a group of obsequious disciples.

14. The extent of this help is displayed in Allen T. Hazen, *Samuel Johnson's Prefaces and Dedications* (New Haven, Conn., 1937). The story of Johnson's assistance to Percy is given on pages 158–168. A fuller account will appear in Bertram H. Davis' forthcoming biography of Percy, previewed, so to speak, in his *Thomas Percy* (Boston, Mass., 1981).

15. See the references indexed under "Percy, *Reliques*" in *Johnson on Shakespeare*, ed. Arthur Sherbo (vols. VII and VIII of The Yale Edition of the *Works of Samuel Johnson*, 1968).

16. Tyers, "A Biographical Sketch of Dr. Samuel Johnson" (1785), in *The Early Biographies of Samuel Johnson*, ed. O. M. Brack, Jr. and Robert E. Kelley (Iowa City, 1974), p. 67.

17. See Donald Greene, "Samuel Johnson, Journalist," in *From Newsletters to Newspapers: Eighteenth-Century Journalism*, ed. Donovan A. Bond and W. Reynolds McLeod (Morgantown, W. Va., 1977).

18. This and future references are to Macaulay's review of J. W. Croker's edition of Boswell's *Life* (1831) in his *Critical and Historical Essays Contributed to the Edinburgh Review*, ed. F. C. Montague (New York, 1903), I, 347–396. On the *Life* generally, see Donald Greene, "'Tis a Pretty Book, Mr. Boswell, But—," *Georgia Review*, XXXII (Spring, 1978), 17–43.

19. A detailed analysis of the content of the *Life* is given in Donald Greene, "Do We Need a Biography of Johnson's 'Boswell Years'?," *Modern Language Studies*, IX (Fall 1979), 128–136.

20. The depressing story of Boswell's last years is found in the

final volumes of *The Private Papers of James Boswell from Malahide Castle* (18 vols., privately printed, 1928–34), ed. Geoffrey Scott and F. A. Pottle; this material has not yet appeared in The Yale Edition of the *Private Papers of James Boswell.* William C. Ober, M.D., in "Boswell's Clap" (*Boswell's Clap and Other Essays* [Carbondale, Ill., 1979]), argues that Boswell's death at the age of fifty-five was, extraordinarily, the result of his many bouts of gonorrhea, not normally a fatal disease.

21. Superbly presented in *The Correspondence and Other Papers of James Boswell, Relating to the Making of the Life of Johnson*, ed. Marshall Waingrow (New York, 1968).

22. *Boswell's London Journal*, ed. F. A. Pottle (New York, 1950), p. 292; *Life*, I, 423–434.

23. See the references indexed under "Monarchs and monarchy: SJ and" in Donald Greene, *The Politics of Samuel Johnson* (New Haven, Conn., 1960).

24. *Life*, IV, 284–285.

25. A spectacular example is the concluding sentence of the article on Gibbon by the eminent historian J. B. Bury in the eleventh edition of the *Encyclopaedia Britannica*: "It is worthy of notice that he [Gibbon] was in favour of the abolition of slavery, while humane men like his friend Lord Sheffield, Dr. Johnson [!], and Boswell were opposed to the anti-slavery movement."

26. Boswell set the precedent for making ignorant gibes against the "comic" definitions in the *Dictionary*. Various college anthologies of English literature used regularly to include a selection of these in their sections on Johnson, for instance ascribing to Johnson's "pedantry" an account of "thunder" containing much scientific terminology—which in fact is given in the *Dictionary* as a quotation from the Dutch physicist Musschenbroek. By way of correction, Lane Cooper published a learned article (*PMLA*, LII [September 1937], 785–802) tracing the long lexicographical tradition of noting that in Scotland human beings eat oats. The "hard words" in the definition of *network* come from what might be called the definitive treatise on the subject, Sir Thomas Browne's *The Garden of Cyrus* (see Donald Greene, *Notes and Queries*, CXCIV [December 10, 1949], 583–589). A denunciation similar to Johnson's of *excise*, a very hot political issue during the

eighteenth century, is to be found in that orthodox textbook for law students, Blackstone's *Commentaries*. Boswell's account of Johnson's method in compiling the *Dictionary*, though still repeated in modern works on linguistics and the history of lexicography, is, as Thomas Percy wrote long ago, correcting it, "confused and erroneous" (*Life*, ɪ, 188, n. 2). James H. Sledd and Gwin J. Kolb, *Dr. Johnson's Dictionary: Essays in the Biography of a Book* (Chicago, 1955) clears away much of the nonsense written about the work.

27. *Life*, ɪv, 395–396, 552. Maurice Quinlan, *Samuel Johnson: A Layman's Religion* (Madison, Wis., 1964), p. 128, comes to the conclusion "The view that Johnson had an obsession about dying was created largely by James Boswell." Even more incredibly, in this supposedly affecting "deathbed" section, Boswell appends a footnote beginning "Johnson's wishing to unite himself with this rich widow [Mrs. Thrale] was much talked of," and then quotes his own near-obscene "Ode to Mrs. Thrale by Samuel Johnson, LL.D., on Their Approaching Nuptials," with such stanzas as "To rich felicity thus raised / My bosom glows with amorous fire; / *Porter* no longer shall be praised; / 'Tis I myself am *Thrale's Entire*." "Porter" was a variety of ale as well as the name of Johnson's dead wife; "Thrale's Entire" was a competing variety, a specialty of the Thrale brewery.

28. "Ernest Jones's Freud: A Dissenting Opinion," *The New Leader*, xlɪ May 19, 1958), 12–16. Bettelheim begins with a quotation from Freud, "Whoever undertakes to write a biography binds himself to lying, to concealment, to hypocrisy, to flummery, and even to hiding his own lack of understanding." Bettelheim quotes Jones's "The English translation of Freud's works . . . will be considerably more trustworthy than any German version," an absurdity irresistibly reminiscent of George Sherburn's remark (in A. C. Baugh *et al.*, *A Literary History of England* [New York, 1948]; still a standard reference work for students in English): "From the Malahide Papers [Boswell's earlier notes and journals] we now learn that frequently Johnson's talk is more characteristically Johnsonian in the final form Boswell gave it [in the *Life*, 1791] than it was in the first form—that in which it very likely fell from Johnson's lips" (pp. 1065–1066).

29. Virginia Woolf, "Middlebrow," *Collected Essays* (London, 1966), I, 196–203.
30. Donald Greene, *The Politics of Samuel Johnson* and Johnson, *Political Writings*, ed. Donald Greene (New Haven, Conn., 1977; vol. x of The Yale Edition of the *Works of Samuel Johnson*) attempt to provide an account of Johnson's extensive political involvements and to place them in the context of modern historiography of the political scene in eighteenth-century Britain. In his *The Achievement of Samuel Johnson* (New York, 1955) W. J. Bate followed Macaulay in dismissing this aspect of Johnson in one sentence, "He never turned much thought to the subject of politics, at least in written form" (p. 165). In his *Samuel Johnson* (New York, 1977), Bate devotes a full chapter and more to the subject. It is gratifying that erosion of at least part of the Macaulayan myth is possible, even though it may take a long time.
31. "Of foreign travel and of history he spoke with the fierce and boisterous contempt of ignorance" (Macaulay, *Critical and Historical Essays*, pp. 391–392). The comment on foreign travel moved Hill to include in his edition of the *Life* a twelve-page appendix (III, 449–460), detailing the evidence of "Johnson's Travels and Love of Travelling." A book-length study of Johnson's involvements with historiography is in preparation by John A. Vance of the University of Georgia.
32. The obesity of the "Dr. Johnson" of the Addams cartoon follows the tradition of the most often reproduced of Reynolds' many stylized portraits of Johnson, that of 1778. Though Johnson in later life did tend to put on weight (and sometimes adopted a dietary regime to reduce it), he was basically a tall, muscular man—a "mesomorph" rather than an "endomorph." The semi-nude statue of Johnson in St. Paul's Cathedral by John Bacon reproduces his muscularity with probable accuracy.
33. Macaulay, *Critical and Historical Essays*, pp. 370–371.
34. *Ibid.*, pp. 395–396.
35. For a brief account, see Donald Greene, "A Bear by the Tail: The Genesis of the Boswell Industry," *Studies in Burke and His Time*, XVIII (1977), 114–127 (a review article on David Buchanan, *The Treasure of Auchinleck: The Story of the Boswell Papers* [New York, 1974]).

36. See F. A. Pottle, "The Life of Johnson: Art and Authenticity," in *Twentieth-Century Interpretations of Boswell's 'Life of Johnson'*, ed. James L. Clifford (Englewood Cliffs, N.J., 1970), pp. 66–73, and Clifford's comment, pp. 8–12.
37. William R. Siebenschuh, "The Relationship Between Factual Accuracy and Literary Art," *Modern Philology*, LXXIV (February 1977), 288. Christopher Fox (*Biography*, IV [1981], 268–272), reviewing William C. Dowling, *The Boswellian Hero*, remarks, "Dowling's attempt to read biography as fiction tends to blur the important distinctions that make biography the unique genre it is. We would not ask, 'Pray tell me, Sir, where in Westminster Abbey do we find Lear?' We would ask this about Johnson. And in even the most 'literary' of approaches to the *Life*, the 'real' Samuel Johnson—as elusive a figure as he is—must be taken into account."
38. *The Correspondence of James Boswell*, ed. Waingrow, p. l.
39. *Adventurer* No. 92 (The Yale Edition of the *Works of Samuel Johnson*, II [1963], 424).
40. *Life*, IV, 65.
41. *In Defence of Reason* (Denver, 1947), p. 565.
42. "Johnson as Critic," in *Samuel Johnson: A Collection of Critical Essays*, ed. Donald Greene (Englewood Cliffs, N.J., 1965), pp. 70–71. First appeared in *Scrutiny*, XII (1944), 187.
43. "Re-examining Dr. Johnson," *Johnson: A Collection of Essays*. ed. Greene, p. 13. First appeared in *The New Yorker*, November 18, 1944.
44. Introduction to *London* and *The Vanity of Human Wishes* (London, 1930). First reprinted in *English Critical Essays: Twentieth Century*, ed. Phyllis M. Jones (London, 1933), p. 308.
45. As well as the review of Croker, Macaulay wrote the article on Johnson published in the eighth (1856) and subsequent editions of the *Encyclopaedia Britannica*, replacing the excellent one by George Gleig that had first appeared in the third edition in the 1790's. Though soberer in tone than the Croker review, it perpetuates the same myth, and was often reprinted, for school use, along with the 1831 piece. Timid modifications of it began to take place in early twentieth-century editions of the *Encyclopaedia*, but it was not until the fourteenth in the 1960's that it was replaced by a wholly new

article, by Sir Sydney Roberts, with the assistance of James L. Clifford. I have an offprint of this with the marginal annotation by Clifford, "Thank goodness, at last we've got rid of Macaulay!" But it took more than a century to do so.

46. *Early Biographies of Johnson*, ed. Brack and Kelley.

47. Described in Bertram H. Davis, *Johnson Before Boswell: A Study of Sir John Hawkins' 'Life of Samuel Johnson'* (New Haven, Conn., 1960).

48. The monumental task of reconstructing Fanny's original diaries and letters was undertaken many years ago by Professor Joyce Hemlow of McGill University and her associates. Numerous volumes from the later period of Fanny's life have been published by the Oxford University Press; the early journals, containing the Johnsonian portions, are in progress.

49. *The Letters of Samuel Johnson*, ed. R. W. Chapman (3 vols., Oxford, 1952), and Mary Hyde, " 'Not in Chapman' " in *Johnson, Boswell, and Their Circle*, ed. Mary Lascelles *et al.* (Oxford, 1965), pp. 286–319.

50. In his review of Joseph Wood Krutch's excellent *Samuel Johnson*, 1944, the first full-length biography to make use of modern research on Johnson, Edmund Wilson complains of Krutch's "entirely unnecessary apologies for having played down the figure of Boswell. The truth is that he has devoted quite enough attention and given a quite favorable enough account of Boswell, and his nervously apprehensive glances in the direction of the Boswell fans are simply a part of that continued tribute which one dislikes to see exacted to that point by the vain and pushing diarist" ("Re-examining Dr. Johnson," *Johnson: A Collection of Essays*, p. 12).

51. *The Reades of Blackwell Hill . . . with a Full Account of Dr. Johnson's Ancestry*, 1906; *Johnsonian Gleanings*, vols. I–XI, 1909–52.

52. Since 1958, eleven volumes of The Yale Edition of the *Works of Samuel Johnson*, the first accurately edited collection, have been published; perhaps another dozen volumes are still to come. Unfortunately, the least known part of Johnson's writing, his voluminous miscellaneous journalism, is low on the scale of its priorities for publication. For a list of dozens of new attributions of writings to Johnson since Boswell's time,

see Donald Greene, "The Development of the Johnson Canon," in *Restoration and Eighteenth-Century Literature*, ed. Carroll Camden (Chicago, 1963), pp. 407–427.
53. *Life*, II, 46–68.
54. A most harsh judgment on the discussion of Johnson's psychology in one of the most highly praised recent biographies is passed by Bernard C. Meyer, M.D., Clinical Professor of Psychiatry, Mount Sinai School of Medicine, New York, in his "On the Application of Psychoanalysis in W. Jackson Bate's *Life of Samuel Johnson*," *Journal of the Philadelphia Association for Psychoanalysis*, VI (1979), 153–161.
55. "Verses on the Death of Dr. Swift, D.S.P.D.," lines 115–116.


## 2    John Butler Yeats: *William M. Murphy*

1. Frank Wadsworth, *The Poacher from Stratford* (Berkeley, 1958).
2. It survives as an essay, "Thirty-six Plays in Search of an Author," in the Union College *Symposium* (Summer 1964), pp. 4–11.
3. Vivian Hopkins, *Prodigal Puritan* (Cambridge, Mass., 1959).
4. Published by Dolmen Press, Dublin, in 1971 (New Yeats Papers Number One).


## 4.    Joseph Conrad: *Frederick R. Karl*

1. The benchmark for biographical analysis and criticism which is precisely the opposite of my own is found in Edward Mendelson's "Authorized Biography and Its Discontents," which is perhaps the most thorough of the pieces in *Studies in Biography*, ed. Daniel Aaron (Cambridge, Mass., 1978). Mendelson's attitudes are colored by his position as Auden's literary executor and his desire to be both truthful and honest with Auden's life. What he resists is what he diagnoses as the modern trend: "Recent literary biographers [Ellmann? Edel? Painter?] perceive their subjects as complex sets of internal psychological relations, which cast up signs of themselves in the form of literary works" (p. 20). As an antidote, he suggests that we "turn away from the recent styles of internalized biography and attempt instead to write bio-

graphies that focus on the *effect* of literary works on their author and the world around him, not the internal *affects* that may or may not have shaped those works" (p. 24).

Wittingly or not, Mendelson has joined the semioticians, who deny that biography can even exist, that only the work matters; to which a philosopher of the idealist school could reply he denies *their* existence. The proposal is self-defeating, since when we read a work worthy of attention we immediately begin to speculate about what in the author's life suggested or nourished that book, scene, character. We always look to the writer behind the work, even when we concentrate on text, word, author–reader relationship, narrative devices, *et al.* Behind the story (or whatever passes for it) lies the story-teller, however disguised, self-conscious, buried. With that, we have entered a biographical process, and all of Mendelson's disturbance over "internalized biography" cannot overcome the fact that intellectually we desire a seamless web between author and work, and biography at its best—the very examples he rejects—tries to do just that.

2. Norman Holland, *The Dynamics of Literary Response* (New York, 1975; [Oxford, 1968]), p. 242.
3. Frederick Crews, *Out of My System: Psychoanalysis, Ideology, and Critical Method* (Oxford, 1975), p. 4.
4. Joseph Conrad, *The Mirror of the Sea* (New York: Kent edn.), p. 71.
5. "But it [psychoanalytic investigation] cannot help finding that everything is worthy of understanding that can be perceived through those prototypes, and it also believes that none is so big as to be ashamed of being subject to the laws which control the normal and morbid actions with the same strictness" (*Leonardo Da Vinci: A Study in Psychosexuality* [New York, 1947], pp. 3–4). Several papers on applied psychoanalysis in Volume 4 of the *Collected Papers of Freud* are useful for the biographer, among them: "The 'Uncanny,' " "The Theme of the Three Caskets," "The Relation of the Poet to Day-Dreaming."
6. Bernard Meyer, *Joseph Conrad: A Psychoanalytic Biography* (Princeton, N.J., 1967).
7. Efforts have been made to find in Conrad's work after 1910 a pathological etiology for the so-called decline. One such theory is that after his 1910 collapse, Conrad, no longer able

to confront the inner demons of creativity, turned to a lesser, sentimental type of fiction. The latter was, in this theory, far inferior to his earlier work. Yet the theory must ignore the hardly inferior *Victory*, parts of *Chance*, the carefully crafted *The Shadow Line*, and aspects of other later work. Psychoanalytic theory here seems aesthetically naive and shortsighted.

8. Although in the present state of methodology I do not see how Lacanian theory can aid the biographer in this area, the future may lie here. For Lacan made distinctions—between word and language, signifier and signified, conscious and unconscious language—that will, very possibly, help us understand that seamless line between the artist's mind and his work. Lacan is concerned with recovery of language at its primary level, and if we can learn to read a text as, somehow, this primary form of communication and then associate it with the writer's life, we have linked what are, still, unbridgeable areas.

9. I am extending my remarks on inertness and passivity developed rudimentarily in "The Novelist: 1899–1904," in *Joseph Conrad: The Three Lives* (New York, 1979).

10. The letter is at the Berg Collection of the New York Public Library and is used with the Berg's permission. In an article called "Letters and Biography: Conrad as Subject and Object," *Conradiana*, 10 (1978), I have quoted this passage, but within a different context.

11. The most sophisticated of such analyses is Dr. Bernard Meyer's. He identifies Conrad's condition as falling clinically under the term "Infection–Exhaustion Psychoses": a severe physical ailment weakens the individual so that an emotional storm, present but quiescent, suddenly explodes, and the individual suffers a psychotic breakdown. Following this collapse, which Meyer ascribes to the loss of Ford's friendship, Conrad could no longer confront the deepest recesses of his imagination, and this inability explains the decline of his post-1910 work.

12. The *Leonardo*, cited above, shows the faultiness of Freud's method, although the three papers listed in note 5 are helpful.

13. Walter Strauss, *Descent and Return: The Orphic Theme in Modern Literature* (Cambridge, Mass., 1971), pp. 12–13.

**6  Thomas Mann:** *Nigel Hamilton*

1. Thomas Mann became resident in the USA in 1938, after the Austrian *Anschluss*; Heinrich Mann in 1940, after escaping from Vichy France via Spain and Portugal.
2. Norman Kiell, ed., *Blood Brothers* (in press).
3. It was eventually sold to McGraw-Hill.

**7  Wyndham Lewis:** *Jeffrey Meyers*

1. See Jeffrey Meyers, "The Quest for Katherine Mansfield," *Biography*, 1 (Summer 1978), 51–64.
2. After my book *The Enemy: A Biography of Wyndham Lewis* I found the corrected proofs of Campbell's book (which had passed through the hands of the Rare Books librarian at my university, though he never told me about it). I have introduced and annotated an edition that will be published in 1985 by the University of Natal Press.
3. The ban was lifted after Schiddel's death and in October 1982 I was allowed to examine the Iris Barry material. See Jeffrey Meyers, "New Light on Iris Barry," *Paideuma* (in press).

**10  T. S. Eliot:** *Lyndall Gordon*

1. All details of Mary Trevelyan come from her unpublished memoir, "The Pope of Russell Square." I am grateful to Humphrey Carpenter for allowing me to read it.
2. *Milton Graduates Bulletin*, 3 (November 1933), 5–9 and the *Grantite Review*, 24, No. 3 (1962), 16–20. Copies are in the Eliot Collection, Houghton Library, Harvard University.
3. Letters in the Berg Collection, New York Public Library.
4. Huntington Library, San Marino, California.
5. Bertrand Russell papers, McMaster University, Hamilton, Ontario.
6. This letter, dated July 25, 1914, comes from Marburg, Germany, just before Eliot went to Merton College, Oxford, to complete his graduate study of philosophy.
7. Stephen Spender, "Remembering Eliot," *T. S. Eliot: The Man and His Work*, ed. Allen Tate (New York, 1966), p. 54.

8. "Tradition and the Individual Talent," *The Sacred Wood* (1920; rpt. New York, 1960), p. 53.
9. *Ibid.*, p. 54.
10. "Preludes": IV, *Collected Poems 1909–1962* (New York, 1963), pp. 14–15.
11. "Sweeney Among the Nightingales," *ibid.*, pp. 49–50.
12. The Eliot–Pound correspondence is in the Beinecke Library, Yale University.
13. *Selected Essays* (New York, 1960), p. 166.
14. "How Pleasant to Know Mr. Eliot," *T. S. Eliot: A Symposium*, ed. Richard March and Tambimuttu (London, 1948), p. 16.
15. Letters to Virginia Woolf, Berg Collection.
16. W. H. Auden, Introduction to *The Faber Book of Modern American Verse* (London, 1956), p. 18. See "Tradition and the Individual Talent," p. 49.
17. "The Custom House," Introductory to *The Scarlet Letter*.
18. *Paris Review* interview with Donald Hall, rpt. *Writers at Work*, ed. Van Wyck Brooks, 2nd series (New York, 1963).
19. Eliot wrote this to Bertrand Russell. See *The Waste Land: A Facsimile and Transcript of the Original Drafts*, ed. Valerie Eliot (London, 1971), p. 129.
20. Subtitle. The full title is "Fragment Bacchus & Ariadne: 2nd Debate between the Body & Soul."
21. "Truth: Balade de Bon Conseyl."
22. Helen Gardner, *The Composition of Four Quartets* (London, 1978), p. 228.
23. "Silence" is in the Notebook, Berg Collection.
24. "Little Gidding": I, *Collected Poems*, p. 200.
25. "The Classics and the Man of Letters" (1942), rpt. *To Criticize the Critic* (New York, 1964), p. 147.
26. Virginia Woolf, *The Waves* (London, 1931), p. 169.
27. *Ibid.*, p. 181.
28. *Ibid.*, p. 169.
29. Trevelyan, "The Pope of Russell Square." This was a celebration of St. Lucy's day.
30. Virginia Woolf, "The Letters of Henry James," *Collected Essays* (London, 1966), I, 286.
31. "The Old Order," *ibid.*, p. 276.

## 13  Albert Camus: *Patrick McCarthy*

1. Leon Edel, *Literary Biography* (Toronto, 1957), p. 22.
2. Conor Cruise O'Brien, *Camus* (London, 1970).
3. For the psychological effects of tuberculosis see Walter Pagel, F. A. H. Simmonds and N. Macdonald, *Pulmonary Tuberculosis* (Oxford, 1953) and Harold I. Kaplan, Alfred M. Freedman and Benjamin J. Sadock, *Comprehensive Textbook of Psychiatry*, vol. 3 (Baltimore and London, 1980).
4. Herbert Lottman, *Albert Camus: A Biography* (New York, 1979).
5. Much of this material had already been gathered by Jacqueline Lévi-Valensi and André Abbou in their edition of Camus' pre-war journalism: *Fragments d'un combat: Cahiers Albert Camus, 3* (Paris, 1978).
6. Alfred Kazin, "Rebel and Stranger," *New Republic*, November 29, 1982, pp. 33–35.
7. Clearly this will not satisfy Camus' hero-worshippers nor Frederick Brown whose article on my book ("The Rebel," *New York Review of Books*, November 18, 1982, pp. 10–14) reads like a parody of Camus' most self-righteous outbursts.
8. Edel, *Literary Biography*, p. 50.
9. Alain Costes, *Albert Camus ou la parole manquante* (Paris, 1973) and Jean Gassin, *L'Univers symbolique d'Albert Camus* (Paris, 1981).
10. Robert Gittings, *The Nature of Biography* (Seattle, 1978), p. 54.
11. Norman Podhoretz, "Camus and his Critics," *The New Criterion*, November 1982, pp. 74–83.

# Select Bibliography

Altick, Richard. *Lives and Letters: A History of Literary Biography in England and America*. New York, 1965.

Atlas, James. "Literary Biography," *American Scholar*, 45 (1976), 448–460.

Clifford, James, ed. *Biography as an Art*. New York, 1962.

Clifford, James. *From Puzzles to Portraits*. Chapel Hill, N.C., 1971.

Cockshut, A. O. J. *Truth to Life*. New York, 1974.

Edel, Leon. *Literary Biography*. Toronto, 1957.

Ellmann, Richard. "Literary Biography." *Golden Codgers*. New York, 1973. Pp. 1–16.

Epstein, Joseph. "Literary Biography," *New Criterion*, 1 (May 1983), 27–37.

Garraty, John. *The Nature of Biography*. New York, 1958.

Gittings, Robert. *The Nature of Biography*. Seattle, 1978.

Johnson, Edgar. *One Mighty Torrent: The Drama of Biography*. New York, 1937.

Kendall, Paul. *The Art of Biography*. New York, 1965.

Maurois, André. *Aspects of Biography*. New York, 1929.

Mendelson, Edward. "Authorized Biography and Its Discontents." *Studies in Biography*. ed. Daniel Aaron. Cambridge, Mass., 1978. Pp. 9–26.

Nicolson, Harold. *The Development of English Biography*. New York, 1928.

Pachter, Marc, ed. *Telling Lives*. Washington, D. C., 1979.

Petrie, Dennis. *Untimely Fiction: Design in Modern American Literary Biography*. West Lafayette, Indiana, 1981.

Schorer, Mark. "The Burden of Biography," *Michigan Quarterly Review*, 1 (1962), 249–258.

# Index

248 *Index*